Insights for Self-Transformation

A Treasure Map to Peace, Wisdom, and Love

EVELYN BUDD MICHAELS, PhD

VITAL VERITE PRESS

Copyright © 2022 by Evelyn Budd Michaels
Email: evelynbuddmichaels@gmail.com
Web site: insightsforselftransformation.com

Vital Verite Press
P. O. Box 359
4804 Laurel Canyon Blvd
Valley Village, CA 91607

ISBN 979-8-218-11717-7 (Paperback)
979-8-218-086879 (e-book)

Book cover by Mary Anne Smith
Book editor: Marie Timell
Print book designer: Robin Krauss, Linden Design

DEDICATION

This book is dedicated to You, dear readers. May you find the knowledge to help you transform your life and illuminate our world with wisdom, love, and peace.

CONTENTS

Insights for Self-Transformation

INTRODUCTION

Welcome to the Journey

People have eyes, but many cannot see what they are creating in their lives. You are different. You were drawn to this book because you know there is much more potential in your life beyond what you are currently living. Somewhere inside, you are capable of being brilliant, loving, kind, successful, happy, wise, and peaceful, but you just may not be living this amazing potential YET. It doesn't matter why.

You may see glimpses here and there of progress, but you know that you still have things to learn, experiences to shed, and new directions in which to grow and stretch. You could be afraid of actualizing the incredible being you are inside.

I've been there, in your shoes. *Insights for Self-Transformation* includes all the wisdom that I opened to on my own journey toward peace and love and is a guide to inner and outer change. It delves deeply into the reality of who you are and will teach you how to handle life with wisdom, love, and serenity.

Most people are identified with their bodies, jobs, education, or something they do, which does not reflect the truth of who we are. We are not our bodies or our minds. We are consciousness, the part of us that can observe what we are doing and knows the truth. This book will help to pull back layers of negativity and pain and reveal the light of our true inner selves.

For 35 years, I have coached people on how to deal with their problems, which means helping them with both inner and outer transformation. All of the work that I have done has a spiritual foundation. My work is based on the principles of service, truth, wisdom, and love. I am not perfect, but the energy and love from

God are perfect, and it is this that I tap into helping others. Every day, I ask for guidance to see the truth and that my heart be filled with God's love. I believe we are all connected to one other and that we can love everyone. To do that, we have to heal our fears and negativity. I pray that all the people in the world are happy and peaceful and we all work together for the good of everyone.

Insights for Self-Transformation presents some of the most successful techniques I use with my clients to work out the many issues that come up in life. I work with individuals who are often successful people, yet who are stuck in some aspect of their lives.

It takes time for our consciousness to fully accept the changes we want to make. Beliefs, excuses, not paying attention, unconscious habits, poor self-image, needs, and many other areas must be dealt with and adjusted to make change lasting and consistent. Sometimes, we even go backward in the process and don't even realize we are doing it. Even with a strong desire for change, old habits may be so strong that they do not relinquish their patterns easily.

To make lasting changes requires effort in many areas of yourself. It is a continual *process* of growth and the peeling away of layers of pain until you discover a comfortable way of being. It is not about an outward destination but about an inner journey, one that is measured by your day-to-day well-being.

Some people are willing to work on themselves more diligently than others. I have found that the clients willing to take responsibility and follow my directions get amazing results. Those who make excuses and work less diligently get the results measured by their efforts. I cannot make anyone do the work; that is up to each individual. Only you can decide what you do about your life. This book gives you the necessary information and guidelines to make changes. I show you the steps and explain how you can take them; the rest is up to you. The results will depend on your desire and effort.

In this book, I extend my hand to you and invite you to join me as I share insights with you that may open you up to a new way of being. I thank you for opening your mind to knowledge that will illuminate you and, in doing so, everyone around you. Read it, digest it, try the techniques for yourself and make up your mind about its value and truth for you. Some of it may inspire you, while other parts may not ring true for now but may make more sense in a few years during a second or third reading when you are in another stage of development.

About This Book

In January 2020 I had a vivid dream and woke up knowing that it was time to share all I know about transformation. I started writing *Insights for Self-Transformation* the next day.

This book teaches you about the many ways you can improve and transform your life through spiritual development. It will show you the process of embarking on a spiritual path and how to progress on the journey. Such a process can result in a profound shift in how you have been approaching your life. In it, you will learn how to dislodge negativity so that you no longer attract what you do not want. You will also learn to make better choices by aligning them with your spiritual goals. Readers may find that, when they follow the book's suggestions and practice the techniques in it, their lives are transformed and they become calmer and freer of problems. For those already involved with a spiritual path, this book offers many useful insights and ideas that may be new to them.

Part I, Transformation and Healing the Past, discusses the foundations of transformation and what may block it. This part teaches how to get in touch with feelings and fears and provides techniques to transform your emotional world. It guides you on how to use the Energy Transformation Technique to dismantle the feeling of being stuck by recognizing, processing, and releasing your fears and other negative emotions. A chapter on negativity illuminates how problematic it is. This section points out the defensive behaviors people use to keep their fears buried beneath the surface.

Next, Part II, The Ongoing Process of Transformation, shows us that life provides us with many opportunities to grow. It reveals how to have a deeper understanding of your thinking, beliefs, attitudes, and behavior. I cover how to move past limiting beliefs, transform your self-talk, and align your thoughts and actions for success. Readers will also learn various ways to sharpen their minds, including meditation and concentration exercises.

In Part III, Living Our Best Lives: Insights on How to Thrive, readers benefit from wisdom on thriving in daily life. There are sections on how to deal with worry, habits, and crises as well as improving focus, goal setting, and clarifying life purpose. Also discussed are patience, a good attitude, and life balance.

Who doesn't want better relationships? In Part IV, Actualizing Our Best Social Selves: Opening the Heart to Truly Loving, the perspective widens even further to relationships of all kinds. This part teaches how love is best expressed through acceptance and letting go. Here are insights on handling problems in relationships, resolving pain, setting healthy boundaries, and communicating effectively.

The last part of the book, Part V, Reaching Out to Spirituality, further addresses the spiritual self and what leads someone to a spiritual path. In addition, Part V discusses all the benefits resulting from living life from a spiritual center such as authenticity, elevated consciousness, and the capacity to extend love and peace to humanity.

Throughout the book are illustrative stories from some of my clients, though their names and some details have been changed for privacy reasons. I also offer some stories about my own life experiences and what I have learned along the way.

Before anyone embarks on a journey of transformation, it is important to understand that everything that has happened or will happen in your life is a gift. When contemplating our lives, it may be tempting to feel discouraged and see life as filled with shortcomings and trying episodes. But in fact, **life is a perfect gift**.

The purpose of any experience is to help people grow in understanding. Due to my own spiritual journey, my view of my early life changed considerably as can be seen below.

Life Is a Gift, No Matter the Gift Wrap

I was born in 1930 during the Great Depression. There was a shortage of jobs, money, and just about everything, including food for most people. My family lived in a small town, Mount Pleasant, Iowa, which had a population of 8,000. I was the oldest child and had two younger brothers, Kenneth and Melvin.

Although my father earned money by shearing sheep, picking corn, and doing just about any odd job he could find, my family was on relief all the time. We lived in a rented house with no refrigeration or inside toilet. Meals were mainly rice and beans. I had to wear socks with holes in the heels the size of a silver dollar and felt embarrassed wearing them to school.

By the time I was eight years old, I had begun to look for work to earn some money. Going door to door, I'd ask neighbors if they had any jobs I could do. Gradually, I lined up work—picking fruit, raking leaves, shoveling snow, babysitting, and washing cars. I also worked for a man who owned a photography business, scrubbing the floor inside the store, the windows and sidewalk outside, and scooping snow in front during the winter. I walked alleyways to collect coke bottles for the deposit and metal for scrap. The Air Force had a training camp in town, and I would wash and iron the soldiers' uniforms.

Later, when I was 11, I used to help out at a fairly large restaurant in town. At the time, I looked mature for my age. One summer, when the dishwasher went on vacation for two weeks, I got to do her job. In those days, dishes were done by hand. I made full salary those two weeks and felt rich.

World War II was in full swing by this time, and the war had created many new jobs. An ammunition plant opened up 15 miles away, and my parents got jobs there. But then, right around the same time, my parents divorced. My mother, brothers, and

About to go to work at the ice cream parlor

I moved thirty miles away to the town of Burlington, population 30,000, where our mother remarried. We lived there for nearly two years. The house in Burlington had a bathroom and most of the modern conveniences of the time. My father moved to Bettendorf, Iowa, near the Tri-Cities. He got a job at an aluminum plant, where he worked until he retired. He kept in touch with me by phone and letters, and we usually saw each other once a year.

During the two years I lived in Burlington, I worked at an ice cream parlor, the kind where customers were served at booths and tables. I worked nights and evenings while going to school, six days a week. I remember liking that job very much.

Where my family lived when I was a teenager

Then, when I was 13, my mother and stepdad decided to buy a farm in northern Iowa near Charles City, a small town of 5,000 people. The farm was 189 acres and was located nine miles outside of town. We had electricity, but there was no running water, gas, or inside toilet. The family had a telephone that hung on the kitchen wall, which was on the same phone line as all the neighbors. The type of ring would signal which household was re-ceiving a call—ours was one long ring and three short rings. Since the phone line was shared, all the neighbors could listen in on our calls.

Living on the farm was a completely different way of life. We got up at 4:00 a.m. Monday through Saturday, and on Sunday, we slept until 5:00 a.m. My brothers and I were given daily chores and couldn't go to school until all of them were done. My chores were to feed the chickens, carry in all the water from 100 feet away, cook, wash the dishes, clean the house, and tend to the garden.

My brother, Melvin, working at the farm

My family grew nearly all its food and had many fruit trees. The vegetable garden was 150 by 200 feet. It had to be planted, weeded, and harvested during the year. My brothers fed and took care of the farm animals and milked the 12 cows. They also worked in the fields planting, plowing, and taking care of the crops. During the summer, they helped bail the hay and pick corn. I sometimes helped in the fields, shucking corn, plowing with the tractor, and gathering the hay.

In northern Iowa, the winters are very harsh. In the fall, the ground freezes and doesn't thaw until spring. Sometimes when it snowed, you couldn't see the roads, and the snowdrifts were as high as a two-story house. When there were heavy snows, my family would not be able to leave the farm for two weeks. It would get as cold as 35 degrees below zero. The

The barn at the farm

house had a kerosene stove for heat, but my stepfather turned the heat down so low that it was practically off. During the winter, the buckets of water that I carried to the house were frozen solid in the morning. Climbing out of bed during the winter was like stepping into a refrigerator. It was a shock zone, and I woke up in a hurry.

There were also some fun times. I loved to go to school. I played on the girls' basketball team—we got to travel on the school bus and play games with teams from other towns in northern Iowa and Illinois. My brothers and I received an allowance of fifty cents per week. On Saturday nights, we'd go see a movie in town. That was one of the highlights of the week. Another thing that made me happy was when my mother would sew me a new dress. Chicken feed used to come in colorful cloth bags, and my mother, who sewed well, made my dresses out of the bag material.

My school

Overall, though, these happy moments could not make up for my unhappiness living on the farm. I used to think that the farm, and having to work so hard, was like living in prison. I hated it and couldn't wait until I was done with school so I could leave.

I share the story of my early years because, today, I wouldn't trade the experience for anything. Despite how unhappy I had been living there, I have since been able to appreciate it. I now believe that my brothers and I were lucky to grow up on a farm. The fresh, clean air, physical work, and time outdoors made us strong and healthy. As children, we felt at one with nature and the seasons. We played and interacted with different animals, which was educational and fun. We ate wholesome, fresh food that was uncontaminated by pollution and chemicals.

My farm experience was filled with important life lessons for me. I learned to work hard, value community, and help others. In the town where we lived, people helped each other bring in their crops, bale hay, and do whatever else was needed. I learned how to work, be disciplined in getting things done, and the value of routine. I was taught that you have to work for what you want and not expect to be given anything. Both literally and figuratively, I learned that you reap what you sow—someone can be self-sustaining by growing their own food, like fruits and vegetables, and raising animals.

Living without running water, an inside toilet, adequate heat, and many other conveniences taught me not to take anything for granted. And today, I appreciate all the inventions, conveniences, and benefits I have been blessed to witness unfolding before my eyes over the decades.

Thanks to my earlier years, I found it pretty easy to adapt during the coronavirus lockdown. Compared to my childhood, I couldn't help but acknowledge how many benefits I had during the lockdown: TV, Internet, radio, good food, a nice house to live in, a comfortable bed, a cell phone, an iPad, running water, heat, air-conditioning, an inside toilet, and a car and gas for it. Having lived without these things growing up made it possible for me to be grateful for each and every thing I had during the lockdown.

Now, I realize that all of the problems and challenging experiences in my life were meant to teach me something. After I learned what I needed to learn from each of them, the problems and feelings associated with them did not persist. They vanished from my life.

I appreciate every experience that ever happened in my life, even though many of them contained a lot of fear and pain. I wouldn't know what I know today and wouldn't have found as much happiness and peace if all those experiences hadn't happened.

Our life is a gift, no matter the gift wrap.

The journey of being alive can be a happy one as we experience the gift of life and the many opportunities it presents for inner and outer transformation. Whether you are just embarking on a spiritual journey or have been on one for some time, I offer a prayer that these pages will uplift your consciousness and facilitate you to experience a new way of being. No human knowingly chooses despair and unhappiness. Let's dig beyond the illusory façade and the defenses so that you can open your heart to love and open your mind to the light of higher consciousness.

With much joy and love,

Evelyn Budd Michaels

PART I

Transformation and Healing the Past

CHAPTER 1

Are You Ready for Transformation?

Every person has had painful experiences that have affected their life and who they are. Many of these are from childhood and involve pain, grief, sadness, and fear. If that rings true for you, you're certainly not alone. Many people carry around the weight of past events and may feel doomed by them. However, you are not your past, even if it is influencing you today. No matter what type of experiences you have had until now, it is important to know that it is you who gives your past meaning, and you who can heal from it. Later in the book, I will be showing you techniques, methods, and exercises to heal from painful experiences. You can learn to shed the pain of negative emotions through acceptance and love.

For now, I'd like to introduce you to Benny, my husband. Benny had a childhood and life riddled with crises. How we cope with the events of our lives either makes us weaker or makes us stronger in the long run. As hard as it may be, a crisis offers a prime opportunity to adapt, learn, and grow. Benny's life experiences underline the idea that humans have an amazing power to remain resilient even in the most extreme circumstances and that our past does not have to define us. We *can* transform, heal, and thrive.

Benny's Experience in World War II

Benny Bilgrai was born in Holland in 1936 to Herman and Clara Bilgrai. Benny was the youngest of six children. Benny's family lived in Holland in Europe. In 1939, the two oldest brothers, Sidney and Freddie, left on the last boat to the United States together with a friend of Benny's dad.

The Nazis invaded Holland in May 1940. By September, the war had started, and an airplane fell on the roof of the house next to Benny's. By 1941, the Nazis announced that Jewish people could not own factories, so Benny's father was forced to sell his coat factory for very little money. He had had more than two hundred employees. In 1942, the Nazis began arresting Jews and wanted to send Benny's father to forced labor on the railroad. Deciding it was time to get out, Herman paid some smugglers to help the family cross the border to Belgium. They planned to try to continue on to Paris from there. However, they encountered a roadblock at the border between free France and occupied France. The family was swiftly arrested and put on a train with a thousand other people to the south of France. Because French and German soldiers were using the trains, they had to change trains often, and it took them two-and-a-half days to get there.

The Bilgrai family, just before World War II, from left to right: twins Sonya and Joseph, Chaim, Herman (father), Benny, and Clara (mother). Not pictured are Sidney and Freddie.

Benny and his family were put in a camp in Rivesaltes, a town near the border of Spain. It was empty because all the former prisoners had been killed. Every Sunday, during the six months the family stayed there, they were taken to the train station where they waited to see if their names were called to board the train to Auschwitz, to the gas chambers.

Ben's father knew he would soon be sent to Auschwitz, so he banded with a group of other men to escape to Spain. The four children stayed behind with Benny's mother since the trip across the dangerous and snowy Pyrenees mountains would be impossible for them. Benny never saw his father again. Herman died from a heart attack trying to cross the mountains. He was fifty-two.

With Herman gone, one day, Benny, his mom, and four remaining siblings stood at the station and heard their names called to go to Auschwitz. Luckily the train was already full. Benny's mom, Clara, and her children were taken off the train because the Nazis prioritized sending men to Auschwitz over women and children.

The Catholic priest, D.E. Stegge Johnna, who saved the lives of Benny and his family.

Back at the camp, Clara was able to get in touch with the Holland consulate and, because they were citizens of Holland, the consulate helped them leave the camp. Still, they didn't know where to go. Then, the consulate put Clara in touch with a priest, D.E. Stegge Johnna*, whom she coincidentally knew in Holland before the war. Benny's parents had been very well off and had donated money to the priest's charity, so she knew him well.

The priest decided to hide the family in various Catholic organizations in Toulouse, France. Benny's mother was placed in a retirement home run by Catholic nuns and worked in the

* The book *Dictionnaire de Juste de France* by Lazare (2003) includes a brief history of D.E. Stegge Johnna's life and his important role in helping Benny's family.

kitchen there. The twins, Sonya and Joseph, were placed in a Catholic boarding school; however, Joseph didn't stay long in Toulouse. He joined the French underground to fight against the Nazis. Benny and his two-years-older brother, Chaim, were sent to live in a Catholic orphanage located in the basement of a monastery. They didn't see their mother again until after the war.

Benny and Chaim lived in the orphanage with 30 other children of different nationalities, all speaking different languages. Only the priest and nuns knew they were Jewish. Inseparable, Chaim protected his little brother. With no adults to take care of them, they were often cold and hungry. There was no milk or meat. They were given the potatoes normally fed to the animals. For two-and-a-half years, Benny and Chaim survived by eating out of garbage cans. There was no school. During the day, they played in the fields and searched trash cans for food. On good days, they could eat from fruit trees or crops in the fields. They were often idle for hours on end. Once in a while, the brothers would have to hide out because the local Gestapo, which was headquartered in a nearby castle, would randomly search the monastery. They never found Benny and Chaim.

Benny was almost nine years old in August 1944 when the Allied Forces arrived in France and the war ended. Ben's mother and Sonya reunited and found the kids. They all moved to a castle in Toulouse for three weeks that was run by the Israeli Youth Organization. Benny hadn't had a bath during the entire time he was in hiding during the war. When he finally had a bath after being reunited with his mother, he cried and cried because he didn't know what it was.

Benny (age 8) on the left and Chaim (age 10) on the right, shortly after World War II ended

Food was still very scarce. Then, when Benny's brother Joseph, who had gone back to Holland after the war, said that conditions were not good there, the Israeli Youth Organization offered to help them go to Israel. They had no other choice but to go.

In 1945, the family arrived by ship in Israel. Clara, Chaim, and Benny were sent to live on a different kibbutz near Jerusalem called Ma'ale HaHamisha. Joseph and Sonya went to live on a kibbutz in northern Israel called Deganya Alef. Eventually, Sonya met her husband, Victor, there.

Clara went back to Holland in 1949 to see if she could retrieve some of the money the family had lost before the war. She hired an attorney, and with his help, she had some success. Clara bought a condo in Ramat Gan, Israel with the money and lived there for the rest of her life.

Benny's two oldest brothers, Sidney and Freddie, who had gone to America before the war, served in the US Air Force during World War II, both as pilots. While his unit was stationed in Australia, Sidney's plane was shot down over the ocean by the Japanese on his last mission.

Benny's older brothers, Sidney and Freddie

Joseph became a general in the Israeli army, married, and had three daughters. In 1963, Sonya and Victor moved to Belgium, where they had a son and daughter, and both became judges. Chaim lived in Israel for the rest of his life. Chaim became an account-ant (CPA) and worked for the government until he retired. He married twice and had a daughter and two sons. Chaim and Benny remained very close throughout the years and talked on the phone at least once a week. Chaim passed away in his sleep at the age of 86 in 2021.

Benny lived and worked on the kibbutz until he was 17. He struggled in school there since he had had so little schooling during the war, so he went into the Israeli army. After serving, he worked at different jobs—as a diamond cutter, a shoemaker, and in a department store. In 1960, Benny immigrated to the United States. He eventually started a fire extinguisher business, which he still operates today.

Although Benny had had a very tough childhood—being separated from his parents and siblings, moving around, and having to eat out of garbage cans—he doesn't complain about it. Benny is grateful to be alive. If asked whether the experience of hiding from the Nazis had had a negative impact on his life, he replied, "I realized that I am not going to be alive forever, so I want to enjoy life while I am here. I let the past go. I live in the present and have had a very good life. It is up to you how you deal with what happens to you." This is profound wisdom that he applied later in his life when he had cancer.

In 2003, Benny was diagnosed with stage 3 melanoma cancer. He had surgery to remove the melanomas on his left leg just above the knee and on his lymph nodes up to his waist. Chemotherapy is not a treatment option for melanoma. In 2006, the doctors found more melanoma on Benny's right leg just above the knee, and he had surgery again. In 2009, tests showed melanoma in his intestines just below his stomach, and the CAT scan revealed he had a spot of melanoma in his throat. By this time, it was stage 4. More surgery removed some of his intestines. The doctor told Benny they could offer no treatment and that he

Benny on a cruise after the "Melanoma Miracle"

only had about nine months to live. Living with the pain and sadness of the diagnosis, Benny and I decided to look for alternative treatments.

We turned to Healers Who Share, a group of natural healers who infuse water with certain vibrational frequencies designed to counteract a disease's vibration. Benny started taking a personalized regimen of waters for several months. He also began taking a special formulation of anti-cancer herbs recommended by an acupuncturist.

In 2011, after he had completed his series of remedies, Benny went in for his regular CAT scan. It showed that Benny was free of melanoma. The doctors were shocked.

One doctor asked Ben what he had been doing. Ben told him about the remedies and the cancer herbs. The doctor told him, "Well, whatever you are doing is working, so keep it up."

Benny has now been free of melanoma for thirteen years, which is a *miracle*.

Life offers challenging experiences. Each can be met with sadness and negativity or can be seen as an opportunity to learn and practice life skills by facing problems and obstacles. **It is not what comes in your path but *how* you deal with it that matters.**

How We Got Here

In my work with clients throughout the years, I have asked myself: "Why is it that a person does not understand the cause of the problems in their life?" "Why can't they clearly see the solutions that would allow them to find freedom from so much pain and trouble?"

People are in pain without knowing why. They point the finger at externals such as the spouse, job, family, or society. So many people face numerous problems, which make them feel unfulfilled, depressed, or anxious. Yet they flounder in dealing with them because they only have old behavior sets to help them—but the behaviors never do help.

We form beliefs and learn to do things based on what we learned in childhood and by imitating others. We pick up habits and learn to perform behaviors unconsciously without realizing we may be creating some long-term problems.

In school, we're taught to obey the teacher, complete our lessons, and pass tests. We're told that passing the tests means that we've learned what we were supposed to and that this would lead to a good job and a good life. It seems that the real focus of education is on acquiring rewards (e.g., grades, money, or a job), which requires us to cooperate with and submit to forces outside of ourselves.

Meanwhile, at home, we are given rules and guidelines. Each child learns and obeys the rules at different levels of obedience. With what was learned in childhood in place, once we reach adulthood, the *ego*—the part of self dedicated to ensuring the physical body's survival—leads us down a pathway of external focus based on wanting approval. The ego doesn't want to be wrong, look stupid, or not know the answer in front of others. After all, any of these situations could cause someone to be ostracized and cast out, thus compromising physical survival.

We Don't Take Opportunities for Growth

It's human to make many mistakes and face a variety of problems. Most people learn to get up, dust themselves off, and keep trying to make progress, despite their problems or the weight they are carrying. Yet, life keeps offering challenges. Every challenge provides a prime opportunity to learn and grow. For many, this is not obvious, and few people are equipped to truly learn from their experiences or navigate their inner worlds in a way that helps them to cultivate peace, love, and illumination. School curriculums don't cover this. Thus, most people are not aware of the nature of their emotions, fears, feelings, beliefs, and how to quiet the mind to connect with the wisdom within. Instead of coping with challenges, they just allow their fears to take over.

People deal with their fears in numerous negative ways and with a multitude of defenses. Some individuals are aggressive and steal, fight, kill, abuse, argue, criticize others, bully, and are destructive to avoid their fears. Then others try to escape from their fear and pain by using alcohol, drugs, deception, and isolation. The levels of these behaviors vary from mild to extreme. Most people consistently return to a repertoire of defenses to deal with their problems, annoyances, and challenges. They learned this repertoire over the course of their lives and are so accustomed to using it to handle life's challenges that they are not even aware of it.

When people are exposed to a new approach to dealing with their fears and problems, it often passes in one ear and out the other. It is *not* always acknowledged as, "Wow, this is something new that could really help me." The information may not penetrate deeply enough into the unconscious mind to cause any real behavioral change. It is easier to reach for the old methods and habits than exert the effort needed to transform. It is easier to be defensive than to engage in change.

The information gets blocked because people are using the same mental pathways that they have been using their whole lives. They are stuck in their habits. Often, they are unaware of their defensive behaviors and avoid seeing and dealing with problems. They are not aware of how they are causing their pain. It can be scary to do things in new ways. The old habitual methods of handling situations seem to be the easier and more comfortable way, so people continue to turn to them. Yet, eventually, if someone carries all the baggage from the past—memories of sad experiences and trauma—with them, the burden becomes too much to handle and they don't have any time or energy to deal with the present, let alone change.

A Willingness to Change

This book discusses the transformation brought about by someone's *willingness* to live a life dedicated to spiritual growth and the achievement of true knowledge. Are you ready to empty out the garbage can of old habits and pain and create space for a new kind of energy, new emotions, and a new way of thinking? You may feel that it is not possible to change. The hardest part is believing that we can let go of our fears and live in peace and happiness.

Whether or not, in your heart, you believe change is possible for you, you can still find the willingness. Examine the attitudes, beliefs, and habits that are not getting you what you want. What kind of thoughts and feelings are you expressing to others? Do you complain, blame, and criticize? What kind of a look do you carry on your face? Be willing to live a life of integrity and be completely honest with yourself. Then you must be determined, dedicated, and focused on what you want to do differently each day.

Refuses to Change

Ruth is a woman that is very unhappy with her life. She is fortunate that she is a multimillionaire and can have nearly anything that money will buy. Ruth dresses beautifully, and her hair is professionally cut and nicely styled. She drives a luxurious car and has a lovely home.

The rest of her life is a different story. She has four children, and none of them will see her or talk to her. She doesn't have any close friends and doesn't get along with her family. She often cries about her loneliness. Ruth does not have a clue that these problems could be her fault. She blames other people when things don't go to her liking. She is unwilling to look within herself. She is opinionated, judgmental, inflexible, outspoken, and thinks she is always right. Her behavior drives people away from her.

Ruth can't understand why her life is so miserable. She finds excuses for what happens and blames other people. She will not seek help or make any adjustments. Until Ruth is *willing* to look inside herself and make some changes, she is destined to have a lonely unhappy life.

Transformation Requires Patience, Focus, and Openness

Transformation may not happen overnight. It's a process and requires patience. Even in our pursuit of happiness and feeling good, we often want instant answers, instant learning, and instant knowledge. We want to achieve the goal *now*, and have it done and settled. After all, who doesn't want to stop suffering right away? This is unrealistic. Instant moments of transformation have happened for some, but usually when a previous accumulation of experiences created a fertile soil for it to germinate.

Transformation requires considerable effort and practice in the form of discipline and dedication, just like learning a new skill or earning a degree. If you truly want change, decide on what to do differently each day. Put down your defenses, stop focusing on others' behaviors, and start to focus on yourself.

Often when people hit an obstacle or roadblock, they get discouraged during the journey and may begin to feel that transformation is not possible for them. Feeling spouts of resistance and taking some steps forward and other steps back is a normal part of the journey. Everything begins with a first step, and each step after that can lead to greater success.

I want to show you a way of responding to life that leads to more peace, resolution, and happiness. It requires, on your part, some awareness, desire, effort, time, and practice. Most importantly, it requires an open mind.

A Story of Being Open

When I was 12 years old, my two younger brothers and I got impetigo. Impetigo is atopic dermatitis, a skin infection that causes red sores and can be very painful. It broke out on my face, chest, back, arms and legs and itched badly in the very hot, humid summer weather. Scratching only made it worse. My brothers and I were just miserable. It went on for a month as our mother took us to several doctors who prescribed medicine and creams to alleviate the infection, but nothing helped. The doctors told Mom that sometimes it affects people for the rest of their lives.

My brothers, Kenneth and Melvin, and I after being healed of impetigo.

At her wit's end, our mother drove us kids to see a healer on a farm close to where she had grown up in southern Iowa. The healer was well known for his successful healings of people and animals. After arriving at his house, we sat in the living room for half an hour while the man went out back to his fields.

When he returned, he brought some small branches with him. He rubbed the branches on our impetigo sores while he spoke in a language I didn't understand. Three days later, my brothers and I were healed. The impetigo was completely gone and never returned.

This story shows the importance of approaching life with an open mind, and how it enables us to learn new ways from new people. Openness is a prerequisite for transformation when what we've been doing is just not working.

Do You Want to Be Aligned with Ego?

The ego, the part of us we call "I," sees itself as a separate self from the rest of the universe. Its primary motivation is to sustain its own survival. It makes decisions in accordance with this goal. When someone identifies with their ego, more attention is paid to *me* and *what I want* than to others—unless others are instrumental in helping the person achieve their egoic motivations, like ensuring their social and physical survival.

The ego aims to keep the body alive, and it runs on the belief that power, competition, combativeness, and selfishness are necessary to achieve this goal. Ego satisfaction demands fame and material abundance to ensure physical survival. It wants to take advantage of others and sees them as prey for its own goals. There is less respect for the law and limited adherence to principles when people are in service of the physical body alone. The person who lives to serve their ego has an unreal view of reality that constantly changes to protect the body. A life lived to fill one's ego can never be completely happy, peaceful, and healthy because the body is riddled with limitations. Thus, the ego is never satisfied. Its desires produce numerous conflicts, challenges, losses, disappointments, and failures.

The Road to Transformation

To transform ourselves, we have to first examine what is happening in our lives now. Then we choose what we want to change and work on one area at a time. We are either getting better or getting worse each day, nothing stays the same.

People often say they want to change something and then take no action to make that change. Examples of this are to lose weight, exercise more, be a nicer person, stop drinking, or stop losing their temper. Do you want to be in charge of the kind of changes you are making, or would you rather be surprised by fate? Do you want the ego to run your life? Look at what caused you to change before in your life. Was it actually you?

When you are ready to transform your life, you need an action plan. Decide what you want to change and make a plan of what you are going to do to make that change, one step at a time. This requires discipline, dedication, work, time, patience, awareness, and determination. There are techniques in this book to help you take these steps. The rewards will be well worth your effort. Time is passing by and you are getting older each day. Do you want to be in charge of what kind of changes manifest in your life?

CHAPTER 2

The Foundations of Transformation

Self-Examination

Every human is conscious, but not aware. It is through the inner self that pure awareness is found. Spend some time each day going inside to ask how you are feeling. Train yourself to recognize when you are upset. When you get upset examine your feelings as soon as possible.

When people get upset, they usually focus on a person or situation that is bothering them. They blame the person or situation for causing their problem as their anger grows stronger. Sometimes the anger turns into yelling, or even physical altercations such as holes punched in the wall or objects thrown at human targets. It takes two people to fight. You have to be a willing participant. I want to show you a way to respond to upset that leads to more peace, resolution, and solutions. This requires more awareness, effort, time, and patience from you.

The goal from now on is to be aware of when you become upset. Notice what is going on inside of you and the temptation to react with the old behavior. If you are not aware, you won't be able to make better choices about what actions to take. As you notice yourself becoming upset, keep focusing within. Accept your feelings and process your emotions. (I will show you how to do this in chapter 5.)

To transform our beingness we need to know who we are. Most people complain about the things they don't like about themselves, but do not spend any effort in doing anything about them. There are some things we can change about ourselves and things that we can't change. We can't make ourselves taller, change the color of our eyes, or have smaller feet. Look at what you have the power and ability to change and work on those things. The most important things to change are on the inside.

Nothing physical or mental can give us freedom. We have freedom once we understand our bondage is caused by our own self and we stop creating the chains that bind us.

The things we can change are within ourselves and include:

Thoughtfulness	Being helpful to others
Giving and forgiving	Being productive
Non-violence	Compassion
Discipline	Truth
Courage	Cooperation
Tolerance	Discrimination of truth from falsehood
A pure heart	Kindness
Gentleness	Patience
Humility	Reverence
Friendliness	Understanding
Wisdom	Selflessness
Generosity	Faith
Sharing	Empathy
Honesty	Love

Understanding Energy

Inner transformation means realizing that you are not the body, understanding that you are not the mind, and knowing that you are not the intellect. Inner transformation means knowing that you are the spirit—you are consciousness. Consciousness means knowing it is inner consciousness that makes the body functional; it is consciousness that makes your mind think, your intellect to discriminate, your body work. Consciousness is one and the same.

—Sri Sathya Sai Baba

There is an energy flowing through us, which some call qi energy. This energy is connected to everything in the universe. We know that we use the energy of food for the body to function. Yet it is difficult for some people to realize that the body consists of energy and vibrates at a certain level. All thoughts and emotions reflect a vibration of energy.

Everyone's energy vibrates at a different frequency. Thoughts help to produce our energy and emotions. Emotions become manifested and experienced in our bodies as energies that vibrate at certain frequencies or levels. Our brains interpret these energies as our experience of specific emotional sensations. Some are peaceful and harmonious (higher vibration), while others are disturbed, turbulent, and fearful (lower vibration). We attract experiences, people, and things that match the energy we have inside of us (either by being similar or providing contrast by being dissimilar).

You might think of the energy that runs through the body as spiritual fuel. Previous thoughts and feelings determine the type of fuel. The fuel might consist of sadness, depression, hurt, anger, rage, feeling unloved, or loss. Most people fluctuate between being positive and negative in their thoughts and happy or unhappy to some degree.

The state of our current energetic field is determined by how we have handled all of our past experiences. It is important to be aware that human energy fields are influenced in many ways, both within and without. Some of these influences include unresolved feelings, emotions, and traumas from the past; childhood and current environments; and our current thoughts, emotions, and behaviors. These are discussed below.

Influences on Human Energy

We reside in the body for a limited time on a rental basis. So, rent may need to be paid. What is the rent? It is not money, but sickness, ailments, conflict, anxiety, anger, and diseases. Sometimes such pain can be postponed but never canceled. Pain is the direct result and consequence of our actions. If actions are vile, then misery follows. If one has done undesirable things and been guilty on several counts, one must suffer the pain and pleasure caused by one's deeds. Some call this *karma*.

When a person has fears and feelings such as guilt, shame, and rage, it affects their energy field. It begins to sag and becomes heavy, dense, and vibrates at a very low level. Similarly, when someone thinks negative thoughts or about committing a crime, their vibrational level is lowered. On the other hand, people who consistently experience unconditional love have energy fields that are light, uplifting, expansive, and vibrate at the highest level. Their energy fields reflect their higher consciousness.

What is important is that our vibration draws to us *matching* experiences and people. For example, if an individual feels jealous, they will attract experiences and people that cause them to feel the energy of jealousy. The same is true with all fears. This is why there are no accidents. Our energy is mysteriously and magically set up to perfectly attract experiences that allow it to manifest.

If we have angry energy, we will attract a situation into our lives to cause us to experience anger. It doesn't matter what is causing the anger; it could come from an insect, stubbing a toe, the weather, a body ache, another person, a vehicle, or anything. We respond with our matching energy because it resides within our cells and in our bodies. The energy and the event provide the context through which energy can leak out. The same is true if we have positive energy within. We will attract experiences of abundance, kindness, beauty, generosity, happiness, and love to the degree that those energies match ours. Keeping one's energy field clear requires resolving negative or painful thoughts and emotions so they don't stay with us and give us a prime opportunity to process and eliminate past negative energy.

Besides our current thoughts and feelings, our bodies and energy fields can also reflect the culmination of past thoughts, feelings, and behaviors, which helps to determine the quantity and quality of the life force that flows within and through us right now. Especially important are negative experiences and traumatic events that have not been healed and forgiven. These experiences are stored in our energy field and drain our energy like a leak in a water pipe, even if the individual is not consciously aware of it.

A blockage in energetic flow due to resistance or unprocessed emotions can disrupt energetic well-being and manifest itself in psychological or physical problems. It is critical to heal these leaks and blockages to ensure optimal energetic flow. Seeking the help of an experienced counselor or psychologist is beneficial to help identify and move past trauma and emotional blockages.

The human energy field is also influenced by the environment. This is especially true in childhood when our energetic fields are like sponges. The thoughts, beliefs, and emotions prevalent within a child's environment from parents, grandparents, teachers, neighbors, religious leaders, the media, school, friends, and care-givers form a deep and lasting impression on children. All ultimately influence how children view the world and react to it.

Even as adults, people are considerably influenced by the energetic fields of other people and social environments. Being surrounded by negativity can spur similar emotions in us if we have not learned how to direct our own minds and emotions.

On a deeper level, many people recognize that there is an interchange of energy between people without fully understanding the process. Here is an illustration. Once, I was playing three-card poker in the casino on a cruise. Playing nearly every night, I had unbelievably good luck, getting straight flushes and three-of-a-kind cards and winning quite often.

Noticing my streak, several people at the table came up to me to rub my back or arm for luck, hoping it would rub off. It seems that, without necessarily being aware of it, those people understood the principle of energy exchange. Energy can be siphoned like that to some degree, but it is best to not interfere with another person's good vibrations. People are better off becoming more positive on their own by transforming their energy.

Besides letting go of energies from the past that are still being carried, it is vital to learn how to manage day-to-day energies. Most people fluctuate between positive and negative thoughts and positive and negative emotions, rarely dwelling on the same kinds of thoughts and emotions all of the time. Positive energy is always within us, but selfishness, envy, pride, jealousy, and greed can also exist like clouds covering the shining rays of positivity.

The effective way for an individual to allow positive energy to shine forth from within them is to reduce thoughts and behaviors that are egoistic, envious, proud, pompous, and boastful and not indulge in self-glorification or self-aggrandizement. Engaging in negative actions can also create density in our energy fields, like calcium deposits in a water pipe that makes it difficult for energy to flow freely through the body. For example, robbery, battery, murder, gluttony, gossip, stealing, and behaviors that intentionally hurt others lower the doer's energetic vibration and create density in the energy field. These lower vibrational energies then attract experiences that produce fear, guilt, pain, suffering, and loss.

It is possible to transcend these negative behaviors and their effect on your spirit to climb to a higher energetic plane. One way is to tune into more positive and uplifting energies. For example, helping others, expressing gratitude, thinking positive thoughts, smiling at people, and focusing on what makes you happy all generate positive energy.

A more intense way is a process of emotional self-awareness, healing, and forgiveness. It can also be seen as unraveling the yarn of untruth, which led the person to act negatively. This requires a journey of learning and evolution, as described in this book, and the help and guidance of those that have gone before. To be ready for this transformation, one needs to be willing to take responsibility for oneself, face one's fears, and live in humility.

Take Responsibility

To start the transformation process, let's look at where you are now. Pause and honestly consider each of these questions.

- How much fun are you to live with?
- What kind of thoughts and feelings are you expressing to others?
- What kind of a look do you carry on your face? If you aren't sure, ask someone to take pictures of you going about your daily routine.
- How much do you complain about people and criticize others?
- Do you feel sorry for yourself and blame others for your failure?
- Are you ready to potentially accept your pain when emptying the garbage of the past?
- Are you ready to create space for a new kind of energy, new emotions, and a new way of thinking?

The goal from now on is to be aware of when something or someone is upsetting you. Stop ignoring it or trying to push it away through avoidance of any kind. Notice what is going on inside you and the temptation to react with the old behavior. If not consciously aware of what is going on, you will behave the same way as in the past. When you notice yourself becoming more upset, keep focused on what is *inside* you. The temptation is to focus on the other person or situation and think *they* are the reason you are feeling this upset energy. **Instead of placing the blame on the outside, redirect yourself to accept total responsibility for what is going on inside of you.**

Take responsibility for the pain, anger, and fear you are experiencing. Own your own emotions and pain. Blaming another person for your pain is a way of portraying yourself as weak and powerless and at the mercy of others. This is simply not true. Your pain is yours and emerges because you consented to experience it in relation to your behavior or another person's behavior.

If we approach others with compassion and understanding, instead of coming from our own whirlpool of pain, we can see their negative behaviors as a cry for help and love. We can empathize with these people, who are expressing their fear, pain, and learned behaviors. When we allow our pain to get in the way of our compassion, it only hooks into their pain. In this way, two people engage in a pain battle with each other. If suffering is cleared from each person's psychological world, they will interact from a place of love and compassion, not from a place of pain. This is our natural state.

We are responsible for the energy we are emitting out in the world. Our emotions and thinking are constantly affecting others. What we feel emotionally is picked up by all types of beings as we move through life. People may try to hide their emotions in various ways—behind their smiles, words, expensive clothes, or fancy cars—but it is challenging to keep up the front for long. Our emotions leak out via our energy fields, our handwriting and drawings, the choices of what we surround ourselves with, who we socialize with, and what we are drawn to. It is also most noticeable in our nonverbal behaviors and body language. We cannot hide them. That is also why even animals can see us and read us very well.

When we take responsibility and change, either the people around us change too, or they choose to exit our lives. Another possibility is that the behavior of people who remain in our lives no longer bothers us. Either way, life has improved.

Find the Courage to Face Your Childhood Fears

Our childhood plays an important role in how we act as adults. By the time we are seven years old, we have a defensive structure in place to protect ourselves. A defense mechanism is a behavior used to cope with our fears and reduce the chances of experiencing overwhelming anxiety. Defenses are learned through our interactions with the social world. Children have an amazing capacity to internalize their social environments and learn by imitating and observing people, including parents, family members, caregivers, friends, and characters they are exposed to through stories, books, or television. Fears and defenses developed through social interactions in childhood and adolescence may be carried into adulthood and manifested in many situations.

Peter Feared Being Inadequate

An example of someone who carried childhood fears into adulthood is Peter, who has had an ongoing fear of inadequacy since he was a child. His brother was handsome, popular, and a star athlete who won a prestigious athletic scholarship to college. When Peter was growing up, his parents had always shown great pride in his brother's abilities and showered praise on him. Peter was relatively uncoordinated and disinterested in sports, preferring to stay indoors and read books. He had grown up in the shadow of his athletic brother, often feeling unimportant and inadequate.

At 38, Peter started an advertising agency with his partner, Earl. They were quite successful. The problem was that Earl only wanted to work when he was in the mood. This pattern began early in the relationship and got progressively worse. Earl liked to take a day or two off each week. Peter was hardworking and wanted to build the business to be even more successful. Peter continually solicited new business. When Peter gave Earl a task to perform, Earl would complain. The work at the advertising firm had tight deadlines, so when Earl neglected his work, stress would abound. He continually promised to complete his work on time, but he was generally late.

Peter became frustrated and upset when Earl kept taking a couple of days off even though he had not completed his projects as promised. Peter felt angry because he could not get Earl to do his work and complete his projects on time. Whenever Peter complained to Earl, Earl would again promise to do better but continued to grumble about the workload and be late. Peter rationalized why he should keep Earl as a partner, telling himself that he could not find someone else as good and that everyone comes with baggage. He thought that a new person could be just as irresponsible yet may not be as talented. After all, Earl had a lot of creative talent and a great imagination. He was charming and easily built rapport with clients, often making people laugh with his witty and quick humor. He was easy to get along with and performed his job wonderfully well *when* he did it.

Peter wondered if he was the one doing something wrong, "Was he expecting too much?" "Was it his fault?" Even though their working relationship was erratic, he concluded that it was worth working on to see if he could improve it. The problem continued for five years, and Peter could not get Earl to change. Finally, Peter was fed up with feeling frustrated every day and decided to get some help.

With help, Peter became aware that on a deeper level, he had felt inadequate and helpless for years. He learned that his fear of inadequacy had been causing him to be stuck in the same place, powerless to resolve the conflict. Peter was stuck in a constant loop of blaming Earl, believing the only solution was to get Earl to be conscientious about work and deadlines. Other solutions did not occur to Peter because of his fears.

Peter feared what would happen if he discontinued his partnership with Earl. How would he cope with clients by himself, without Earl's charm and creative ideas? Only after Peter dealt with his feelings of inadequacy and helplessness did he realize that he had other choices in managing his relationship with Earl and their advertising business.

Gradually, Peter stopped blaming Earl for his work ethic and accepted his positive and negative traits. Once Peter was free from the loop of constant blame running through his mind and being stifled by his fear of being inadequate without Earl, he had the mental and emotional space to examine his options honestly. He decided that he could either accept Earl and continue on as they had in the past or negotiate with Earl and delegate the work differently. Earl could take time off as he wanted, only be paid less so that projects could be delegated to someone else. Earl agreed, and Peter found another person just as capable as Earl yet willing to do the work. Their business grew enormously, and Peter now feels he is in command of his life.

Understanding the Power of the Unconscious

The conscious mind consists of the thoughts, feelings, and be-haviors that we can call into our minds *at will*. However, most of our thoughts, feelings, and intentions occur *outside of* our conscious awareness and contain layers of programming resulting from our experiences with the world. Most of our negative energy and fear comes from this place, the unconscious. In the example above, Peter's fears of being inadequate were buried in his unconscious so he had no idea how it was influencing him whenever he dealt with Earl.

Unconscious fears and feelings can lead people to be stuck in loops of scenarios with the same themes (e.g., fears of inadequacy), but with different actors and content. This is how powerful the unconscious can be. These scenarios arise as opportunities for becoming aware of deep-seated fears. Healing occurs when we are willing to change both the conscious mind and the unconscious.

Recognize that unconscious directives come from within us from our past or present experiences or can be funneled through us from the outside world, such as other people or television and other media. If we do not tell the unconscious mind what we want it to do, it will respond and react according to past programming or take its directives from the outside.

Do you want to direct your mind? To do this, you must be very attentive to how you react to the world outside of yourself. Any reaction becomes infused with your energetic vibration, which plays an important role in your life.

How to face fear is discussed in detail in chapters 4 and 5, which present this practice as a foundation of change. When we learn to respect the power of the unconscious mind enough to delve into it and release what we find there, we can:

1. Improve our relationships
2. Create more harmony and less conflict
3. Unleash creative abilities
4. Cultivate the capacity to reach higher vocational goals
5. Release anger and hostility
6. Achieve more peace and happiness
7. Allow love and compassion to flow through us

Approach Life with Humility

People often focus on their self-centered concerns about problems, frustrations, and challenges and talk about life's negative side. However, events, objects, and people are usually not completely good or bad. They come into our world and awareness for reasons we often do not understand.

A fatal flaw is to think we know how things work or that we are right when the fact is there is so much in life that we cannot see and simply do not understand. Recognizing this is humility. **Having humility automatically makes you open and willing to learn and change.** If you go to a large university library, stand at its center, and slowly scan the shelves, it is easy to be awed by the volumes of knowledge that exists. This is one way to cultivate humility. Realizing how much we do not know opens the mind to the wonder of life, causing us to search for answers and see things in different ways.

Despite what humankind has achieved, the profound truth is that there are limits to science and our intellectual knowledge. Science provides valuable insights, yet it cannot fully account for the complexity of the universe and human experience. The universe is filled with mystery. Humility allows us to say, "I don't know, and I want to know. I am open to growing and learning the new."

Seeking Help

We are now living in an age where people have access to such an unprecedented amount of spiritual, emotional, and intellectual information that it is possible to make leaps and bounds in our evolution. There are now more people on our planet who are evolved to the point they can help others through this journey than ever before. It is a gift to be born during an era where such rapid evolution of our spiritual lives is possible. **Living in humility means we are open to learning** from those who have walked the path of transformation, whether a counselor, therapist, pastor, or the authors of books on the topic.

Meditation and Emotional Healing

Transformation is facilitated by the twin pillars of meditation and emotional healing. Meditation is an important tool to transform your mind as you learn to quiet your thoughts and become more consciously aware. Emotional healing consists of processing and eliminating negative energy, allowing the natural flow of positive energy to transform and illuminate your being. In the following chapters, I will teach you meditation and emotional healing techniques that you can implement to support your transformation. Both of these processes facilitate your awakening, like the metaphoric caterpillar turning into the butterfly. Emotional Healing is discussed in more depth in chapters 4 and 5. Meditation is discussed throughout this book. To learn meditation, take a class or find one on YouTube. Chapter 7 on the mind includes a meditation technique and in chapter 12, I share my meditation technique.

Other Basics of Transformation

Once you have made a real choice for change and spiritual awakening, the foundations of transformation outlined above will support and assist you in the process and enable you to:

1. Decide that you want to change.
2. Be willing to put the time and energy into learning how to make the changes.
3. Become more consciously aware of what you are doing by learning to meditate.

4. Take full responsibility for your actions and the results of your behavior.
5. Give up blaming yourself and others, judgment, and ego.
6. Give up being needy.
7. Listen to others' feedback earnestly and with an open heart.
8. Accept that transformation is possible for you.
9. Be willing to deal with the pain of your emotions.
10. Give up negative defenses.
11. Identify your fears and examine how you are defending and feeding them.
12. Live in the present. Let go of the past.
13. Review your behavior each day and note what you want to change.

It is up to us how much we would like to learn and grow. We are responsible for our actions and can choose when to change. It can be now, years from now, or we can choose to stay the same. A prime opportunity to escape from pain and suffering is available when we come to an understanding of our transgressions and can genuinely see the error of our ways. When we recognize the poor decisions we've made, then we create the space to experience the presence of a Higher Power.

Ask for help, guidance, and to be open to learning new ways of doing things. This is the primary path to profound change. When you let go of the resistance to life and stop creating havoc, you will slowly unravel the past and the untruths. In this way, you can start to climb to a higher vibrational energy level and to love.

CHAPTER 3

Negativity

What Is Your Outlook on Life?

Imagine that positive energy is the sun and negative energy is the clouds in the sky. When clouds are present, they can block the rays of the sun, even to the point where the sun doesn't seem to exist. It is there, but it's not visible or accessible to the naked eye. Similarly, clouds of negative energy can block all that is positive. But, it is possible to blow negativity out of the way by aligning with positive energy. Positive energy is summoned when we are happy, joyful, kind, smiling, helping other people, and thinking about the things in life that make us feel grateful, thankful, and appreciative. This book can teach you how to do this.

Our thoughts have a way of finding their own path when we don't know how to control our thinking. Some people see the future as bright and full of opportunities and possibilities. Then others see a darker road filled with strife, problems, sadness, fear, and unfulfilled goals. What is your outlook on life? If it is the latter, then your outlook is pessimistic, which is an attitude of negativity. (Often a main cause of pessimism is due to the use of alcohol, drugs, nicotine, and medication. These all have side effects that cause mood changes such as depression and sadness.) Chapter 8 delves further into beliefs and attitudes. For now, realize that a negative outlook can block your progress.

Optimism or Pessimism

There is a story about a woman with twin sons. She took the boys to a psychologist and told him she was concerned that one twin,

Dick, is a pessimist and cannot see the good in anything. On the other hand, she explained that the other twin, Rick, is an optimist who finds something to be happy about in everything he does. The doctor told the mother to bring the boys back to the office the following week for an experiment.

The next week, when the mother arrived at the doctors with the boys, he took Dick to a room filled with all kinds of toys. He put Rick in another room that contained only a huge pile of hay. He left the boys alone in the room for 20 minutes. When the doctor and mother went back to Dick's room, they found him sitting in a corner crying. Then, they opened the door to Rick's room, and Rick was singing and playing with the hay. They asked him what he was doing and he replied, "With all this hay, there has to be a pony around here someplace."

Through desire, work, and practice, we can change the way we see the world.

Negative Thinking

Focusing on what you want to avoid is unproductive. Every thought creates an emotion, and when you think about what you do not want, like worrying, it causes you to have negative feelings. The next time you feel "down" check your thinking. Thinking habits are learned in childhood, and they can be changed with some work. Ninety percent of most people's actions happen unconsciously. The way you think is also a habit. If there is a behavior that you no longer want then you can change it. It takes desire, time, awareness, and practice to change a habit.

Examine how much you are thinking about problems, fears, worry, anger, and disappointment. If you keep thinking the way you have been, you will get the same results. When your thinking is negative, it causes you to be unhappy and you communicate this to others. Sometimes this is called, nagging, whining, and complaining.

A mind that is not disciplined is scattered, vague, unfocused,

and lacks direction. Achieving the ability to concentrate with clarity requires training and practice. It requires discipline to gain the ability to think clearly and direct your thoughts with precision. If there is a problem focus on the solution and direct your actions to resolve the issue.

Most people's heads are filled with chatter, which causes confusion and distraction and reduces productivity. Sometimes it takes the form of worry, dwelling on the past, wishful thinking, or something they want to happen in the future, but they take no action to create it. Negative chatter is a waste of time and energy because it builds more negative energy and attracts more problems.

You Are Not Your Past

Have you noticed how often you have felt the same unhappy feelings and thought the same negative thoughts in different situations?

Some examples are:

I'm not good enough.

My body is fat, tall, skinny, ugly, light, short, or has too many freckles.

No one loves me.

I'm not as smart as other people.

I'm treated unfairly.

These feelings exist because an event happened in the past, which created fear, negative thoughts, and feelings. If negative thoughts and feelings are not dealt with, they remain with us, influencing us and blocking our energy. Often old emotions will erupt inappropriately and sabotage the present. Therefore, the answer is not avoidance, repression, or suppression of our negative thinking or emotions.

It is of utmost importance that we look squarely at ourselves and face our mental and emotional worlds—head-on—with the courage of a lion, no matter what it brings. It is only when negative emotions are embraced—like when a parent soothes a crying child—that people can allow the density of their energy fields to dissipate and lighten so that the rays of the sun of positivity can shine through. In this chapter, negative thoughts and behaviors are discussed, as is the importance of developing awareness of your mind. In the next chapter, I discuss the negative emotions, particularly fear, that create resistance.

Bruce's Past Means He Feels Unsafe

Bruce's story exemplifies how old feelings can make life more limited. Bruce's house caught on fire when he was eight years old, and he barely escaped. Two of his younger sisters died in the fire. Since that time, Bruce has had a fear of danger in his home. Sometimes he wakes up with nightmares about the fire. He often thinks about his sisters.

Unless Bruce resolves and heals the feelings that emerged from what happened in his childhood, the fire, the feelings perpetuate and are carried into other situations. Bruce does not feel safe at home and doesn't like to go to unfamiliar places in case he finds himself in a dangerous situation. He won't go hiking because he is afraid of being attacked by a bear or getting lost and dying alone in nature.

Negative feelings and fears not only become activated in other situations, but they help to attract even more experiences that match the emotions that we have inside. These new experiences, while seemingly negative, actually provide prime opportunities to process and heal the feelings that came from the past *if* a person can look within at their inner storm with awareness. Yet, more often than not, individuals do not take the opportunity to heal when a new situation activates an inner storm from a previous life event. People run away from a problem by looking externally for its source and finger-pointing others. This further energizes and feeds the inner storm, causing it to grow in magnitude.

Even a Simple Task Can Trigger Old Feelings

An example of how a seemingly simple task activates an inner storm of negativity may help to drive this idea home. Let's say Mark is trying to put together an IKEA desk and is having a hard time screwing two pieces of wood together. He wipes the sweat from his brow and thinks, "I am worthless at putting together furniture." This thought will likely make him feel awful and frustrated, which then deflates his energy. Mark ends up slumped down on the floor in the middle of the room, looking around hopelessly at the dozens of pieces of wood, screws, and tools scattered around him.

Those negative feelings then spur Mark on to more negative thoughts and memories about other times in his life when he felt worthless because he failed at tasks. Now his thoughts go back to childhood when his sister was better at keeping her room tidy, and his mom gave *her* approving looks, which made him feel jealous and worthless. Then his mind flashes to a presentation at work when his colleagues asked so many questions that he couldn't answer that he felt worthless. Thoughts and memories stream into consciousness in a split second. They're about what no longer exists, but like uninvited guests, they intrude into the present and compound the current situation. They create strong emotions that bubble up in Mark's chest and spread throughout his body, affecting his energy field. After his reverie, Mark is now in such a state of worthlessness and depleted energy that he gives up on the task altogether.

In short, the act of simply screwing two pieces of wood together incited a blizzard of thoughts and emotions that affected Mark's energy field. This has not happened by chance. When people do not process their experiences and take steps toward healing, a seemingly unrelated situation, like putting together a desk, can trigger an intense blizzard of emotions like worthlessness.

Pent-Up Negativity Triggers Eruptions

The feelings were already within Mark, and the situation just triggered them to come into expression. A person with a lot of pent-up negativities such as hate, anger, and fear may have their energy tied up, thereby making their energy field dense and heavy. In this state, it is difficult to be consistently productive or express kindness and love to others. These feelings, from childhood or other past events, represent old pain and many triggers are due to it.

Often triggers lead to emotional eruptions. It usually takes a certain situation—perhaps even an eruption—to wake you up and help you realize that something is not going right in your life. Usually, it is only through experiencing a great amount of pain that someone becomes willing to change. Sometimes, a person has to reach rock bottom before they seek help. The timing has to be right.

The first step is to decide that I do not want to continue living as I have been—enough is enough! At this point of dissatisfaction with present circumstances, it is easier to stop doing things in the same way and take responsibility for feelings and actions through self-examination. It is important to be open and willing to receive help. Things *can* be different when you are ready to change.

Next, ask yourself, Do you have the power to change a situation? When you get upset about people, experiences, or things, ask yourself if you have the power to change them. If you don't have the power to change something, then why would you continue to be upset about it? That is like expecting the weather to always be a certain way and then being unhappy every day because it's not. If you can't change a situation, then your job is to accept it. Find peace in allowing it to be the way it is. Use your time, energy, and thoughts to focus on what you do have the power to change, which is constructive rather than negative.

Healing is letting go. It is about the deep healing of negativity to free one's energy from its density. We can learn how to let go of negative thoughts, feelings, beliefs, and behavior and invite more peace, happiness, and love into our lives. This can be learned in the same way that we progressed through school—in stages. We didn't learn everything in the first or second grade. This is why spiritual development is a *process*.

You will know you have graduated when your life is peaceful, happy, and full of love. Imagine a world where people want to help one another. They act with kindness and consideration and are a joy to be around them. This world can be invited into your life by starting the transformation process within yourself.

Blocks to Positive Change

There are many blocks to well-being and a positive outlook—some are fears, some are emotions, and some are behaviors and habits. These blocks, indicating the presence of fearful and defensive energy, need to be brought to healing. For example, ever since Simon was in a car accident, he has been afraid of driving, and takes an Uber everywhere. He has a block, and to remove it, he could seek help, or even take driving lessons.

As long as blocks are operating in any form in a person's life, it will be difficult for the person to come to a place of full well-being. Even though there may be improvements in some areas of a person's life, the presence of any blockage will cause them to vacillate back and forth from positive energy to negative energy. It is as if they have their foot on the gas pedal and the brake pedal simultaneously. The low vibrational energy of blocks will continue to attract problems until they are resolved and will prevent the vibrational level of someone's energy from increasing. The person will have to dig deeper, sometimes into the past, to figure out what created the blocks. Some blocks to positive changes are:

Closed-mindedness doesn't allow us to think about new possibilities and ideas. It keeps us stuck and prevents humility and transformation.

Vanity enables people to pat themselves on the back and tell themselves that they are wonderful. It is used because of an underlying self-image problem.

Anger is used to hide from fear and feel more powerful and in control.

The need to be right is when someone wants to be stronger and better than the person they are interacting with or fighting with. Underneath the need to be right, they feel inferior and uncertain. If they can convince others they are right, it provides an assurance of certainty and comfort in their own selves.

Inflexibility/rigidity is a fear of change. Someone clings to the way things are as a way to feel secure and in control. They are frightened about what change may bring and if they will be safe and well after the change.

Stubborn is being opinionated, unchangeable, and unreasonable. A stubborn person does not want to be confused by facts. There is black-and-white thinking and blind grasping at ideas. They are rigidly for or against something because they are unwilling to adjust their thinking, be flexible, or even admit that they are wrong.

Fear is the anticipation of pain, a threat, or unfavorable results.

Ego-driven behavior focuses on the self and its aims at the neglect of considering others.

Negative habits are unproductive behaviors that diminish the success, quality, and happiness in someone's life (e.g., laziness, lack of focus). It is important to identify what negative habits affect one's quality of life and learn how to change them into positive ones.

Not listening is a way to avoid hearing something annoying or painful. It can be a way to dismiss others so that the listener doesn't have to pay attention to them or do what they want.

Lack of awareness can be caused by poor habits and improper training. Meditation and concentration exercises can help to increase awareness immensely by stilling the mind. Also, what helps is paying attention in the moment.

Focusing on other people's problems can be a waste of time and energy, especially if there is no actual way to help them. All we can do is just listen to someone without judgment, yet in full acceptance; often, this is enough to help them feel better. It is best to stay focused on knowing what can be done and what can't be done.

Fighting verbally or physically is a way to deal with fear but only creates more problems.

Rebelling is where a person takes a stance for or against something just to defy another person or organization, usually perceived as an authority. There is a failure to use reason, flexibility, and understanding to cope with the issue.

Lying is a trait used to try to hide something, avoid pain to self or others, or gain something without merit. The person doesn't take responsibility for their actions.

Addictive behaviors are compulsions to overindulge in alcohol, drugs, gambling, shopping, or eating. They can be a way of escaping negative psychological states or undesirable circumstances in favor of a more pleasant reality. The problem is that the pleasant reality is short-lived and usually comes with a hefty price tag, such as financial, physical, or psychological issues.

Needing approval is a fear of disapproval while wanting to feel more secure, confident, and strong. There is a need to be supported and propped up from the outside to feel more confident, usually involving abilities, the way someone feels and looks, or what is owned.

Low self-esteem is a lack of belief in one's worth and value and usually includes underestimating what someone believes they can achieve. As a result, an individual sets lower goals due to this self-doubt.

Enablers

Enablers are those who help people with problem behaviors to continue their negative actions. For example, they might give the alcoholic money, buy liquor for them, make excuses for their behavior, or drive them places to buy or drink alcohol. The enabler also helps the drug addict, overeater, abuser, or person with any other addiction. They might say, "They are actually a nice person. They don't mean to be like this."

The enabler makes excuses for others. They tell themselves they are helping, but they are only adding to the problem. Because they make it possible and easier for the problem to continue, they are, in fact, a negative influence. Unconsciously, they are assisting someone with a problem to order to make *themselves* feel better. The enabler is not willing to see and admit the truth that they are part of the problem. Enablers are blocks to progress.

It's Futile to Blame the Past

When we look at what gave rise to our negativity and blockages, it is futile to blame past circumstances for our present reality. This type of thinking just keeps us stuck in the past and can cause more negativity. It is equally pointless to wallow in complaints about our lives. This keeps us stuck in negativity.

You may be thinking, well, I couldn't help it. I acted in ways based on what life dished out to me. It is true that everyone is not born on an equal footing. Through the complexities of the universe, humans are born with different genes, physicality, and propensity toward diseases. People are born into varying geographical locations and experience unique environmental, social, political, family, community, and financial situations.

Some experience extreme hardship growing up and others less so. Certain philosophies explain this through the concept of karma; others see this as due to chance. Regardless of how or why someone got here, it doesn't help them *now* to lament their past or overfocus on past actions, right or wrong. If someone has blocks and pent-up negative emotions from the past, they are affecting the person now. It is important to deal with them and move toward healing. Living in the past just keeps people stuck in the past. What about the present and the future?

Channel the energy that you would use to blame or complain about your life into a more positive direction by asking yourself these critical questions:

- Who do I choose to be within my current life circumstances?
- How will I rise to the occasion of actualizing my highest potential in these life circumstances?
- What goals can set me on a path to change any of the circumstances of my life that I am unhappy with?

Thoughts Sow Seeds

Ultimately, what people think about and say to themselves plays a major part in directing the unconscious mind. We may not always be aware of our thoughts and emotions, particularly if we are in avoidance and distraction mode. It is critical to cultivate the ability to be aware of the contents of one's mind.

Become mindful of what you think because you will attract and create those things into your life. If you feel inadequate and talk about how you can't pass a test or get a good job, you will manifest these events in your life. The more aware you are of your thinking and expectations, the more control you have over your internal and external world. Awareness enables you to be intentional about what you would like to invite into your life.

Learn To Observe

Many of our negative actions and thoughts are habitual. We are unaware of the seeds we're sowing and what we will harvest from them. We have much more power than we realize once we become aware of the kinds of thoughts we are having, the energy we are manifesting, and our actions. Before anyone can take steps to change, they must first become consciously aware of where they are and what they are doing.

To become conscious in each moment of the thoughts, energy, and action you are putting out, turn on your observer mode. Everyone has one. Simply observe yourself as though you're another person. As you observe, ask yourself, Is what I am putting into the world what I want to be reflected back to me in return? For example, if you yell at your children's misbehavior, be ready to have that returned to you in a different package. Soon, you may see them yelling when they feel anger, either at you or other children. Your life becomes a mirror of how you have acted.

This is one of the reasons meditation is so helpful. When meditating you learn to not only observe your thinking but to stop your thoughts from jumping from one subject to another and to remain focused in the present. When your mind is still, it is easier to project your thinking in a specific direction—away from negativity. By practicing positive affirmations, you can choose how you want to direct your thoughts. Affirmations are a good way to change habits and negative beliefs. Chapter 8 discusses affirmations in more detail. For now, here are a few examples:

> I am staying focused in the present.
> I handle any issue that comes up with patience, understanding, and confidence.
> My life gets better and better every day.
> I see only the good and the positive in life.

The saying, "You reap what you sow" is very true. When you plant corn, you get corn. When you plant an apple tree, you get apples, and when you share positivity, you receive positive energy in return. **Your life is a mirror of your thoughts and actions until now**. But it does not have to define you or the potential of who you can become.

It is possible to tap into the never-ending stream of universal positive energy that is the True Self when we learn to allow kind and loving thoughts to flow through us and choose to live a life of service focused on helping others. This is only possible when we become aware of and take responsibility for our negativity, regardless of how it started in our lives, and consistently allow our negative feelings to be healed.

Benny in the Israeli Army

At 17, my husband, Benny, joined the Israeli army and served for two-and-a-half years. For training, he was sent with other soldiers to the desert with enough rations for one month. They had to learn to get water by digging a hole in the sand at night and putting a can, covered with a cloth, in the hole.

Benny in the Israeli army

One night, the soldiers were marching in the dark. Two soldiers were in front of Benny, and another soldier marched beside him. Suddenly, the two men in front of Benny fell off a cliff. Then, Benny and the other soldier fell off the cliff. One of the first two men that fell died. Benny and the other three men fell into a tree, which saved their lives. Still, he broke both of his arms and was in casts for over two months. The breaks were never properly set, and to this day, his arms are permanently bent. He was fortunate to live through that experience.

Benny had another close call in the army in the middle of a gun battle. He was grazed by a bullet leaving a quarter of an inch indentation across his entire chest. Again, he was very lucky to be alive. Benny spent the rest of his time in the army being a policeman.

Life can give us unexpected experiences. *How* we handle them is what matters. Will we be negative and let them scar our lives or will we move forward positively?

It is vital to keep reminding yourself that no matter what the past looked like or even where you are today, it is possible to strive toward positive transformation and work toward improving your well-being. You just have to start now.

CHAPTER 4

Feelings, Fears, and Resistance

Emotions Are Important

Emotions play a critical role in all aspects of life—physical survival, decision-making, health, goal achievement, and how to navigate the social world successfully. The ability to be aware of emotions and manage them in yourself and others is called *emotional intelligence* (Goleman, 2005). When you know how you feel about a person, situation, or thing, you can relate to others with more warmth, empathy, and love.

There are times when it is appropriate and useful to be objective and cerebral. For example, if you need to decide whether to accept a new job, make a large purchase, or get married, it is important to access your thoughts and analyze the situation before taking action. Analyzing your thoughts, utilizing your experience, and connecting to your feelings give you more resources to make sound decisions.

However, if we only plug into our thoughts, we remain disconnected from our feelings and limit our access to crucial data provided by emotions. Some people habitually disconnect from their feelings and operate out of their thoughts. If asked how they are feeling, they will express what they are thinking. Here's an example:

Question: How did you feel about Jeff's comment?
Answer: He shouldn't have behaved that way.

This answer is a thought, not a feeling. An answer expressing emotion is, "I felt hurt, like he didn't care about me."

Let's consider another example.

Question: How does it make you feel when Doug acts that
          way?
Answer: He should be more thoughtful and polite.

Again, this comment describes the person's thoughts. An answer describing emotion would be, "I felt humiliated and upset."

Emotional Intelligence

Emotional intelligence can be developed in several ways. One is the practice of *emotional self-awareness*, which is consistently and consciously bringing attention to our emotions and what we are feeling and experiencing in our bodies. At times, this may be difficult because we may have layers of excruciating feelings that are difficult to face, and there may be a temptation to escape or resist those feelings.

Be aware of what you are feeling. Practice by asking yourself, what am I feeling? What's going on in my body? When someone has been disconnected from feelings for much of their life, learning how to access feelings will take practice. State to yourself, "I now want to be aware of what I am feeling."

Our emotions manifest and are experienced through our physical bodies. Notice any tightness, shallowness in breathing, aches, hurt, uncomfortableness, or pain you are experiencing. Set aside a few minutes each day to practice checking in with your body because it can tell you when you have feelings that you aren't acknowledging.

Begin to develop an understanding of how your emotions feel to you. Do you feel any of them in your body? How and where? Consider the following:

Worried

Uncomfortable

Upset

Angry

Unloved

Sad

Depressed

Treated unfairly

Uptight

Helpless

Not good enough

Anxious

Nervous

Afraid

A compulsion

During the journey of emotional self-awareness, you may go back to pushing your feelings away. Train yourself to become aware when you are doing this. For example, it may be particularly tough to deal with feeling unloved, and there may be a temptation to push this feeling away and not face it.

Some feelings may be associated with a painful childhood experience, a traumatic event, or years of accumulated experiences. These feelings may have multiple layers, which sometimes need to be unraveled like a ball of yarn. Overcoming the resistance to facing these feelings and finding the motivation to do this work may be the most significant obstacle to healing these feelings.

To further help you examine your feelings, you may want to ask yourself: What percentage of the day do I experience any of the following feelings?

Peaceful	Unhappy
Calm	Upset
Happy	Worried
Joyful	Sad
Balanced	Angry
Confident	Confused

Awareness of what feelings we are carrying around or are being triggered by outside events is the first step to healing and releasing them. With the pain inside dealt with, often outside problems clear up. It requires practice and patience. It may take time to become more aware, heal painful emotions, and align with a lifestyle of accepting what is.

Avoiding Emotions with an Outer Focus

One way of avoiding our painful emotions is to look outside ourselves for *who* and *what* "caused" this pain. It is best to avoid this temptation at all costs. Allowing our minds to loop and reloop blame weakens us and can act as a distraction from doing the work of healing these painful emotions. Instead, it is essential to develop the strength to look at the feelings, no matter how painful. In the beginning, it will take considerable redirection of one's focus from outside of ourselves to inside.

With steadfast effort, you can overcome the tendency to focus outside of yourself and finger-point to check out of your feelings. Instead, do a check-in of your feelings and become aware of your emotions. Once you have identified the emotion you are experiencing, say to yourself, **"This is not about X or the other person; this is about what is going on inside me. The cause of these feelings and unhappiness is located within me, as is the solution."**

Marilyn Focuses on Carl

Marilyn wanted her boyfriend, Carl, to be more loving, talk to her more, and show her how much he cared for her. Carl could be warm at times. At other times he was distant, secretive, and undemonstrative. When Carl was distant, Marilyn felt that Carl didn't love her and she wasn't important to him. While there was the temptation to blame Carl for how Marilyn was feeling, this never helped. Marilyn needed to recognize that her pain was, in fact, *not* about Carl. Marilyn's feelings came from an accumulation of past experiences. Carl did not cause Marilyn to have these feelings. Marilyn attracted Carl because his energy matched hers. Carl was the catalyst that triggered Marilyn's pre-existing, deep-seated emotions.

Marilyn felt unloved and unimportant, and she wanted to feel loved and important. Even if Carl had been more attentive, made her the number one priority in his life, was consistently warm, and told her how much he loved her, it still would not have been enough. Marilyn told herself that she felt unloved and unimportant because of the way Carl was treating her. She blamed him and was convinced that it was his fault that she was unhappy.

Take the Focus Off Others and Put It on Yourself

Just as Marilyn's story shows, it is crucial to recognize that we are responsible for how we feel, not anyone else. Our negative feelings are inside of us and not outside. Since the pain resides within, only we have the power to release it. We won't have lasting feelings of being loved, important, or happy in our interactions with others as long as we feel unlovable and unimportant inside. This may be a bitter pill to swallow at first. But, with practice and acceptance of this principle, we can become free of the perception that people are responsible for making us happy or have power over us. We are much more powerful than we know if only we are willing to take full responsibility for ourselves—our experiences, thoughts, emotions, and behaviors.

Once you recognize that you have been looking in the wrong place—for someone or something to fix the pain and discomfort—you can adjust your focus. The more emotion you invest in someone, the more power they have to upset you. When you feel you need someone to be in your life or act a certain way, the more power you give them to affect your world.

You will achieve healing and empowerment when you focus within. The work is first on the inside and not on what others are saying or doing. As long as your inner emotional suffering remains unresolved, you will continue to attract people, situations, and things into your life that trigger old, negative feelings. Only by looking within and not outside can hurt, fear, and negative emotions be healed.

One of the most important emotions we all need to connect with is fear because it is the fundamental cause of all problems.

How Fear Works

Fear is the anticipation of pain or unfavorable results. The keyword is *anticipation*, meaning that someone is afraid of something that *might* happen in the future. What is feared is not real, it has not happened, but the person is afraid it might occur.

Fear helps to protect us when we feel threatened. When fear is present, the physical body goes into a heightened response to allow faster reactions for survival. The problem is fear is anticipation, not real fear, so, when we are fearful, our body can be in a high-alert state much of the time. This causes stress and can have a debilitating effect on the body due to the overproduction of adrenalin.

Hiding from Your Fear

Common fears can become activated by everyday life and this compounds negative energy. Typical day-to-day fears are of disapproval, helplessness, or not feeling good enough. Interactions with others often trigger fear.

For example, Jane often-played cards with her friends. One day, one of the women dealt two too many cards to a player. Then there was a discussion about how the two extra cards should be removed. The women could not agree, and an argument ensued about what was the right way to remove the two cards. Jane thought the cards should be removed at random. The woman holding the cards disagreed. Jane became very angry and said she never wanted to see her again. She also blamed her other friend for not backing her up and decided not to stay friends with her anymore either.

This incident is not about the cards, it is about fear disguised as a need to control. Jane felt she needed to control the situation her way to feel more secure. She was also afraid of her pride being wounded. In a game that is for fun, does it really matter how two cards are removed?

The reason small issues like this create bigger problems is due to fear, in this case, represented by Jane's need for control. That was the energy that fueled the argument and ended the friendships. The two extra cards were only the channel, not the real problem.

Fear creates anxiety and affects judgment and decision-making. When someone reacts emotionally, they perceive their feelings as justified and real. The position is defended by coming up with seemingly valid reasons to think, feel, and behave the way they do. Jane also felt they didn't respect her, or her opinion by rejecting her solution. Becoming angry served to protect her ego from sadness and fear. The root of this fear will not be healed until her feelings are processed and she understands what she is doing.

When Jane makes a commitment to identify and face her fear, she will be in an ongoing process to give up denial, blame, and getting angry instead of giving up her friends. As the fear energy unravels and dissolves, she will find there are more layers to be healed. It requires sustained motivation to continue the healing process until all the negative energy is gone.

Fears are very painful and if you don't know how to identify the source of the problem, it can be overwhelming and confusing. The problem is often blamed on something outside yourself, and blaming what is happening on the outside hides the real problem. It is through self-examination, connecting, and letting go of fearful emotions that one can live free from fear.

Neediness Is Fear

Neediness is a fear of not having something in your life that you feel you have to have to be all right. The fear is an illusion and, unless it is seen for what it is, it will always be there pressuring you. Often the thoughts switch to needing something else. The solution is to identify the needy feeling. What is the fear that causes the need? Check for any negative beliefs connected to the need. By accepting the feeling, you can give up the struggle. This does not mean you can't improve your life and have what you want. It means your life will not be filled with wanting things that make you unhappy because you don't have them.

Neediness causes unhappiness. We have needs because we fear we are lacking something and not having it often creates sadness and a helpless feeling. The belief is if we had what is lacking, we would be happier. Some people have a very long list of needs. Here is an example of things that people tell themselves they need.

> A mate
> A friend
> To be in control
> To be smarter
> More money
> To be better looking
> To be younger
> To be right
> A new car

Once you have healed your neediness, you have the freedom to choose and enjoy the things you want.

The Cycle of Fear

Fear bubbles up from the unconscious and attracts situations that make us experience what we fear because this allows the energy of the fear to express itself. The fearful energy we have inside and anchored in our bodies is like a magnet that attracts experiences to match. Thus, to avoid attracting more fearful situations and stop the cycle of fear, it is important to face fears and release their negative energy.

Here is how the fear cycle works. An event evokes a perception of a threatening situation in someone, which elicits fearful thoughts and feelings. The person formulates mental pictures of the anticipation of pain. This elicits negative emotions and attracts experiences that match the negative energy. Most people try to cope with such an unfortunate situation by escaping, avoiding, and becoming angry. This allows the fear to remain unprocessed until the next time another event triggers it and causes the whole cycle to reoccur. Each time the same fear is triggered without healing, the fear is energized, allowing it to grow more.

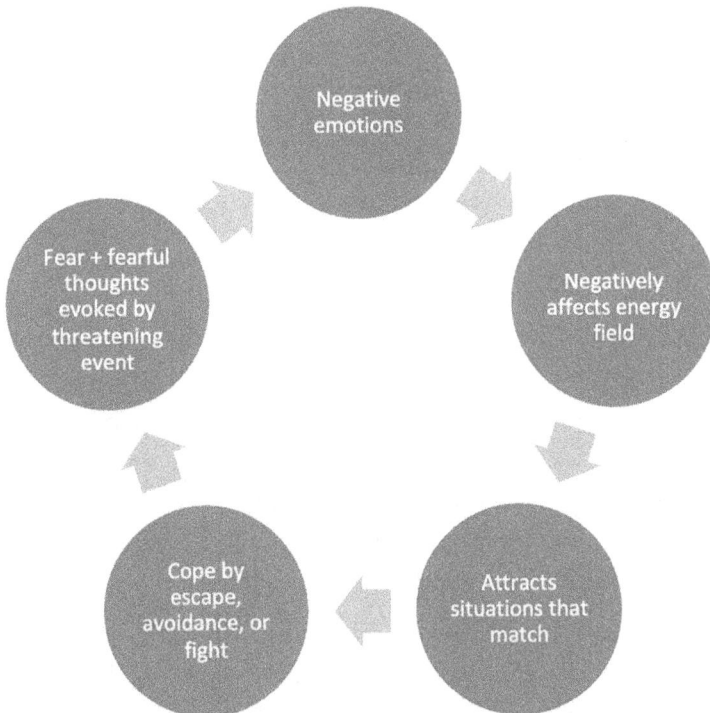

Negative emotions

Negatively affects energy field

Attracts situations that match

Cope by escape, avoidance, or fight

Fear + fearful thoughts evoked by threatening event

Toni Fears Helplessness and Disrespect

An illustration is the case of Toni. Toni often thinks about how much she feels disrespected and treated unfairly by her landlady because she doesn't respect her boundaries and enters her apartment with her key whenever she wants. The landlady yells and criticizes Toni. Toni gets upset and angry and complains to her friends about it, yet she does nothing to resolve the situation. This has been an ongoing problem with other people in Toni's life and weighs on her. She has had roommates who complained about her, stole clothes from her, and criticized her.

Toni never dealt with feeling hurt over people disrespecting her and continued to have similar experiences with other people. Until Toni does deal with these feelings, she will attract more experiences that cause her to get angry and feel disrespected. Her anger is a defense to shield her from coping with her feelings. To release her anger, she needs to acknowledge when she feels disrespected and accept her feelings. Instead, she becomes consumed with anger and blames everyone else for their behavior. She has angry thoughts about how people mistreat her. She feels helpless and confused and doesn't know what to do. If she asked me, I would tell her to get in touch with her fears.

Common Fears

There are times when someone knows they are afraid, but they typically try to fight or run away from facing the fear. Usually, however, fear works in our lives at an unconscious level and causes resistance. Strong emotions and resistance in relationships land us in the Pain Pit (more on this later).

Below is a list of the most common fears. Later, we will discuss the defenses most often used to cope with fears.

Helplessness is the feeling of being incapable of doing what we want to do. We fear feeling powerless, weak, dependent, and unable to take care of ourselves.

Lack of confidence is feeling self-doubt and that we don't have the ability to accomplish what we want to do.

Betrayal is to be disloyal and deceive someone. Here the fear is that someone will be treacherous in the way they deal with us.

Rejection is refusing to accept someone or something. This involves being afraid that we will be denied or refused by someone, thrown back, or be unwanted, pushed away, and cast off.

Inadequate is the feeling of not knowing how to do something properly—like we are not enough or sufficient. It is usually related to fearing failure.

Unimportant feels like we are not getting as much attention as we want or are ignored and treated as insignificant or less.

Unloved is feeling like we are not wanted, not desired, and not cared for, or feeling coldness from others. We fear feeling unloved because it feels threatening to our existence.

Humiliation is when we feel embarrassed, put down, made fun of, and mistreated. We fear humiliation because it reflects a loss of pride.

Disrespected is being discarded as not having value. We fear being treated with rudeness, insulted, or unworthy.

Incapable is fearing that we don't have the necessary qualifications or lack the experience, knowledge, training, education, or ability to do something successfully. This fear is a close cousin of the fear of failure.

Unworthy feels like we are devalued in life and not deserving of the best. We fear not being enough to merit all the good life has to offer.

Abandoned is when we feel left alone, told to go away, or taken away. We are afraid of being unwanted, relinquished, discarded, forsaken, and deserted.

Not appreciated is to fear being cast aside, our efforts belittled and ignored, considered unimportant, and not noticed or acknowledged. It is the fear of being given too little regard or value.

Guilt is feeling we've done something wrong. We have not lived up to what we believe we should have done. We have committed a violation or offense and feel remorse for it. We fear being punished and being "bad."

Out of control is when we have lost our strength and power over some aspect of our lives. We fear that we aren't in charge or capable.

Lack and neediness are feeling like we need more than we have, such as abundance, food, love, or people. We are afraid that we can't get more of what we want.

Not good enough is when we feel we do not measure up to what we compare ourselves to. We fear that we don't live up to standards and are viewed as lower quality for various reasons.

Taking advantage of (used) is fearing that someone is being unfair in the way they treat us and take more from us than they give.

Fear of loss is when we feel insecure, fearing that we cannot hang onto what we have. We feel inadequate about knowing how to prevent losing things. We fear losing a person, love, money, home, or job.

Fear of death is the fear of dying or of someone else's death. The thought of life ending is unbearable because we do not know what will happen. This is a fear of the unknown.

Overwhelmed is a state of confusion and feeling overloaded and unsure of ourselves. It can feel like too much is going on, and we fear we are incapable of making appropriate choices to accomplish our goals.

Competition is a fear of not measuring up to someone or something else. We doubt our ability to succeed and feel threatened. There is a fear of rivalry, and there may be a fear of not having sufficient skill or knowledge.

Loss of freedom is the fear of restraint and the loss of liberty and the ability to do what we want, including our freedom to make our own choices.

Evaluation is being afraid we may be perceived negatively or rejected by others during a future evaluation, one where it is important to us to achieve goals or look good such as in public speaking, acting, tests, interviews, or sports. Another way to think about it is *performance anxiety*. We may be afraid that we won't perform adequately, forget important aspects of our performance, or act in stupid or incapable ways that cause us to feel embarrassed, humiliated, or shy. There may be the related fear of social consequences such that we may be rejected, ostracized, removed from a valued position, or perceived as incapable. The fear of being evaluated often comes up during interviews, submitting a paper to a professor, or taking a test. Other related emotions are not feeling good enough, self-doubt, and fear of rejection, disapproval, or humiliation.

Being homeless is a fear of losing money, a job, or the ability to work so we can't pay the rent or mortgage and don't have a place to live.

Jealousy is the fear of loss from competition. Often this fear is caused by experiences with siblings or close friends.

Fear of failure is lacking confidence in our ability. The result of this fear is that we often set lower goals because we don't believe we have the ability to be successful. We play it safe and avoid challenges.

Fear of responsibility is the fear of taking on a heavier load. The word *responsible* means being able to respond to a situation appropriately. We fear that taking on more responsibility will cause us to have less sleep and less leisure time to have fun and enjoy our social circle. It also may mean the fear of having more problems to solve.

Fear of saying the wrong thing is a threat to our egos. Saying the wrong thing can be embarrassing and humiliating. We may be perfectionists who allow no room for making mistakes or not knowing everything.

Fear of commitment is the fear of having to make a choice. We fear losing our freedom and becoming stuck permanently in a situation we'll be unable to escape. There may be a fear of losing our identities and what we already have.

Indecisiveness is the feeling that we lack the ability to decide what we want and don't want. It involves a fear of taking a risk. We fear making mistakes and any resulting problems. We are unable to weigh the consequences of a decision and what we may gain or lose. This fear blocks our thinking and the ability to see clearly.

Understanding Resistance

Resistance is a way to avoid experiencing overwhelming fear and anxiety. We become resistant because of fear and other strong emotions, which make us attempt to get away from something or feel we want something we don't have. Either way, there is a struggle, so resistance signals that we are not all right where we are.

People put up a wall to keep something they do not want out of their lives. There is a lack of acceptance and cooperation in dealing with outside issues, ideas, or people. Resistance wastes energy and keeps us in a defensive mode of action. Resistance causes disease, unresolved problems, cruelty, fighting, and unhappiness. Most people aren't aware when they are resistant, as it has become an unconscious way for them to live.

Resistance blocks someone from getting what they truly want. We can live our lives with resistance or be fully accepting.

A person is in resistance when they are feeling uncomfortable, avoidant, negative, unhappy, or are pushing or pulling for or against something.

The paradoxical secret to understanding the outside world is that we must look within and strive to understand ourselves first. We cannot understand ourselves until we are connected to our thoughts and feelings. Unfortunately, most people have not learned how to understand their inner world and how it directs their behavior. They may be intensely focused on their interactions with the outside world, which means they may be prone to employing resistance.

Am I in Resistance?

Let's dig a little deeper into the important topic of resistance. Often, we can come to greater clarity and understanding by asking ourselves the *right* questions. To determine whether you are in resistance, honestly ask yourself:

- **Am I angry or frustrated?** The anger may be directed at ourselves or someone else. Anger is a symptom of trying to mask fears by asserting power. It can give the illusion of power and control, but when allowed to take expression, the temporary feelings of power often lead people to behavior that later results in regret.
- **Do I feel confused?** Someone wants something different from the way it is, but they don't know what they want or, if they do, they don't know how to get it. Trying to decide between what they want, what they need, and what they are not getting upsets them. Their thoughts keep going over and over the problem, trying to make sense of it.
- **Am I unhappy, worried, depressed, and fearful?** Any time we feel uncomfortable, it is an indication that we are struggling with something outside of ourselves and resisting what we do not want.

- **Am I pushing my feelings away rather than accepting them?** Humans fight, resist, avoid, and blame as a way to escape what is happening.
- **Am I trying to escape my life or feelings through distractions?** Escaping through distractions includes the use of alcohol, drugs, sex, food, shopping, TV and movies, social media, the Internet, or being a workaholic.
- **Are my thoughts about events or people in the past or future, rather than being focused on the present?** Unprocessed feelings from the past may lead someone to keep dwelling on the past. Also, having fears, anxiety, and uncertainty related to what might happen in the future can lead people to overly think about it and how to control negative outcomes.
- **Am I deceptive with myself or others?** People may try to hide their real feelings and the truth of their lives from friends or family by presenting a false image of themselves. If you do not know the answer to this question, ask yourself if someone filmed my behavior for one week from waking until sleep, would my close friends or family be surprised at what they would learn about me? What are you hiding?
- **Do I have impossible expectations of others?** Expectations often lead to disappointment. When someone is accepting rather than resistant, they can deal with each moment without unrealistic expectations that people or events should turn out a particular way. They go with the flow.

Moving Out of Resistance

If you answer yes to any of the questions above, it is time to move out of resistance. The first step is to develop a *strong desire* to stop resistance. Recognize that resistance is a recipe for unhappiness because it is an attempt to protect the painful and uncomfortable feelings that we hold inside. Yet all it does is keep us stuck in the same place.

When you decide to change, consistently ask yourself the questions above in every situation to determine if you are being resistant and defensive. Be self-aware and stop resisting, face your fears, and do whatever it takes to practice *acceptance* of yourself and others. For this, your ego must get out of the way, which means learning to live in humility. Accept that you do not have all the answers and are not always right. Focus on your own choices.

Avoiding Resistance through Self-Awareness

To avoid falling into resistance and find acceptance more easily, learn to incorporate awareness as an ongoing practice. Regularly check in and observe your feelings as you interact with various people throughout the day. Whenever you notice any upset, uncomfortable feelings, or negativity coming up within you, it is time for you to take a breath, decide to be non-reactive, and observe what is going on.

In situations where it becomes apparent that you have uncomfortable feelings, reflecting on the following questions may help shift you into a state of **self-awareness and observation**:

- **What am I feeling?** Identify the fear. Become aware of what is going on and how you are feeling. Taking a moment to do this is essential because people are easily distracted by the outside world and don't notice when they begin to be affected by upset energy. To notice how you are reacting to your experiences requires training and practice. This includes daily meditation and observing your mind instead of getting swept away by the tides of your thoughts and emotions. (See chapters 7 and 12.)

- **Why does this not make sense to me?** When something is not making sense, it means there is confusion. This can be coming from different sources. For one, your thinking is not clear and is out of harmony with your feelings. Strive to identify where the disconnect exists and what needs to change to iron it out. Confusion may also emerge from not having enough information to completely understand a situation at hand. Sometimes, the data needed for you to see the full picture may not even be attainable. Are you all right with living with uncertainty, or do you feel the need to control the situation? You may need to process your feelings about fear of the unknown.

- **What is threatening me?** When you feel a sense of threat, focus on what is triggering you. Your emotions and body are picking up on a real or imagined danger and alerting you to pay attention. Is this a physical source of danger and threat? If so, it is time to act. Or, it could be an emotional threat—no physical danger is present, but you feel triggered. Did someone walk into one of your emotional landmines? If so, identify what type of fear is activated and connect to that feeling. Disconnect from the outside situation and stay focused inside. Notice where the feeling is in your body, and then proceed to face and process it (see chapter 5).

- **Am I blaming the other person?** If you are in a blaming or defensive mode, then stop to seek within for what is causing the problem; otherwise, your energy will be thrown out of balance. What is the fear? What was the trigger? Is there an emotional landmine? If you weren't feeling threatened, there would be no need to blame. Identify your fear and examine your feelings. Once you are balanced on the inside, you can see if you need to handle anything outside.

- **Do I need to be by myself to deal with my feelings?** Anytime you have upset feelings or fear, take time for yourself to take care of your emotional world. If you are in public, you can visit the bathroom to check into your emotions or take a quick trip to your car.

Self-Acceptance Keeps Us Out of Resistance

Once you are regularly focusing on your inner life and settled into more self-awareness, you may start to become uncomfortable with what you are discovering about yourself and others. This is a critical time to practice acceptance of your feelings, ideas, and other people. Without acceptance, someone could easily return to the space of resistance, so there can be no healing and no progress.

As we continue to embrace what is within ourselves, we can make it all right by facing our feelings head-on and focusing on our fears. Accepting these emotions will help eliminate negative energy. I will show how to do this in more detail in chapter 5.

If we recognize something about ourselves that makes us unhappy, ashamed, embarrassed, and angry, it is important to remember that we can heal these feelings through processing, acceptance, and a Higher Power. Living life will become increasingly easier when we consciously choose to deal with what comes up for us.

Ask yourself, Do I want to continue going through my life having these painful feelings, or would I rather acknowledge, own these feelings, and do the work to eliminate them? Some steps to acceptance are:

1. Focus on what is going on inside of you.
2. Allow yourself to feel your pain and accept it.
3. Identify, process, and accept your feelings of fear.
4. Change negative beliefs.
5. Recognize your needs.

Soon, as we discover something outside ourselves that seemingly disturbs us, we can use these steps to look within and move toward acceptance. Eventually, we will be healing years of pain that have been held inside. This is the path of acknowledging our negative emotions and allowing them to dissipate through acceptance and unconditional love for ourselves.

Self-acceptance gives us power over our beingness. It allows us to attract the positive things that match the new, balanced energy within us. It is all a process of cleansing, healing, and evolving. Once we have mastered this process, we even learn to appreciate and be thankful each time an experience gives us an opportunity to do this work. We feel grateful to all the people in our lives who are helping us to *wake up*, move into healing, and get closer to our true selves.

Resistance in Relationships

Resistance often occurs between people. One person pushes someone or something away because they don't want to face their feelings. Our daily interactions with others trigger both positive emotions like joy and negative emotions such as fear and anxiety. Closely examining our feelings when interacting with everyone in our lives—from the grocery clerk to drivers on the freeway, to closer relationships like co-workers, spouses, our children, friends, and relatives—provides important insights into what triggers fear and resistance.

Blaming and Attack

When individuals feel overwhelmed, frustrated, critical, angry, argumentative, or hateful, there are *only* two choices. The ideal choice is to face the feelings and take responsibility for them in order to work toward healing. The other option is to avoid looking inward. This avoidance causes people to look outward to find someplace to put the blame for their feelings. In life, people choose to either resist their negative feelings or face them, let them go, and become happier and more positive. There is no standing still. There is no in-between.

Blaming and attacking are major forms of resistance in a relationship. It may be hard to believe, but some people purposely say and do things to get a negative reaction from others. It may be to protect themselves, that is, to "let me get them before they get me." Some of the behaviors that are used to attack are:

Character attack is when one person draws a judgmental conclusion about someone's character or actions and expresses it in a way that puts them down or seeks to harm them, such as gossiping about them. It is trying to make a person "wrong." The goal is to denigrate the person's self-worth, cast doubt on their morality, or reduce their social standing—for example, accusing a person of being dishonest, lazy, mean, immoral, incapable, wrong, unfaithful, cheap, weak, or indifferent. No one is perfect, and we all make mistakes and engage in less-than-perfect behavior. Pointing out behavior that could be improved is not necessarily an attack if it is intended to be helpful.

Physical actions are highly aggressive behaviors such as hitting and grabbing and taking, stealing, or breaking someone's belongings.

Threats and verbal abuse are saying things to confuse and belittle people and make them doubt themselves. An example is when one person criticizes and finds fault with another person to make them doubt whether they did a good job.

The Pain Pit

When people blame situations, events, or others for how they feel, they will inevitably project their feelings outward, and this energy is apparent in their behavior. It is expressed with a mean look, searing words, sarcastic and biting jokes, tears, yelling, hitting a wall, throwing objects, damaging property, or hurting people. Usually, these outward behaviors start mildly and gradually escalate to higher and higher degrees of harm as more inner feelings are suppressed or projected outward. It can spiral out of control. The end goal is usually destruction to some degree, starting from very mild (a jabbing joke) to moderate (yelling) to the most extreme (hurting or destroying another person's body or a group of people).

Whoever is the target of this negative energy may get sucked in and react by reciprocating with a similar kind of behavior. This only further fuels and energizes the conflict. This is called the **Relational Pain Pit**. Imagine the Pain Pit as a pool of water that contains repulsive, destructive, fear-ridden, and toxic energy. When people in a negative state look outward to blame and project their feelings onto others, they have jumped into the Pain Pit.

Connecting to the Pain Pit contaminates a person's energy, and more destructive words and actions help them sink deeper into the Pit so the energy grows and builds more momentum. When another person reacts to someone already in the Pain Pit, they are connecting to it too and voluntarily jumping into the Pain Pit pool. The person responding to the other's Pain Pit doesn't realize what they have done. They only know that they are upset and their thinking is muddled. People learned to enter the Relational Pain Pit and react this way as children when they watched adults behave this way. It can often be the only way someone knows how to relate.

Look at it more closely. The interaction in the Relational Pain Pit becomes a ping-pong match of negative, upset, and fearful energy being exchanged until some kind of stopping point is reached. After the Pain Pit battle has run its course, both individuals climb out of the Pit, oozing the wounds of guilt, hurt, and anger throughout their minds and bodies. Every time there is a visit to the Pain Pit, it is strengthened with additional energy. Over time, the parties' reactions are quicker to become destructive and less conscious, while the negative energy multiplies. How can this be a healthy approach?

When Attacked, Don't Enter the Pain Pit

While it is vital to handle any inappropriate behavior directed toward us, it is in our highest good to do this without entering the

Pain Pit. It is imperative to stop, wake up, and turn our attention inward.

When people behave inappropriately, it is tempting to point the finger at their behavior, making them wrong and us right. To do so means we must find *justifications* for our emotional responses, like being angry. We may think, of course, I'm angry, they are wrong, how could they do this to me? With a bit of prodding, we may even admit that it *feels good* to be right. Humans frequently use this approach of focusing on what others are doing.

People may not realize that relating this way keeps them stuck on a hamster wheel or a road to nowhere. While on the hamster wheel, relishing and basking in the idea that they are right and others are wrong, they have lost the precious opportunity to understand their feelings of upset, anger, and discomfort. Instead, by only justifying their feelings, they impede their progress on the path of transformation.

With some practice in being aware and processing feelings, you can learn to stay calm and observe without reacting so you don't enter the Pain Pit (getting defensive, arguing, or yelling)—even when attacked. Instead of focusing on the other person, focus your attention on your inner world. Go somewhere to be by yourself as soon as possible. Avoid the temptation to think negative thoughts about the other person. Stop replaying what the other person did or said in your mind. Focus your attention on identifying your fears and processing your feelings.

Nonjudgment

Even when you have learned not to climb into the Pain Pit, your reaction to others in it is of the utmost importance. You can still get sucked in if you react to those who are in their own Pain Pits when you spin negativity or judgment in your thoughts or in your conversations with friends or relatives—even if the person is not physically there. Judgments suck you into a vortex of negativity that multiplies your pain.

When we are able to withhold judgment of who is right and who is wrong, we can clearly see that all that has happened in every situation is that the other person has successfully triggered a response from us that comes from our own fear or insecurity. That is what led us into the Pain Pit—our own emotions. Even if a person's actions are blatantly wrong by all standards, if we become defensive, negative, or judge the person, we have allowed ourselves to be blinded by our fears and emotions.

It is possible to train your awareness to stay out of the Pain Pit or to back out of the temptation of entering this psychological swamp when we are close to entering it. When you are with a person who becomes critical, angry, combative, and sometimes abusive, just mentally step back and simply observe the person. Do not react with negativity and judgment. That is, refrain from thinking or saying things like: "Wow, how horrible that this person is so angry," "This person should not be feeling this way," and "I can't believe anyone would act this way."

Instead of allowing yourself to slide into the Pain Pit with someone, observe the person like you would a leaf on a tree, with complete neutrality. It will take practice at first, and it may feel very uncomfortable. Power through this discomfort and keep steadfast in this stance of nonjudgment. If you can stay relatively still in the storm, you may even begin to feel compassion for this person's plight. You will be able to connect with the idea that they have a temporary inability to take responsibility for their feelings and fears. Their weakness is driving the ugly behavior.

Look at what the other person is doing as a **desperate cry for help**, no matter what form it takes. However, be clear that it is not your job to help the person in the Pain Pit. You are not responsible for others, only for yourself and your dependents. Sometimes, you may be in a position to help, and sometimes you may not be.

The same approach is advised for any media content (television, social media, celebrities, politicians) that depicts people in the Pain Pit or violence of any kind. We can get sucked in if we react with negativity or judgment to the media as well. So, we can take care when choosing what type of media we consume. The more we surround ourselves with people, media content, books, pictures, and objects that are peaceful, loving, inspiring, nurturing, and restorative, the more we will build our capacity to withstand the temptation to enter into the Pain Pit.

Learning how to do this takes training, so practice this with every person you come into contact with, whether in person, virtually, or through media. There is no faking detachment, nonjudgment, or compassion. Your energy must be authentic and consistent; otherwise, you may still fall prey to the Relational Pain Pit yourself.

My goal is for you to build more awareness by reading this book so you never have to go into the Pain Pit again. It takes time and gradual practice to heal negativity and cultivate the ability to be the observer rather than the reactor in the Pit. You can learn how to do this.

If Someone is Physically Abusive

It is important to say that there are times when it is necessary to remove ourselves from a situation. Looking at someone's bad behavior as a desperate cry for help does not mean that we have to stick around and bear the brunt of it, especially if they are unwilling to work on it.

Always avoid a confrontation with anyone violent and physically abusive. If you climb into the Pain Pit with an out-of-control, raging person, there is a good chance that you could be injured or will have to defend yourself physically. Until you have learned how not to react, it is difficult not to be defensive. But under these circumstances, it is dangerous to be combative.

It is best to communicate with the raging person calmly and harmoniously, exit the situation, and put space between you and them as soon as possible. If your or anyone else's psychological or physical safety is threatened, ensure your well-being and that of loved ones, such as your parents or children. In fact, not allowing a person to be psychologically or physically destructive toward you can be an act of love. It not only protects you and your loved ones, but it protects the misguided person from their actions.

If this happens to you, there is a good chance that it is not the first time that it has occurred. These situations can escalate as they are repeated. The best choice is to remove yourself from the building and get to safety, if possible. Call for help. Preplan to make sure your phone is within easy reach and the numbers for helplines and friends are programmed into it for quick dialing or redialing. Have a packed bag ready and within quick access. Hopefully, this will be the last time you will need to get out.

Even if another person is not violent but is angry, it is not a good time to engage in any way until they have calmed down. When a person is verbally attacking you, it is best to remain the observer and be calm. In this situation, you have three choices: stay calm and observe what is happening, leave the scene, or fight in the Pain Pit.

Self-Focus is the Answer

When we are triggered with emotion, turning inward to do self-examination is where all healing unfolds. The key is to examine ourselves to see what emotion has been activated and move toward wellness rather than focus on the outside and allow ourselves to become defensive, judgmental, or blame the other person. There is a detailed section on how to do this in chapter 5. For now, it is essential to emphasize that **focusing on oneself is the most profound act of love and compassion** that someone can take.

First, show yourself love, compassion, and acceptance. This will eventually be projected outward to others. Then, you will be able to address the person you are interacting with on the outside in a calm, compassionate, and composed manner instead of from a place of pain and anger.

Remember, to move into a space of acceptance, we need to let go of our old behaviors of defensiveness, judgments, and blaming as a way of life. This means redirecting the mind every time it focuses, with anger and fighting, on what someone did to us. The mind will do this a lot at first, but this calls for steadfastness in focusing inwardly on our feelings.

Often disagreements are caused by different beliefs and motives. Examine your motives when dealing with others. Are you attempting to change someone's mind? Is the reason that you fear losing something—for example, their company, fun, or money? Consider how you are being selfish and look for opportunities to negotiate and find agreement. Be willing to let go of something having to be a certain way. Often it is possible to compromise, be flexible, and find a happy solution.

Acceptance includes allowing other people to make their choices about their lives and to have their feelings. Someone may have a different opinion or perspective, and it does not mean they are wrong. Come from the belief, "I want to be harmonious and agreeable whenever possible and allow others to make their own choices."

With consistent efforts to transform over time, others will no longer have power over us. When we take responsibility for all our triggers and deal with them, upset ends. The actions of those around us will no longer throw us off our game, and if they do, it won't be for long because we have the tools to get back into equilibrium.

What Happens to Manure?

One day, I asked a client, "Have you ever seen a fresh manure pile?"

The client responded curiously, "Yes."

"What happens to that manure," I then asked, "when the sun shines on it day after day?"

The client thought for a minute and, with a grin on her face, jokingly replied, "Does it smile at you?"

After we shared some laughter, I continued, "Wouldn't that manure begin to dry up?"

The client then nodded in agreement and added, "That is the compost I put in my garden to help my vegetables and flowers grow."

"Right," I said, "and what would happen to that manure if it stayed in the dark?"

The client thought for a while and replied, "I guess it would stay pretty yucky."

Nodding, I explained, "But, the same way sunlight transforms manure into compost so it can help beautiful things to grow, the light of consciousness mystically transforms the 'yuck' of our emotions into beautiful, harmonious, and more powerful energy." And that is what the next chapter is about.

CHAPTER 5

The Energy Transformation Technique

A Path of Healing

The *Energy Transformation Technique* (ETT) is a method of allowing healing to take place by fully facing our feelings and fears with an open mind, open arms, and an open heart. It is about moving into what is present within and accepting it. As discussed, this requires that we observe our negative feelings, accept them, and allow them to be present. During any painful experience, we hold ourselves with the same compassion, love, and nurturing as we would a baby crying in our arms. When we approach our fears and feelings this way, we will be living in a state of acceptance.

Acceptance means giving up denial, avoidance, struggle, and resistance. Instead, we accept negative emotions, allowing the feelings to be present until they have dissolved. It is not a sign of weakness to acknowledge the presence of our vulnerabilities and negative feelings.

What happens when we master the ability to accept?

Problems decrease.

People around us act differently.

We become more peaceful.

Life seems more magical and filled with wonder.

We become happier.

We are able to connect with others on a deeper level.

Why Does it Work?

Imagine you are holding a hose that is spraying energy in all directions. The energy from the hose is landing on various things that you are involved with in life. With certain people and situations, you may be able to adjust the energy from the hose to some degree. Now realize that the energy from the hose is *your* energy and that you go through life spraying your energy everywhere without realizing it.

Some people do not activate your anger, fears, and negativity, so they may not be sprayed as directly as others. But the negative energy is still there all of the time, waiting to be triggered. When this negative energy connects with the targets of your hostile energy, it affects every aspect of that relationship or situation. If you are spraying sadness, anger, fear, blame, criticism, and sometimes abuse on your relationship with your partner, fellow employees, children, parents, teachers, siblings, and friends, what effect will this energy have on them? Of course, this will affect how they feel, respond, think, and how they treat you. Now imagine you are spraying kindness, love, compassion, understanding, helpfulness, and happiness on everyone you meet, wherever you go. How will this affect how they feel and behave with you?

When we avoid or block negative feelings, they only persist, usually at an unconscious level. In fact, they snowball and build up. They then come up time and time again in different situations and are expressed in different ways in our energy field. As the above paragraph illustrates, they get sprayed around at what we encounter in our lives. If we suppress, deny, or resist our feelings, the energy of the emotion stays stuck in our physical bodies, and it can wreak havoc on our psychological and physical health.

Using the ETT, we move *into* our fearful feelings. This can be painful and sometimes seemingly unbearable for a time. The temptation is to avoid this unpleasantness. The paradox is that if we allow ourselves to feel the discomfort, the pain will decrease as the feelings subside from our bodies. Why does this happen? The ETT works because **negative energy dissipates when resistance**

to it is given up. By fully embracing our feelings, there is no more negativity energizing them.

Think of it this way. Feelings usually arise as a response to something external in our experience. Examples are when someone feels frustrated over traffic because they will be late for a job interview or a mom feels annoyed when her son does not listen to her call to come down for dinner the first time.

Feelings that arise in response to the outside world happen to give us a message. Are we willing to listen to the message? We need to observe and allow the emotion to play out. Instead, we focus on the outside world, thinking thoughts like: Why is there always traffic when I have an interview? How many times do I have to call him to eat? Why won't he listen to me? I want him to stop playing video games. Then we aren't able to process our feelings. Processing requires mindful attention to our inner experience of the outside world. It requires listening to the message that emotions are telling us.

The message is saying, I have feelings that need to be healed. Start by defining the fear. For example, If I don't make it to the interview on time, I am a failure. If my son doesn't listen to me the first time I call him for dinner, he doesn't love me.

Even further underneath the fear—the hidden gift for growth—is: I could improve my planning for interviews. I could learn new and more effective ways to communicate with my son.

But instead of seeing these situations as opportunities for growth, many people would be frustrated by them and unable to pinpoint their fears. They would suppress, deny, or resist their feelings. By checking out of their feelings, they keep themselves stuck on the pause button.

Embracing negative feelings gives someone the freedom to accept and welcome all facets of living—the good and the not-so good. When they do, their life expands and deepens.

Peeling Away Layers of Ego and Pain

It takes time to let go of our illusory, egoic self, which is based on a separate identity from who we are as spiritual beings. It requires consistently facing our fears, which are rooted in the ego, and is a process of peeling away the layers at its core. Even when fears from the past have been dealt with, they may need more work. It's just about continuing to move through negativity until all the cobwebs of fear have been cleared up. This is the path to transformation because fear is the main obstacle to love and peace.

Daily processing of negative emotions will bring you to a place of healing. Catch yourself when you are defensive, angry, and resistant so you don't create additional negativity. Be patient with yourself and others. You may vacillate back and forth at points. Stay steadfast. Move into this task with self-compassion, dedication, faith, determination, and perseverance. Take as long as you need.

In embracing and facing our fears, we allow more of our spiritual self to emerge and a state of peace and love to blossom. Eventually, it is possible to transcend the ego, but it will take time.

God's world is a perfect world. Why not reside in this perfect world?

Get Out of the Way

Now that you understand *what* you are doing and *why* you are doing it, you are ready to learn *how* to put the Energy Transformation Technique to use in your life. First, let us review some points already discussed having to do with getting out of your own way.

1. Stop blaming other people for your feelings.
2. Realize that other people behave badly because they have negative energy inside that is feeding their outside behaviors.
3. Do not spend one ounce of energy thinking about or trying to change another person. You cannot change anyone else

unless they ask for your help. You can only work on changing yourself.

4. Remember that it takes two people to fight. When one person refuses to get involved in the negativity, the battle can't continue. Only each person can decide when they are ready to change.

5. Focus on yourself because you have profound work to do for yourself.

6. Realize on a deep level that anytime you have negative feelings about a person or situation, you are playing a part in the problem. It is up to you to examine your feelings and actions to discover the part you are playing.

7. Bring your focus back to yourself.

8. Notice that as you change, your relationships change.

How to Process Feelings and Find Freedom

Below, we outline the steps of the Energy Transformation Technique. It is a very useful approach to processing your feelings. Before you engage in the technique, you must first focus on and identify what you are feeling.

1. When upset with someone or something, say to yourself: This is not about X; this is about me. It will help you look at yourself rather than the other person or situation. Take responsibility for feeling the way you are feeling. Examine what you are feeling. Look at the fear list to help you label a fear. Here are some questions you can ask to help you identify and connect to what you are feeling. Do I feel:

   - That there is something I want that I'm not getting?
   - Put down?
   - Unloved?
   - Out of control?
   - Disrespected?

- Threatened (unsafe)?
- Used (taken advantage of)?
- Loss?
- Helpless?
- Lonely?
- Inadequate?
- Grief?
- Betrayed?
- Rejected?
- Mistreated?

2. Sit or lie down, and close your eyes. Keep looking inside until you can label what you are feeling. More than one feeling may emerge. Just focus on the main feeling for now. (This technique is best when you work with one emotion at a time.) You can deal with the other feelings later. Notice *where* in your body it feels like the painful emotion is located.

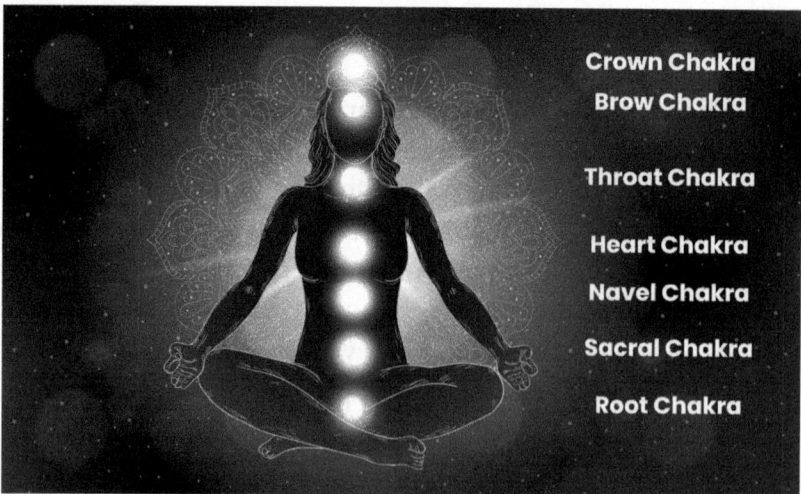

Crown Chakra
Brow Chakra

Throat Chakra

Heart Chakra

Navel Chakra

Sacral Chakra

Root Chakra

3. The body has chakras or energy/spiritual centers responsible for helping it function in an optimal state. Many

painful emotions are located around two chakras—the solar plexus, right below the sternum, and the throat chakra—but be prepared because they can pop up anywhere in your body. You can do this same exercise when you feel afraid—pinpoint the area where you are feeling fear and label it (e.g., loss, betrayal, humiliation).

4. Next, focusing on the area in your body where you seem to feel either the emotion or fear, ask yourself some questions to help you fully connect to it:

   - How deep is the feeling?
   - Is it sharp or dull?
   - On a scale of 1 to 10, with 10 being the most intense, how intense would you rate the feeling?
   - What shape is it?
   - Is it moving or still?
   - If a color, what would it be?
   - Is it smooth or rough?
   - Is it hot or cold?

5. While going through the above process of thoroughly describing the feeling (size, color, texture), see if you can enlarge the feeling in your mind's eye. This allows you to dig more thoroughly into the feeling and experience it with more acute intensity. It gives you the ability to stay focused on embracing your feelings.

6. After you have described the feeling for yourself, take a deep breath, focus on the upset feeling, stay with it, and lean into it fully. A part of you may be averse to experiencing negative emotion in the same way as you would avoid touching a hot stove. Your feelings are not a hot stove. Accept that it is entirely all right that the feeling exists within you.

7. Accept the feeling without any resistance. It helps to think of embracing the emotion in the same way that you would

lovingly hold and comfort a crying baby. As a child, you may have been told to "stop crying," "stop being angry," or "cheer up." It's time to let go of this programming and allow yourself to authentically feel whatever you are feeling. Allow yourself to build the confidence that you can handle it, one negative emotion at a time.

8. Keep breathing deeply and imagine that the feeling, in whatever shape and color you envision it to be, is growing even larger. Make the feeling as large as your body. Then make the feeling as large as the room.

9. Notice if the shape and color have changed. Take some more deep breaths and stay with the feeling. Watch for any changes that are occurring. What number is the intensity of the feeling now?

10. Imagine now that the feeling is getting gradually larger, as large as a city block, then imagine it is a square mile, then 10 miles, then the size of a city, state, country, continent, planet, and then the universe.

11. As you go through the enlargement process, you may notice that the intensity of feeling lessens, or its color or shape changes. Once the color has turned white and the intensity level is reduced to zero, you can stop and open your eyes. The energy has dissipated. If it has not, go through the technique again until it does.

When an emotion is resisted or suppressed, it becomes frozen and anchored within us. The Energy Transformation Technique is a very good method for processing our negative feelings once they come to our attention. It works because rather than resisting the feeling (or fear), we allow it to be there. We move into it and not away from it. In this way, the energy isn't healed as much as it just disappears because we no longer hold on to it by avoiding it.

Bringing our attention to the emotion gives it the space to run its course. When we allow the expression of the emotion, we connect to a space that enables the feeling to dissipate to a Higher Power. Like a soap bubble, it floats in the space of consciousness until it bursts and disappears. We let it go, along with the fight, blame, and control.

The more this technique is practiced, the easier and more automatic it becomes. When you regularly use it to process negative feelings, more and more fear and hostile energy will be emptied from your body. Eventually, there will come a day when you notice that you are not negatively reacting to what is said or done anymore. You feel lighter and can connect to yourself more profoundly because so many emotional landmines will have been removed. You have become an observer of what is going on rather than a reactor.

Avoiding Feelings through Defenses

If you find it difficult to get in touch with your feelings, it may be helpful to look at what defenses you have employed to keep your fears in place. Defenses are used to avoid fear and other uncomfortable feelings. Most people use defenses. Until a person can become aware of theirs and stop using them, they will continue to suffer because defenses keep them from getting in touch with their feelings and solving problems.

People acquire certain defenses in childhood. Children watch their parents use defenses and then copy them when protecting themselves from their own fears and painful feelings. Sometimes, a child will observe a parent using a defense, and the child will consciously decide that they don't want to act that way. Instead of arguing, the child will resist fighting or not stand up for themselves just to avoid a fight. In other words, the child sometimes chooses the opposite behavior from that of a parent.

Defenses are usually unconscious. For example, Connie called a friend on the phone to ask about a problem she was having with her landlord. As her friend was giving her some ideas about how to handle the situation, Connie changed the subject. When

Connie's friend called her attention to it, she didn't even realize she had changed the subject. Connie used an escape defense to avoid her feelings about dealing with her landlord.

Identifying Defenses

People avoid dealing with their fears and other feelings by not being consciously aware of them as problems. Alternatively, someone may occasionally think about when they are hurt, feel the discomfort, and visualize their fear, but they do not think about how to resolve their problems. The person may feel their anger, feel their negative feelings, and want to feel better, yet does nothing to address the situation. It is just easier to shut down and avoid having to deal with anything.

When someone is defensive and uses excuses to avoid unpleasant feelings, there is no way they will be able to change. No one can transform their lives until they are ready to give up their defenses. Usually, people use either more hostility defenses or more escape defenses. Most employ some of both but consistently uses the same ones.

Examine the lists below and identify which ones you use.

Hostility Defenses—Fight

Anger	Rage
Resentment	Irritation
Annoyed	Frustration
Hurt	Bugged
Upset	Defiance
Sarcasm	Aggression
Impatience	Rebelliousness

Escape Defenses—Flight

Lying (rationalization and making excuses)	Alcohol, Drugs, Smoking
Procrastination and Indecisiveness	Escape by using food, sex, work, shopping
Daydreaming	Distractions
Deception	Denial
Fantasizing	Sarcasm
Excessive sleeping	Hiding

Other Ways to Escape

Intellectualizing

Rationalizing

Making excuses

Saying they don't have time

Refusing to work on the issue

Denying they are part of the problem

Staying addicted to past behaviors (habits)

Being lazy

Refusing to listen

Blaming others

Isolating

Giving Up Defenses

To change defensive behaviors, sometimes it's necessary to do the opposite of what you have been doing. Some examples of this follow.

Instead of:

Looking outside yourself, examine what is going on within you

Talking, be quiet

Thinking, still your mind
Blaming, take responsibility
Hating, be loving
Trying to be powerful, be humble
Needing to be right, admit you do not know
Wanting to get even, get over it
Procrastinating, take an action
Expecting others to make you happy, make yourself happy

One thing we can do to stop being defensive is to use affirmations to direct the unconscious mind to help us stop being defensive. For example, I am now aware of any time that I am defensive.

Another method to give up defenses is to make a list of your typical ones. Then, each night, take a few minutes to review your behavior that day. Check for when you were upset or uncomfortable because that will give you a clue about when you have been defensive. Next, examine your behavior and make a note of what defenses you used. Then go over what you could have done differently if you hadn't been defensive. For example, you could have:

Stopped the defensive behavior
Listened to what was being said
Kept quiet and examined your feelings
Asked questions to get more information
Examined the other person's viewpoint
Compromised
Faced the truth
Admitted you were wrong
Been kind and calm

It takes some time and practice to give up being defensive. We have employed our defenses most of our lives. As we become more aware, review our behavior, and practice daily, we will become less defensive. This allows us to get in touch with the real problem, our fear. Then we can begin to heal the feelings that were caused by fear. As we progress, the pain and discomfort of daily life diminish, and fewer negative situations come up.

Helen's Rationalizing

Helen often operated out of her defenses, so she either rationalized away whatever happened in her life or she used it as an excuse for her anger. This kept her from taking responsibility and making changes.

Coming from an unhappy childhood, Helen didn't feel loved by either of her parents. Her mother punished her by hitting her with whatever was easiest to grab. Helen felt like she was in trouble most of the time and learned how to lie, rationalize, and distort the truth skillfully. The sad part was that she became so good at it that she no longer knew the difference between the truth and what she was making up.

Helen would rationalize anything—putting off chores, not getting a job, why someone didn't like her and why she didn't have any money, pay her bills, or return phone calls—that she viewed as unpleasant. She became a serial talker and an extremely poor listener. As long as she was talking, it felt like she was dodging a problem. It didn't matter if what she said made sense or if there was a purpose for the words. What she said was uninteresting, boring, filled with excuses, and meaningless much of the time. Due to her unwillingness to let her defenses go, it was difficult to improve her life.

Helen also had difficulty getting along with people, such as her daughter, sister, co-workers (when she had a job), boyfriends, and relatives. She couldn't see that she was the one causing the problems—she blamed everyone else, which fed her anger. It felt normal to her because it was the same kind of conflict as when she grew up.

Still, Helen was unwilling to face the truth of how her behavior pushed others away, kept her from having a good job, and prevented her from having love and lasting relationships. The upsets and issues in these areas kept her distracted as she tried to make sense of what was happening. She didn't have a clue because of how good she was at avoiding responsibility and failing to acknowledge any part she played in problems. It was much later that she learned how much she disliked herself. Helen hid this fact by telling herself and others how smart and capable she was every chance she got.

She would sometimes work on self-improvement and then she'd quit for long periods. She'd do some more work for a while but make little headway. She kept clinging to her protective defenses of rationalization, excuses, anger, and creating confusion. Helen would take one step forward and two steps back. This went on for years and years.

Finally, more recently, she reached bottom and lost all her possessions and friends. The pain became so bad that it caused her to go to professional counseling and slowly make some real progress. She became more aware of her excessive talking and defensive behavior and began to think more about what she was about to say. Instead of trying to protect herself all the time, she started to think about others more. She became more consistent, meditated daily, and stayed focused on what she wanted to accomplish, learning to be more honest and responsible.

Helen's relationships slowly improved because she learned to stop saying things to people that angered them and pushed them away. She stopped manipulating people to get what she wanted and became more straightforward and truthful. Whenever she felt upset, she consistently accepted her emotional pain. Helen finally realized that pain is her friend, which motivated her to be consistent about doing her inner work. Soon she saw her transformation process as a work in progress and was willing to take it one day at a time as she continued to improve.

Common Obstacles to Successfully Using the ETT

Besides the list of defenses above, there are two common obstacles to successfully using the ETT: **staying in our heads** and **being unable to focus on our own emotions**. The first, staying in our heads, means having obsessive thoughts about an upsetting situation at hand. We may be in the habit of relying on our *thinking* processes to solve our problems with other people and find it challenging to shift the focus from the other person back to us. We may be so used to being in our heads and obsessing about what someone did and what they are thinking that it may be a challenge even to identify what we are feeling.

To get out of your head, focus your attention on where you are experiencing negative emotions in the body. If you can't identify the fear, look at the list of fears in this book and examine which fear most closely describes your feelings. With continued practice, you will become good at identifying your fears, even without the fear list. If this part is challenging, get some guidance from a coach or professional counselor.

The second common obstacle to the ETT is being unable to focus on our own emotions. This most often occurs because we are blaming others. This typically happens when emotional triggers are activated during a conversation or other interaction.

Someone is triggered during an interaction because the other person(s) is right there. It seems like the other person's actions are directly responsible for their negative feelings. It's like a cause-and-effect relationship. It appears that others are the cause, so people must blame them for the effect because that is their experience.

Samantha Blames Jorge for Her Feelings

Jorge and Samantha are married, and Samantha does almost all the cooking for the family, except when they go out to eat or order in. Samantha was out shopping with friends one day and lost track of time. It was past dinner time when she came home, and there wasn't much to eat in the fridge. Jorge was hungry and yelled angrily at Samantha for being late and not having his dinner ready on time. Samantha got upset because she felt unappreciated and unloved. She blamed Jorge for her feelings and told herself she would leave him and stop being a "slave in the kitchen" once their children were grown.

Why would it benefit Samantha to refrain from blaming Jorge for her upset feelings in this situation? Samantha has no control over Jorge. No one can change others without their consent. Blaming keeps Samantha at a psychological dead-end of unhappiness.

Blame

There is no way out of this unhappy state without giving up blame. Blaming others for their emotions is one of the greatest illusions entrapping most people in a cycle of pain and suffering. Blame is based on the idea that we are powerless and at the mercy of outside factors that are the cause of our fears and feelings. Logically then, blame leads us to think we have to change people and environments outside of ourselves to feel better. We will suffer in unhappiness as long as we continue to blame others and refuse to deal with our thinking and feelings.

Here's another reason why blame is entirely futile. Blame falsely affirms that we have no choices in situations. We do have choices. We can choose how to react to a situation and how to perceive it. This means that external factors are not the entire "cause" of our experience. Our reaction to the outside world is almost entirely based on how we perceive it. Samantha could interpret Jorge's anger in many ways, including as a cry for help (i.e., he feels unloved and neglected), which could elicit an empathy response from her rather than evoke anger and plans for future relationship dissolution. Her perception is her choice. This means, therefore, that the key to our happiness is inside of us and how we perceive the world.

Look within when you have negative feelings, no matter how difficult and tempting it may be to only look at other people. Refrain from blaming someone else so that you can focus on processing your negative emotions and set yourself free from them. The less you blame others, the less power people and external factors will have over your life. You will no longer be the leaf that is easily shaken by a little wind but the trunk that stands strong and weathers any storm. Instead of looking to change the world so you can feel better, a better strategy is to be a living example of how you'd like the world to be.

To help you redirect your attention away from focusing on and blaming others and connect to your feelings, do the following:

- Examine what happened in your experience that upset you. Identify your negative feelings.
- Ask yourself what fears you have that keep recurring in the relationship.
- Do you have a fear that stops you from doing what you need to do to resolve the problem? What is the fear?
- Do you feel like something is missing in the relationship? What is missing?
- Are you hanging onto an ideal or expectations of the person that are causing you unhappiness?
- What feelings are you having difficulty embracing and processing?
- Are you in denial? Are you refusing to see what the person is doing or who they really are?

Process before Engaging with Others

Why focus on processing our emotions *first* before engaging with others instead of immediately engaging or telling the other person what we think and what they are doing wrong?

It does not help, in a heated situation, to tell people that they are wrong. The behavior of Jorge is a good example. He felt unimportant and unloved because Samantha was late and did not think of him. Instead of dealing with his emotions, he became filled with anger and poured it out on Samantha with unkind words. Did it help? Clearly not. It was like pouring gasoline on a fire. It only made things worse. People have a hard time listening to others when they are angry or upset. They want to protect themselves, often become defensive, and tell you how *you* are wrong. It becomes a contest of who is right and who is wrong as they duel in the Pain Pit. Why continue the argument when it only makes things worse?

We can only work to change ourselves. We are in the situation because we have something to learn. **The energy inside of us is attracting the experience in the first place.** It is not our job to harp on other people's faults. People cannot truly make us feel happy or unhappy. All perceptions and emotions reside within us. We must turn inside to the source of the issue to move toward change and healing.

The source of all the feelings, emotions, perceptions, thoughts, and projections is *you*. Therefore, focus on yourself. Use the ETT. After you have balanced the energy within you, you can then take any necessary actions on the outside to resolve any matter calmly and harmoniously. After you process your feelings, you may find that you no longer feel upset, and it turns out there is nothing to address. It was all in how you were looking at it.

Sometimes, we may find that we do need to discuss a situation with whomever triggered the feelings. But after the ETT, we will find ourselves calmer and more balanced during the discussion. If the conversation triggers us again, there are more layers to work on and more ETT work to be done. We continue to process the negative feelings, releasing and peeling away the layers of fear. Gradually, we notice that the intensity of pain is diminishing as we shift the focus from others to ourselves. One day, we may even notice that the emotional trigger is gone.

Are You a Doormat?

Whenever anyone is criticizing or mistreating us, not respecting us, or arguing, it is our job to observe what is going on and not react.

Do not allow upset energy to get inside of you by reacting. As someone who practices energy transformation regularly, you will become more of an observer of life. In the beginning, you may think it is impossible not to react in the face of someone yelling and criticizing you. If you become the observer and just watch what is going on, you can avoid your negative response. In some cases, you may want to remove yourself from the situation. Don't try to make sense out of non-sense.

This does not mean that we should not stand up for ourselves or become a doormat for people to walk on. No, it does not mean that at all. The point is that reacting negatively only throws *us* off balance and sends us into the Pain Pit. Nothing can be resolved with yelling, fighting, and arguing. The raging person is not able to see clearly and be reasonable. Effective action only occurs when we are detached, balanced, and fully aware of what we want to accomplish

Sometimes it is necessary to change the people we live with or our business associates, friends, clubs, or other groups. This will be much easier to do when our energy is not matching their energy. The truth is that we can only get away from negativity once our energy is no longer a match. When we leave a person or situation yet have not changed ourselves, our energy will only attract the same types of people or conditions. Why would anyone want to deal with people that are continually causing problems?

Most people don't want to hear what they should do or how they need to change. Each person will change only when they are ready. Pain is a huge motivator for making changes. Without pain, we would all keep doing what we have been doing.

Instead of telling people what to do, be an example and let your behavior demonstrate who you are. You can't be a role model by trying to influence or coerce others to change. Wait for others to ask you questions before giving unsolicited advice, and just be an example. Watch your thoughts to see if you are supportive or harmful to others. The goal is to learn to become an observer and accept others.

Moving toward Peace by Not Reacting

Processing negative emotions is a tool to be used as a way of life. When approached this way, people find they have fewer and fewer negative feelings to process in response to life. Eventually, the negative energy within will be emptied and replaced by positive energy such as feeling peaceful. The job is to be aware of feelings and process negative emotions whenever they surface.

The next step in transformation goes to a deeper level than processing feelings with the ETT. The next level involves *observing* everything that happens in life to achieve more balance and harmony. This requires more conscious awareness and more dedication. It requires giving up the need for others to be a certain way. It becomes easier to say, "It doesn't matter," because now there is the realization that no one has the power to do anything about any person or condition in the world that causes upset in the first place.

When energy transformation and being an observer are an ongoing part of your life, your focus and behavior become more about staying balanced, giving to others, being helpful, and extending love. At this level, you learn how to provide for your own emotional needs from within and from a connection to your spiritual life and God. Remember, **like energy attracts like energy**. If we are kind, considerate, and loving, we will attract those qualities. Imagine how the world would change if only half of the people lived this way.

Next are stories of individuals who successfully used the Energy Transformation Technique.

Stories of Using the Energy Transformation Technique

The story of Anne and Ryan is an example of a couple who employed the ETT method. The story also illustrates a typical session, which includes identifying problems and how they are being dealt with, along with suggestions on how Anne could address her behavior. Also, fear and how to process the energy of fear and negative emotions are discussed. Most importantly, this case provides us with an opportunity to see how Anne was able to make changes and deal with her life, resulting in more happiness.

Anne and Ryan Marry Then Disconnect

Anne and Ryan have been married for seven years. Anne is 65, and Ryan is 72. Neither of them has children. They had known each other for many years and used to be close, but they had drifted apart. When they got back in touch again, they really hit it off this time and decided to get married. Anne moved from New York City to Florida to live with Ryan.

Anne was immediately unhappy living in Florida. She hated the hot, humid weather, and she missed her friends in New York, complaining about it every day. Ryan didn't have any sympathy for Anne and thought she should get over it. After all, they lived in a beautiful home overlooking the ocean. Their house was new, and it had air-conditioning, a hot tub, a swimming pool, and all the comforts anyone could imagine.

Ryan had never been married before, so starting a marriage at 72 was a huge change for him. After living alone, he was used to being independent, and it was not easy for him to live with another person.

Anne had been married before for twenty years but was divorced. She had been single for eighteen years before she married Ryan. Moving away from her home and friends was also a huge change for Anne.

Married, Anne and Ryan each have their own bedroom and cook their own food. For the first couple of months, things went fairly well. But soon, Ryan began criticizing Anne for numerous things. He told her he was sorry he married her and didn't love her. Ryan also complained that she wasn't a good cook, didn't put things in the drawers correctly, talked too much, and didn't respect their privacy. All in all, he had thought she would be different.

Anne complained that Ryan was cold, distant, didn't respect her, and was unappreciative of what she did for him. She felt that she couldn't do anything right in his eyes. Anne didn't think that she loved Ryan and looked forward to the time she could leave him and move back to New York City. Due to finances, she couldn't do that right away.

Anne spent her time connecting with her friends through the Internet and telephone and constantly dreaming about being back in New York, going to the theater, and enjoying her friends. When it was hot, Anne complained about the weather every day and talked about how much she hated living in Florida.

Ryan and Anne attracted each other into their lives. Each of them could learn many things from their marriage if they took advantage of the opportunity. The problems they were encountering didn't start when they got married. Both were unhappy before, but they blamed their unhappiness on other things. Ryan was lonely and had problems getting along with girlfriends. Anne had money and relationship problems as well.

They blamed each other, and both felt they would be happier if they weren't married. Neither one was looking for a solution other than to escape from the other. The real problem was within them. Anne wanted Ryan to seek help, but he refused. He believed he had all the right answers and wasn't open to getting any help. Anne asked if I would help her. When I agreed, we began working together immediately.

First, I asked Anne, "Are you ready to make a commitment to work on yourself and, in the meantime, stay in the marriage for at least six months?" Anne readily agreed.

Next, I told her, "I want you to stop blaming Ryan and Florida for your unhappiness and take responsibility for what is going on and how you feel. Focus on working on yourself and realize that this is a process, so it will not change overnight."

Like many people, Anne had never dealt with her fears and the negative energy within her. She had always looked for something or someone outside herself to solve her problems, and it hadn't worked. Her issues won't be resolved until Anne deals with what is going on inside her. When I explained this to Anne, she agreed to work this way.

First, Anne was shown how to meditate and asked to do so every day, 10 minutes in the morning and 10 minutes before bed. At this point, it was also crucial for Anne to avoid thinking any negative thoughts because they create more negative energy. This required her to be aware of what she was thinking.

Anne shared more details about her life, past relationships, and more data about her relationship with Ryan, which was useful when more problems surfaced. Anne was also asked to deal with other people and situations that caused her to feel angry and defensive. Even though she was working to stop blaming and being angry at Ryan, I explained to Anne that if she continued being angry and defensive with other people and situations, it would build more negativity inside of her and would get in the way of making any progress.

Anne was taught how important it is to stay focused in the present, which keeps us in our power. I told her, "We are powerless when we are thinking about the past or the future unless it has to do with some action we can take in the present."

I also shared with Anne: "Anger is a defense we use to avoid feeling our fears. You need to get past the anger and in touch with your fears so you can process them and let them go. If you start feeling those negative emotions again, it means there is more negative energy to be processed. Normally, negative emotions will come up repeatedly. Continue processing all of the negative feelings until they stop coming up. How long it takes depends on how much fear and negative energy you have.

"If you do not stop being defensive and entering the Pain Pit, you will continue to create more negativity and keep having to process those feelings. If you are diligent about getting in touch with negative emotions and overcoming the temptation to climb into the Pain Pit, your progress toward healing will go faster. Don't be concerned about how long it will take, be willing to take however much time is required. It is different with every person and with every situation."

It was a lot for anyone to digest. Anne admitted she would need to practice and go back over these ideas several times. It is natural for it to take time to practice and become familiar with new ways of thinking and responding. It's like learning to drive. Someone doesn't master it the first time they get behind the wheel. I told Anne to be patient with herself and aware if and when she is not practicing the steps correctly.

Just telling herself to stop being angry at Ryan or anyone else wouldn't work. Anne had to learn to accept her fears, anger, and negative energy. It was the negative energy that caused the cycle to continue.

It was not easy for Anne to accept that it was *her* fears, *her* energy, that were causing *her* unhappiness. Anne had to learn that a person's energy attracts situations and people into their life that perfectly matches that energy.

"Our job now is for you to identify the fears and feelings you are experiencing when you are unhappy," I explained. Then I went on, asking Anne, "What defenses have you been using to hide from your fears?" Anne was able to see how she had been using anger, blame, and judgment to escape from her pain.

Anne started to see how she put all the blame on Ryan while telling herself how she would be happy if he were different. She believed that if he would stop criticizing her, be more helpful, more loving, everything would be all right. She kept telling herself that if she lived in New York and could be with her friends, then she would be happy. Anne had to understand that happiness comes from within, it is not in a place, and no one can get it from another person.

One day, Anne admitted, "I didn't realize that I was the one causing so many of these problems." Once Anne understood this, she needed to practice this new way of thinking and behaving. She would automatically want to act and think in the old way for a while. Instead, she had to become consciously aware of what she was doing and thinking. Whenever Anne found herself behaving in the old ways, she learned to stop and spend time alone to go over what she wanted to change. Gradually Anne would be able to let go of her fear and negative feelings. Once Anne understood that she was responsible for her experience, she started identifying her fear.

The following is an example of how Anne and I would dialogue about Anne's feelings. Eventually, **you can do this dialogue for yourself** as your ability to observe within becomes stronger.

To begin, I asked Anne, "Sit back in the chair, close your eyes and focus inside your body. Notice any place where you feel pain or any uncomfortableness. Can you get in touch with what you feel when Ryan criticizes you?"

Anne took a couple of minutes and said, "I feel that I am not loved. It hurts here in my solar plexus."

Next, I asked Anne to give the unloved feeling a number between 1 and 10, with 10 being the most painful?" Anne said it was a 10.

"Stay with that feeling and tell me more. How deep does it feel?"

"It feels like it is about three inches deep."

"Is it hard or soft?"

"It is hard."

"If it had a shape, what shape would it be?"

"It is shaped like a baseball with bumps on it."

"Does this baseball feel like it is hot or cold?"

"It feels very cold."

"If it had a color, what color would it be?"

"It is dark gray."

Then I directed Anne, "Stay with the feeling and make the feeling even bigger. Make it as big as your body in your mind."

"Ok, it is as big as my body."

"Good, now stay with the feeling and embrace the feeling. Make it even bigger, make it as large as this room, and take a deep breath." After a minute, Anne nodded yes. "Now make the feeling as large as a two-story house. Check and see if the color and shape have changed."

"The size is more like a golf ball, and the color has changed to a lighter gray."

"Great, now make it as large as a square mile."

Anne took a couple of minutes and then told Evelyn, "It is that big."

"Now make it as large as five miles square and stay with the feeling." Anne nodded yes again.

"Make it as large as the city of Los Angeles. Has anything else changed?"

Anne said, "Now it is the size of a marble, the color is light gray, and the feeling is becoming more comfortable."

"What number would you give the unloved feeling now?"

"A two."

I answered, "Good, now make the feeling even larger. Make it as large as the state of California." Anne nodded.

"Now make it as large as the United States. How has the unloved feeling changed, and how does it feel now?"

Anne answered, "It's gone, the feeling is gone, and it's a white color." Then she opened her eyes and said, "I can't believe the feeling is gone."

In this way, Anne learned to process her fears and negative feelings. As the weeks went on, anytime an uncomfortable feeling came up, she processed it exactly as she had done with me. Some of the other emotions and fears Anne worked on were feeling unaccepted, unimportant, helpless, worthless, and rejected.

Soon Ryan was a little less critical. When he started to criticize

Anne, she watched him and listened to what he said while observing herself and how she was reacting and feeling. Sometimes, when she got upset, she would start to react by talking back to him. Then, she realized what she was doing and instead went to her room to review what happened and process the negative feelings that had come up. Anne confessed, "The hardest part for me is not to react when Ryan is criticizing me. I get upset and react the old way before I can catch myself."

It started getting easier, but she had to continue to practice. As I explained: "You have been defensive most of your life, and it takes time to break the old habits. It is a process that requires practice to master. Observe yourself closely and notice when you are being defensive and reacting to Ryan. Continue processing your feelings every day when negative emotions come up. Gradually, you will feel less pain and will react less to others. Ryan will notice that you are not reacting emotionally. He will feel the difference. When being critical is no longer getting him the benefit of a reaction from you, he will gradually change his behaviors."

Anne continued to process her feelings and just observed Ryan more and more when he acted out rather than fighting back. Other areas of her life improved as she accepted responsibility and practiced her new behaviors. She knew that her emotional freedom was a work in progress. She made new friends in Florida and stopped daydreaming about being in New York City. Anne couldn't believe that it took her until that point in her life to learn how to deal with her fears. When she learned to keep focused on the present and be more accepting of herself and others, Anne and Ryan became happier.

How Harry Attracted What Matched His Fear

We can tell if our energy is negative or positive by the experiences we are attracting and what we are feeling. Here is an example of what Harry was attracting, how he dealt with it, and how it matched his fear and negative energy.

Harry had a small business and worked in the field most of the time, so he was rarely in the office. He had a secretary, but she wasn't doing a good job. Often, she didn't answer the phone and would let the answering machine pick up the calls. When Harry unexpectedly showed up, she would be talking on her cell phone on a private call. She didn't call customers to remind them to pay their bills. Harry was upset and frustrated with her. It was causing him a lot of stress. He had had similar problems with previous secretaries.

Harry came to see me and explained his problem. I asked him, "How does it make you feel that your secretary isn't doing her work properly?"

"It makes me upset, and sometimes I feel angry," replied Harry.

I explained that his anger was a defense that he was using to avoid feeling his deeper emotions. "What are your feelings under the anger?" I asked.

Harry answered, "I don't know."

I began to use the ETT process with Harry to help him connect to the feelings in his body and tell her what he was feeling. He told me, "I feel tight in my stomach and chest."

"Do you feel rejected, disrespected, unimportant, or helpless?" I asked.

"I feel helpless to get her to do what I want. I feel disrespected."

I directed Harry to go inside his body to where he felt tight and asked, "Can you connect to what it feels like to feel helpless?" He replied, "A little bit."

"Good, just stay with that feeling and see if you can feel it even more." Harry was able to feel the helpless feeling a little more.

Then, I told him to shut his eyes, take a deep breath, and feel that tight and helpless feeling even more. "Where do you feel the feeling?"

"Mostly in my stomach."

"How deep is the feeling?"

"In the middle part of my stomach."

"How large is it?"

"The size of a grapefruit."

"What shape is it?"

"It is round."

"Is it hard or soft?"

"Hard."

"If it had a color, what color would it be?"

After a minute, Harry said, "It is a brownish-black."

I then guided Harry to make the brownish-black, round, hard ball in the middle of his stomach bigger, as big as he is, and let me know when he had accomplished that.

After a moment, Harry told me, "It's as big as me."

Then I asked him to make it progressively bigger in his mind's eye, first as big as the room, then as big as a two-story house, and a square block. Harry nodded yes to each.

"Now check to see if anything has changed," I told him.

"The color is lighter. It's a gray color. It is lighter, and it's the size of a cherry, and it feels softer."

"Good, now stay with that feeling, take a deep breath, and make it even bigger. Make it as large as a square mile."

In a couple of minutes, Harry said, "Ok, it is that big."

"Make it as large as New York City."

Harry nodded yes and said, "The feeling is gone, and the color is clear."

When Harry opened his eyes, I explained that he had gone through an exercise of processing his feeling of helplessness and that helplessness is a fear he had been carrying with him since he was a child. By fully embracing the feeling and allowing it to be there, the energy dissipated and disappeared.

I went on to explain that, sometimes, it may be necessary to keep making a feeling even larger—continuing to expand it to as large as a state, then half of the United States, moving onto as large as North America, enlarging it into two continents, making it as big as the world, and finally, the universe. (I have never had anyone go as large as the universe.) I told Harry, "If the feeling is not gone by then, you are not doing the exercise properly."

"Whenever you are feeling upset, angry, or have any other uncomfortable feeling, then try to be alone as soon as possible, and do this exercise. Identify the underlying feeling. The next feeling, I want you to process is disrespect. Practice the technique on this one as your homework." He left the office feeling more relaxed.

Harry continued to work on processing his feelings. I discovered that Harry had not learned how to direct other people. During his work life, he had either been in positions where he had been told what to do or been self-directed. Harry lacked the right words for giving others directions. Instead, he would ask them questions: "Why didn't you do that?" "What took you so long?" "How come you can't do what I tell you?" These questions only got him excuses as answers.

To help Harry transition to telling his employees what he wanted instead of asking them questions, I role-played with Harry, pretending to be him and talking to him as if he was his secretary. Harry did homework by writing down in advance what he would say to direct his employee to do what he wanted. In the sessions, as role play continued, Harry became very efficient at being able to ask clearly for what he wanted rather than ask questions and complain.

In a few weeks, Harry was feeling more confident and relaxed. One day, one of his customers told him she had a friend looking for a job as a secretary. Harry interviewed her and hired her. She turned out to be excellent. Harry had worked out his fears, and his energy was a better match with excellence now. Harry felt pleased.

Every Relationship is a Gift

Harry had been unable to identify and feel his feelings of helplessness. But this energy and fear were still inside of him. He needed to attract experiences and people into his life to help him release his energy of helplessness. His previous secretary was a match in the things she did to trigger the release of Harry's energy of feeling helpless and disrespected.

Unbeknownst to Harry and his secretary, they were unconsciously a team working together to allow Harry an opportunity to activate and release his energy. Whatever energy and fear Harry had internally would attract people or situations that caused him to express the energy he had within. This is a principle that works in all areas of everyone's life.

Both Harry and Anne's stories show that our most problematic relationships are gifts. If the emotions they engender are processed correctly, they can free us from our blocks and defenses. The ETT offers this process. With practice and awareness, all relationships will eventually be seen as wonderful opportunities for emotional and energetic freedom.

Summary of the Process for Change

Let's summarize what you have learned so far. To enact change, you need to be motivated and direct your desires toward transformation. It requires you to invest time and energy in becoming aware of your emotions so you can clear them away, thereby allowing for the development of your spiritual self.

Daily, focus on what emotions are evoked by what occurs in your life. Stay out of your head, take responsibility for your feelings, and avoid blaming others for them. Allow the fears to be there and process them by facing your fears.

To get started, you can:

1. Identify your most significant problem area.
   - Who or what is causing you the greatest unhappiness and the most pain?
   - What are you afraid of?
   - What fuels your anger the most?
2. Identify your fears and the defenses you are using to defend them. As long as you are using negative defensive behavior, the problems will not be healed.

3. Identify your negative emotions, such as feeling unloved or unimportant, fearing disapproval, or being powerless.

4. Practice processing these negative emotions with the ETT every day for as long as it takes for them to start dissipating from your everyday experience.

5. Take 100% responsibility for what is going on in your life.

PART II

The Ongoing Process of Transformation

CHAPTER 6

Opportunities to Transform Your Emotions Are Everywhere

The transition from living a life focused on the external world to one of looking inward does not happen overnight. Transformation is not about making changes in a day, a week, or even a month. Life is always in flux, and nothing ever stays the same. So, we must ask the question, Is my life getting better or worse? Transformation is about making a daily commitment to learning and improving your life.

Here are some steps that are helpful for the transformation process.

1. Commit to change.
2. Practice awareness.
3. Process your negative feelings with the ETT.
4. Recognize when you are becoming upset.
5. Listen to others and hear them out.
6. Have no judgment and blame toward others because of your negative feelings.
7. Stop reacting, arguing, and defending.
8. Observe your physical, social, and work environment instead of reacting.
9. Strive to be the embodiment of calm and peace.
10. Plan and take action only when you are calm.
11. Meditate regularly.

Here in Part II, I discuss the ongoing work of transformation, how life presents us with many opportunities and lessons that promote this work, and how to look at the mind and its beliefs. The goal is to be able to observe and deal with outside situations without reacting negatively. Instead, strive to consistently respond in a way that brings light, positivity, and healing into every situation and relationship.

Repeating Lessons until We Get It

Life provides the gift of learning and advancement, so lessons for our emotional and spiritual growth come to us in many ways. We may experience the lessons in various ways, through people, places, our children, work, money, the in-laws, cheating, alcohol, drugs, or sex. The lessons can come in the form of any number of situations. The actors may be different, and the context may be varied, but the principles to be learned are the same. Until we know to process our emotions and our thoughts about them so that we understand the reasons for these lessons, we will repeat them in different ways and contexts until we learn them.

In other words, a person will keep attracting experiences until they finally get in touch with and release their negative feelings. The situation may concern money, cheating, criticism, jealousy, or even something different than what was experienced in previous relationships. Yet, they will feel the same level of pain and unhappiness as they did before until their inner fears and negative emotions are transformed. Their internal energy level is what has to change the outside experience. Until then, someone will continue to attract similar situations and be provided with more prime healing opportunities.

A person can pick new people with whom to have relationships, pack up and move to a new house, neighborhood, or even a new country. They can change schools or change jobs. But these changes will not fix what's going on within them. They will only help if they facilitate energy work somehow or if the decisions to change emerged as a result of new awareness, healing, and transformation. If they did not, and someone is changing the outside to run away or engage in avoidance, that person will continue to attract experiences and people that cause them to feel negative energy.

Although we may perceive many of our experiences as unfortunate events, in truth, they are healing opportunities and gifts. We may not completely understand why something keeps happening, and we don't need to since it will be revealed when the time is appropriate.

It is helpful to **have faith that every single thing in life comes to you for your good and as an opportunity for learning and betterment.** There are no exceptions, no matter how bad the outside events may seem.

As the adage goes, you can run away from everything except yourself.

Attracting the Same Energy Over and Over

The outside is a mirror of our insides.

Energy attracts matching energy. This is why we have to repeat lessons until we learn them. The energy of what we attract into our lives always matches our energy frequency. Negativity attracts negativity. Anger attracts anger. This principle is demonstrated daily by how what we attract or experience perfectly reflects our feelings. It is why we must remember that we will continue living at a specific vibrational energy level until we face our fears, thereby causing our energy to vibrate at a higher level.

People in a relationship match each other's energy in certain areas even if appearances suggest otherwise. They came together because they are similar in some categories. Their healing needs are complementary, like a lock and key. The relationship is there to provide healing opportunities for both individuals. It is up to each person to fully embrace and learn the lessons offered by the relationship—or they can choose not to.

For example, suppose a married couple gets a divorce because they argue and fight too much, and the breakup happens without them having learned any lessons from the relationship. In that case, each person will have to face the same lessons about getting along with a partner in a different context. They will still have to face and heal their fears related to marital discord, release the negative energy, and figure out how to get along in a new relationship. Once they have fully embraced the lessons, they will be free from the problem. The couple may or may not choose to continue their relationship. Either way, the relationship fulfills its purpose, and its gift is received.

Also, when we are in a relationship or marriage, the relationship itself has a certain level of energy and consciousness. The type of energy varies according to the two people, time, circumstances, and the situation. The relationship is a unique fusion and intermingling of what the people bring to it. If negativity emerges due to arguing and fighting (entering the Pain Pit), it brings the relationship's energy to a lower level.

Betty Let Go of the Need to Be Loved

Betty and Joe's relationship is an excellent example of how much can be learned from dealing with problems rather than running away from them.

Betty and Joe got married in their mid-30s after knowing each other for three months. It was the second marriage for each of them. At first, everything seemed wonderful. Then, gradually things began to deteriorate as Betty and Joe got to know each other better. Joe liked to drink more alcohol than Betty had realized. He also had problems going to sleep and would often stay up until 4 or 5 a.m., which created a problem in their small apartment for Betty because she had to get up early to go to work.

Joe worked at home so he could sleep until noon or later. A consultant for a sales company, Joe was a good salesman and an excellent public communicator. Betty learned how to become a better public speaker and writer from Joe. As a speaker, he could command the attention of hundreds of people in a room. Joe was funny, original, and successful in his business. Betty was surprised to discover how insecure Joe was behind the scenes and in his personal life. Some of the other problems were more difficult for her to cope with.

After being married for about a year, it became obvious that Joe was jealous of Betty, although he never admitted it. As Betty's talents developed, she became successful on TV, doing shows about celebrities and other famous personalities. Joe started to find things to argue about the night before Betty had to tape a TV show. He tormented Betty all night to make sure she didn't get any sleep. While she was going through the experience, Betty didn't understand why Joe was doing what he did. Years later, she gained more insight.

As Joe was growing up, his father was away from home for weeks at a time due to his work. His father was one of the men who helped build the atomic bomb. Joe's mother, Jane, was lonely with her husband gone so much. Joe and his mother grew closer. She would let Joe skip school so they could go to a movie together. She would visit Joe at his school and sit in his seat with him during class. Joe's sister was excluded from their rendezvous.

Joe loved the attention from his mother and would get very jealous and angry when his sister received any from her. The same type of possessive jealousy would be triggered years later with Betty whenever Joe felt her attention was diverted away from him. He demanded to have Betty's attention and to be number one just like he had been with his mother.

Betty and Joe lived in California, and his parents lived back East. Joe talked to his mother, Jane, privately every day on the phone. One night as they were lying in bed, Joe announced to Betty that his mother was coming to visit them for a week. Joe said, "If you hurt my mother, I will leave you." Joe's remark flabbergasted Betty, as she had never met his mother or talked to her.

Joe's mother, Jane, arrived the following week, and she and Betty were polite to each other. The next day, as the three of them were relaxing in the living room, Joe and his mother talked to each other without looking at Betty or including her in the conversation. They acted as if Betty did not exist, and Betty felt coldness and rejection from them.

Joe's mother went out to the patio off the living room and sat down. Soon afterward, Joe followed and sat close beside his mother. They talked and laughed with each other like they were boyfriend and girlfriend. Joe's mother rolled her pant legs up to her knees and put her feet up. A few minutes later, Joe rolled his pants legs up to his knees and put his feet up, just like his mother. They were mirroring each other as they continued with their private conversation.

For the next few days, Joe and his mother ignored Betty, and she became more and more unhappy. Betty felt completely devastated because it seemed that Joe didn't love her. It wasn't that she thought Joe had stopped loving her; she now realized he hadn't loved her in the first place. He couldn't be treating her this way if he truly loved her.

Betty cried and cried as she felt the pain of feeling unloved, and she immediately started going to counseling. Feeling unloved turned out to be one of Betty's main fears. It was important for her to feel loved by her family and her husband. It was the worst emotional pain she had felt in her life.

Betty continued to go to counseling to deal with her pain for the next year. Sometimes, Joe joined her. Finally, there was no more fighting between them, but they became more independent of each other. After a year passed, Betty and Joe were equally ready to end their marriage. They shared the same attorney, and Joe moved back East. Joe did call a few weeks later to say how much he missed her and would like to see her, but Betty told him she would like to leave things as they were.

Joe and her marriage to him was a catalyst for Betty to learn many things about herself and her unresolved pain. After the divorce, Betty didn't want to return to the dating scene, and it took more than twenty years for Betty to start dating again. She continued counseling. Betty realized how strong her need was to feel loved, special, important, and happy. She learned how to value herself more, process her feelings, and enjoy her own company. Betty finally understood that loving herself and others was more important than receiving it.

Life Changes When We Do

Someone's experience of relationships changes when, instead of focusing on the other party and trying to change them, they look at the source of their discontentment, focus on their own transformation, and do the work of processing their negative feelings. In this way, they can reach a higher level of consciousness by changing their beliefs, thoughts, and habits. After that, it is their choice whether to continue to be in a relationship or not. But usually, the relationship also has to change to match their new state of mind and energy and provide other opportunities to deal with their fears. If it doesn't change, like Betty, the person may choose to leave.

This doesn't mean that people should stay in violent or abusive relationships while doing the ongoing work of processing their negative feelings. It is best not to try to resolve problems that may not be fixable. Individuals in these relationships *should* leave and find a safe refuge to ensure their and their children's physical and psychological safety.

To avoid entering another violent or abusive relationship in the future, the individual will need to closely look within themselves and question *why* they entered this type of relationship in the first place. What fears, emotions, beliefs, and patterns are present? Before moving on to another relationship, healing must take place. Professional counseling may be necessary in this case.

Pain is Our Friend

It is up to you to decide when you have experienced enough pain. You have the power to change. When you have a strong desire to change how you live, you will have the opportunity to do so. It is like the saying, "When the student is ready, the teacher will appear." You will attract a person, find a book, have a dream, or be guided in some way to learn how to change your life. How much pain do you need to experience before you are willing to start processing your fears? What you choose to do *now* matters most.

Without pain, no one would change, so pain is our motivation and friend. Pain is telling us that something is wrong. It is up to you to find out what it is and how to change it.Suffering is due to non-acceptance. The personal self tries to avoid pain. When pain is accepted, the separation between pain and pleasure begins to break down. Physical and mental pain requires action. If the feelings of pain are resisted it results in more pain. If the feelings of pain are accepted, they become joy.

Happiness comes through awareness. Accepting pain, practicing non-resistance, and having courage and determination open the door to real happiness. You can release energies and obstacles by being with yourself, the I AM, the part of you that observes what is happening, understanding rather than judging, and allowing the truths behind the painful feelings to reveal themselves. It requires using your intelligence with diligence and precision to achieve this freedom. The mind can distort, exaggerate, anticipate, and project the past into the future and this results in pain. So, **if your utmost desire is to obtain your freedom from living a life filled with pain, be on high alert about what is happening within you.**

How do you know if something within you is crying for attention and healing? Your negative feelings are the perfect barometer to help gauge what needs tending. The following feelings have a very low vibration and indicate that something needs to be healed.

Guilt

Shame

Anger

Apathy

Grief

Hopeless

Blame

Being demanding

Humiliation

Despair

Jealousy

Helplessness

If you are experiencing any of these emotions, see them as an alarm bell. Process this negative energy by uncovering the fear behind them using the Energy Transformation Technique discussed in chapter 5.

Take Advantage of What Is Presented

Daily life provides numerous windows of opportunity—gifts in disguise—to process emotions and help the negative energy of the ego dissipate. Once someone is in the habit of processing their feelings, they may notice that their fears begin to dissipate, and they may not be experiencing such strong feelings in reaction to incidents as before. Unraveling fears is like going through the layers of an onion—they get smaller and smaller over time if we continue peeling it.

You can choose to transform your approach to life and how you see the world by incorporating emotional energy processing as a way of life. When anything triggers a negative emotion, come into conscious awareness and refrain from looking at it as an annoyance. Look at it as a signal to process what you are feeling and to grow.

Even when fears lessen, processing emotions will still be necessary occasionally because fears may manifest in more subtle ways. At this point, negative feelings and emotions play out in more covert ways and should be watched closely. Notice when you are reacting or feeling tension, unhappy, uncomfortable, or having negative feelings.

Look at everything daily life presents as an opportunity to heal—a magnificent chance to get in touch with your fears, process them, raise your consciousness, and liberate yourself. The ideal is to process any feelings right away because that is when they feel very present and raw. If you face your feelings right away, you can be free from having a cloud of negativity or feeling bad raining on you the rest of the day or beyond.

If circumstances prevent you from processing negative feelings right away, then do your processing as soon as possible or when you are alone. You could even set time aside in your calendar for that same evening to check in on the feelings and do any needed processing.

Processing Emotions as a Daily Routine

Many people have a routine of getting ready for bed when they wash and moisturize their face, brush their teeth, and shave. If we could use the same discipline and consistent effort in caring for our internal lives as we do for our bodies, we could make leaps of progress toward peace. We spend a lot of time caring for our bodies—drinking water, cooking, eating, shopping for food or clothes, dressing, doing laundry, exercising, and grooming. Our emotions and internal states are often left out of self-care behaviors. They deserve the same consistent attention that we pay to our bodies.

By setting aside even five to ten minutes each evening to examine your day and emotional world, you will see marked changes in yourself. Review the day and determine if you had any upsetting experiences, conflicts, or negative feelings. If you did, tune back into those feelings and process what comes up. By making emotional processing a habit and a part of a daily routine like brushing your teeth or shaving your face, you will be calmer, more balanced, and more in charge of your life.

During your evening review, here are some questions to ask yourself.

- Was I angry?
- Did I argue?
- Did I worry?
- Was I judgmental?
- Did I complain?
- Did I talk too much?
- Did I focus on things that I cannot change?
- Was I critical of myself or others?
- Was I kind to others?
- Was I helpful to others?
- Was I positive in my self-talk and in talking to others?
- Did I take care of my health?
- Did I work conscientiously?
- Did I spend money wisely?
- Was I honest and truthful?
- Did I handle my responsibilities?
- Did I process my negative feelings?
- Did I stay in the present?
- Did I practice observing?
- Was I thankful, appreciative, and grateful?

Even Driving Can Be Used for Self-Observation

Staying in awareness even during mundane tasks can help us understand what is going on within us. For example, examining our behavior while driving is an excellent way to determine how we may be unconsciously navigating life.

For many people, driving triggers considerable emotion and anger at other drivers. When driving, people are encapsulated by the car, and it seems like that is a harmless and safe time to allow anger to surface. They swear at the other drivers, yell at them, give them the bird and then speed past them. It is unlikely that they would act this way face-to-face. Their thoughts are about what the other driver is doing wrong—they are driving too slowly, too fast, too recklessly, too closely, or cutting in and out of the lane. Drivers also complain about the traffic, the road conditions, and the weather.

Driving in traffic, in particular, is an excellent way to observe your behavior. How do you react to the mistakes of others? When driving, consider some of the following questions: What fears and feelings are surfacing? Are you patient and kind with others? How do you treat pedestrians? Do you give others the right of way? Are you smiling or angry? Are you anxious in traffic? What thoughts are running through your mind? Once you have some time, reflect on what you learned and process it.

Driving can be an exercise in love, compassion, and forgiveness if you practice on other drivers until you finally feel calm and happy while driving your car.

Media Is a Tool to Check In

Other good situations for observing feelings are when we consume media content such as watching television and movies or looking at the phone, books, magazines, and billboards. Observe yourself, especially when interacting on social media such as YouTube, TikTok, Facebook, Twitter, or even LinkedIn.

We humans often become judgmental when watching a show or a sports game by wanting a certain person or team to win and others to lose, even when there is no particular reason for this. Someone may dislike a player or a character in a movie or a show. The ego likes to see the world in terms of "us" and "them." What is the fear underlying the attachment to one side or the need to exclude the other? What negative feeling or fear has the character or team triggered?

It is common for people to look at the profiles of friends and acquaintances on Facebook, LinkedIn, or other social media and to judge them, putting them down, even unconsciously—starting with their profile photos and the contents of their posts. Are you happy that your former boss is now a CEO? Are you jealous? Do you want their success? Do you feel superior to your former co-worker? Do you have negative feelings about your high school girlfriend and her new life and children? You may be comparing yourself to others and feeling either superior or inferior somehow.

People frequently judge celebrities, musicians, politicians, journalists, models, influencers, and other successful people as they browse social media. Do you wish everyone equally well, or are you secretly happy that someone has gained weight, is involved in a scandal, or has developed crow's feet? Check your feelings in these arenas. They can be very subtle and unconscious as you browse. Own and process these feelings. Are you able to approach people with love, kindness, and compassion?

Become conscious of your reactions as you listen to the news, hearing about politics, leaders, religion, crime, social issues, or other potentially charged issues. What comes up in you? Do you have any resentments? Are you able to approach topics with love, kindness, and compassion? Do you see the world as "us" versus "them"?

When someone is engaged in negative reactions to media, they are not objectively watching television, interacting with social media, or spending time connecting with friends. It means they are in *judgment*. They are in a reactive mode, not an active one. The more someone judges others and reacts negatively in *any* circumstance, the more they feed their ego, making their negativity stronger and themselves more emotionally charged.

To transform yourself and your life, you must bring all aspects of yourself—not just some—into the light and be willing to look at them, no matter how subtle. Media is a good opportunity to process your feelings. When you are engaged with media objectively, without judgment, and as an observer, you will find it is less exciting, reactive, and emotional. You will be calm, won't take sides, and be happy for everyone and their successes. You will feel compassion for other people's losses and wish them well. It doesn't mean that you won't still have a favorite character, leader, or sports team, but you won't feel the need to dislike the "opposition." The game will be enjoyed as a game, and you won't have to be invested in who wins. Instead, you will sincerely wish all the players good luck, admiring their talents and efforts, while you have fun watching the game.

Fears at Work

Work occupies many hours of our day, so it is important to examine any fears you may have about work as they will bring unhappiness, stress, and strife to your life if left unchecked. If you have any fears at all, then pinpoint what they are, and examine your feelings about them. It's a good opportunity to process your negative feelings. Once you have let go of fear, it will put you in a position to be a more qualified and respected employee.

Some common fears associated with work are:

Speaking up for what you want and deserve
Eventually getting fired
Not being as capable as other employees
Not being valuable
Not being accepted
Not having enough self-confidence
Not getting recognition

Do you know your value as an employee? Are you conscientious, diligent, able to get along with others, honest, and dependable? A good employee would have these traits and more like those listed below.

Determined

Honest

Punctual

A good organizer

Good at communicating

Someone with attention to detail

Able to get along with people

Loyal

Good at concentration

Consistent

Clean and neat

An appropriate dresser

Knowledgeable about the job

Willing to learn

Dependable

Respectful

The Pitfalls of Ego and Fear

Despite our commitment to change, even the best of us fall prey to certain pitfalls that may throw us off. One is our ego. It may blind us or tempt us through illusion to lead us astray. The ego emphasizes that our value and worth are measured by external factors such as money, looks, possessions, power, and fame.

This misguided deception may encourage people to live their lives chasing these things as ego food instead of focusing on inner growth. There is nothing wrong with having wealth and material possessions, provided they are not used to serve the ego. When they are used to help others with kindness and love, material wealth and possessions become beautiful. People who learn this early on in their lives are fortunate. They do not allow themselves to be trapped by believing their importance and value are determined by money, looks, possessions, power, and fame.

We are all going to die sometime. When we fear death, it is the ego's fear. We can either deal with the fear or spend our entire lives carrying it so that it affects us every day. We need to embrace the reality of death by processing it, accepting and making it all right that death will occur one day to be free to live our lives fully. It is also essential to accept the death of our loved ones. We have no power or control to determine when and how death will occur.

We can release our fear to God or the Universe and put it in their hands. Whether it is the fear of our death or that of a loved one, the fear of death is one of the most important fears we can examine and process. It is possible to process this fear until it has dissipated.

Focus on the Benefits

To be dedicated requires a belief system that includes a deep knowledge of how it will benefit us to stick to the work—knowing that we will be better off, happier, and healthier. Unless we have an appropriate belief system that drives our motivation, it can be difficult to continue the effort of self-improvement or work on cementing positive habits. We may just follow our impulses instead. Why do we eat a salad instead of a pizza or exercise instead of sitting on the sofa?

The first thing to do is to be aware of and then train the mind to think about the specific benefits that are achievable through self-improvement for when we are losing steam. If we are going to dedicate our time and energy to working on transformation, it is natural (and wise) to want to know how we will benefit from the work. If our investment doesn't appear to yield results, we won't make an effort to do what is required. Of course, the benefits are commensurate with our regular contribution and effort.

When we look at something as desirable and believe it will make us happier and more satisfied, then, of course, we want it. If we truly know how we can benefit from transformation—such as becoming more honest, sincere, loving, compassionate, wise, happy, kind, and spiritual—why would we let ourselves down by not continuing to do the work?

To help you continuously muster motivation and overcome resistance, deeply consider how doing transformation work will benefit you. Write down your thoughts along with the answers to the questions below.

- Why should I bother to make an effort?
- What are the benefits for me?
- What are the benefits to others in my life?
- What are the benefits to society?
- Deeply examine the following list of positives and ask for each one, Do I really want this? If not, why not? What is the source of the resistance?

To Be:

Healthier

Happier

More peaceful

Wiser

Trustworthy

Free of anger

Free of Shame

Free of Guilt

More successful

A better friend

A better worker

A good example to others

Someone who allows abilities to develop

Someone who helps more people

Someone who positively contributes to society

More spiritual

Closer to God

To Have:

> Less conflict
> More friends
> Happier relationships
> More self-confidence
> More capabilities
> Integrity/honesty
> Stronger character
> More respect
> More resources to share with others

What Will it Cost Not to Change?

Next, it is helpful to be conscious of what you will lose if you don't follow through with self-improvement. First, examine the consequences of your choices. If you don't consciously think about why, you make your choices and the consequences of your actions, it is like going through life with your head stuck in the sand while the rest of you is being swayed by life's wind.

Next, look at **what will happen if you don't accept the challenge.** What will it cost you if you don't bother? Examine some of the costs associated with staying as you are in the list below. Be completely honest if any of them resonate with you. What are you resisting? Why are you hanging onto any negativity? Get to the source of the negativity.

If I stay the same, then:

> The pain grows stronger
> It may negatively impact physical and mental health
> I'll stay unhappy
> I'll be a poor example to others
> I'll continue to have problems in relationships
> It will be harder to maintain friendships

I won't be as productive

I may use drugs or alcohol to numb pain and/or self-medicate

I may engage in crime

I may not be motivated to reach personal potential (career, character, spiritual, social)

I may not reach financial goals

I may hurt others

I'll have enemies

I'll feel:

Anger

Fear

Guilt

As though I am selfish

Accidents

Helpless

Like I lack wisdom

A lack of confidence

A lack of respect

One of the best ways to avoid the sabotage of impulse and stick to your commitment to transform is to **keep foremost in your mind the benefits of changing and the probable costs if you don't.**

Energizing the Will

Once we are clear about how and why change will benefit us and the potential costs of not changing, we'll have a strong desire to engage in the ongoing transformation process. Such a strong desire will energize us to have a lot of willpower geared toward goal accomplishment, making us feel like we can conquer the world.

Our energy field fuels willpower—when feelings are negative, and energy becomes low, then will is weakened. The lowest point of willpower is when a person feels so psychologically down that they can hardly get out of bed.

Willpower is weakened when:

Motivation is lacking

There is weak desire and not wanting the goal badly enough

Consequences are not considered

A goal is seen as unimportant or not prioritized

Fears are associated with outcomes

There are negative beliefs concerning goals

There is a lack of confidence

We easily give in to negative feelings or resistance

There is no realization of the benefits received from achieving goals

There is fear of realizing the benefit

Making excuses

There is procrastination, which is a symptom of fear

Self-discipline is lacking

Bad habits hamper goal-related activities

We can energize our will by channeling our determination, dedication, decisiveness, tenacity, self-confidence, faith, positive beliefs, and optimism into our transformational efforts. Cultivating these traits and employing discipline to sustain motivation will enable us to get through the journey's highs and lows. We need self-discipline and positive habits.

Willpower is closely connected to life energy and motivation. When there is a lack of motivation, fear and negative beliefs are involved. Examine your feelings and pinpoint the fear. The fear could be the fear of disapproval and a fear of failure. What defenses are you using to avoid feeling fear? Stop using them, get in touch with the negative feelings, and process your emotions. Examine your negative beliefs to see if they are getting in the way of your success and change them. We show you how to look more deeply at your mind and examine your beliefs in the next chapter.

Even with the best intentions, clear motivations, ongoing emotional processing, and awareness, sometimes, the way we think and what we think about can sabotage us. In the next chapter, we discuss the nature of the mind, how to observe it, and how it works. Then we discuss the power of beliefs and ways to transform the beliefs that don't serve us and keep us from fulfilling our potential. Observing the mind is a vital aspect of the ongoing process of transformation.

CHAPTER 7

Understanding the Mind

Be careful what you think because your thoughts run your life.

—Proverbs: 4:23

In addition to regularly processing emotions, the practice of observing the mind and thoughts is integral to transformation. Emotions both inform thought and result from it. Together they influence our actions. All real change includes having mastery over the thoughts that pass through our minds.

Transforming the mind is like creating a garden. The soil must be made ready, and the plants must be planted at the right time. The fertilizer and minerals need to be placed in the earth to help the plants grow. Then, the plants will need sunlight, water, and care every day. The mind is the same way.

When the mind is ready, a light switch goes on one day, and a person says, "Oh, I am ready to accept these new ideas and make some changes. I think this makes sense." At that point, the mind is fertile and ready to receive new information, and the body will go along with the mind.

Thoughts

Have you ever wondered where all your thoughts come from? Have you noticed how many random thoughts go through your mind when you lie down to sleep? Thoughts are energy and we tend to think thoughts that match the frequency of our energy. If you are worried and fearful, you tend to conjure negative thoughts that match those vibrations.

In addition, every thought that anyone has ever had exists in the universe. Most of us believe that we think our own thoughts. But, sometimes, the thoughts we have are ones we've picked up from the universe, much like how picture and sound signals are transmitted through the air to antennas.

Observe how much of your thinking is about problems, fears, worry, anger, and disappointment. When negative thoughts are streaming through your mind, it can cause you to be unhappy. You communicate this unhappiness to others in several ways, including through body language, facial expressions, what you say and how, like nagging, whining, and complaining, and what you do. This may then generate negative experiences with others. If you keep thinking the way you always have been, you will get the same results.

Good energy and positive thoughts will connect you to even more elevated thinking and experiences. So always remember how important it is to have positive thoughts that generate upliftment and the energy of love.

Mental Chatter

In addition to negative thoughts energized by fear and negativity, people can experience mental chatter flowing through their minds. It can cause confusion, distraction, and reduced productivity. The content is different for each person. Some people often tune in to think about what others are doing, saying, or thinking. This rambling stream of thoughts can be about someone or something they are angry about and about the various ways they would like to punish them. It can take the form of worry, dwelling on the past, or something they have no power to change, yet they take no action to create a solution. This chatter also can be about beating themselves up for something they said or did.

Mental chatter is a waste of time and energy and detrimental because it makes us powerless to resolve our problems. Time and energy are wasted on mentally looping blame, guilts, and complaints about others. If there is a problem, it is more effective to take responsibility, focus on the solution, and direct any actions to resolve it. How can anyone create a happy life with this kind of continuous negativity?

But there is a way out. When people process their fears and emotions by doing the ETT work (or any other method), there is little, if any, fear energy to connect to a stream of fearful thoughts. There is nothing to hook into fearful thoughts and allow them to stream into our consciousness. In other words, the air has been let out of the balloon.

Duality

The way we find meaning and understanding in this world is through duality. Our minds measure things by comparing one thing to another. We cannot know hot without cold, large without small, happiness without unhappiness. Every experience is like a coin, having two sides. We can call one side negative and the other positive. Most people tend to see one side or the other.

Focusing on the negatives of anything dims its positive aspects from our awareness. The same is true when you focus on the positive; the negative is pushed out of consciousness. **Practice expanding your ability to see more perspectives**. Look for the positive side in your experiences. Look for what you have learned and how it has helped you to change your direction. With desire and practice, you can learn to broaden your thinking. The result will be more happiness, better communication, and an improved ability to accomplish what you want.

Always Tired

Years back, I took a class where I was asked to sit and write down my thoughts for twenty minutes every day. At first, I simply observed the thoughts and didn't write anything down because I decided I wasn't thinking about anything important. Then, I realized that I was not doing the assignment and started noting my thoughts.

After twenty minutes, when I read what was written, not only was there nothing important there as I'd guessed, but I was surprised I had written about how tired I felt three times.

Our thoughts direct our unconscious mind. During those twenty minutes, I was just thinking blah-blah thoughts that had no purpose or special meaning—mental chatter. First, the exercise helped me realize the contents of my mind were mostly meaningless. Second, it helped me to stop telling myself how tired I felt. I realized that by saying I felt tired, I was going to feel tired.

Since then, I have made a practice of thinking about having plenty of energy and vitality and focusing on getting enough sleep. I also practice thinking about more meaningful things when I'm not relaxing. Today, I am now more aware, making conscious choices about my thoughts.

Getting to Know Your Mind

To transform our minds, we need to closely examine how we are using them. First, we need to become aware of our thoughts and how we handle them as they arise in our minds. It is important not to underestimate the power of what we think. Thoughts determine the quality of someone's life. They affect people's choices, their actions, and what type of person someone becomes.

Try writing down your thoughts for twenty minutes. Then, go through the questions below to help you become more aware of how you are using your mind, taking note of anything you'd like to change.

Are your thoughts negative?

- Do you have destructive thoughts?
- Do you worry and have sad thoughts?
- Are your thoughts unhappy, selfish, and hurtful?
- Are your thoughts hopeless, rude, and cruel?
- Do you have angry thoughts about yourself or others?
- Do you hang onto many of your thoughts about the past or the future?

- Do you have a monkey mind where your thoughts are jumping around?
- Are your thoughts confusing and unclear?
- Do you examine the inner part of you?
- Do you have mean thoughts about others?

On the other hand, are your thoughts positive?

- Are you consciously aware of what you are thinking?
- Are you generous, gentle, and thoughtful?
- Do you keep your thoughts in the present?
- Are your thoughts calm and peaceful?
- Are your thoughts about being helpful to others?
- Are your thoughts spiritual?
- Do you have kind thoughts about others?
- Do you appreciate the good points of the people you know?
- Do you want to volunteer, contribute, and be productive?
- Do you think about making a difference and your enjoyment of working?

Determine how you'd like to change the way you think. Then, make a plan about it. In the next chapter, we talk about affirmations and meditation as tools to retrain the mind from habitual thoughts and beliefs. But remember that it is *you* who decides what to think. You have the power to pivot away from unproductive or meaningless thoughts. It only takes being vigilant as you observe your thinking. When you notice a thought is dark or mean, immediately replace it with an equally positive one. You can make a decision right now to be proactive about this.

Self-Talk

How we talk to ourselves affects the way we feel about ourselves and the world around us. This is called self-talk, and it makes up quite a bit of our mental chatter. Some people engage in self-talk that is overwhelmingly negative.

Realize that what you say about yourself in your thoughts is equivalent to projecting those same ideas out to the world. Become aware. What is your inner voice saying about you? Is it positive or negative? Some common examples are:

I am stupid.

I cannot do anything right.

They will make fun of me.

I wish I looked better.

My hair is a mess.

I could make a mistake.

I am too fat.

He will not like me.

It's too difficult.

No one loves me.

I will fail.

I'm not good enough.

I'm unworthy.

What You Focus on Matters

Focusing on what we want to avoid is unproductive. Each thought creates emotion, and when we think about what we don't want, it causes us to have negative feelings.

The next time you feel down, check your thinking. You'll notice that you have been thinking about something negative. The majority of people's thoughts happen unconsciously. As with any behavior that you no longer want, you can change this. It takes time, consciousness, and practice to change a habit.

Thinking habits are learned in childhood, and they can be changed with awareness and some work. A mind that is not disciplined is scattered, vague, unfocused, and lacks direction. It easily gets swept up in what is going on in the environment, and it cannot redirect itself.

To achieve the ability to see with clarity, we must expend the effort to train our minds to settle down, concentrate, and focus. Most people understand that they must exercise a muscle to increase strength and ability. In the same way, it requires practice and discipline to gain the ability to think clearly and direct our thoughts with precision.

First, it helps to understand what is happening within the mind and how it works.

Is Your Mind in the Past, Present, or Future?

Are you focused on the past? When you think about the past, there isn't anything you can do because the past is over. If you are thinking about the future, the future isn't here yet, so there isn't anything you can do about that either.

Fears can hijack the mind and keep us focused on the past or the future. The energy of hurt or pain keeps the mind stuck in loops. This prevents us from focusing on the present moment, which is the only time we can be in our power.

When repetitively thinking about a person or situation, ask yourself:

- Why is my mind going back in time?
- Why is my mind looping this past situation?
- Do I have any unresolved issues or emotions from the past that need to be processed?
- Do you have fears about what will happen? What am I afraid of?
- Why is my mind going to the future?
- Am I anticipating a negative event in the future based on past experiences?
- What emotions about the future need to be processed?

It is critical to dig into the past, unearth any fears and pain, process and accept them, forgive yourself and others, and let go and move on into the present. If your mind is spinning with the prospect of future events, process these and set your mind free.

The goal is to keep our minds and emotions in the present by focusing on our inner beings and what we are doing now. The only exception to this is when we are doing something that pertains to the future, for example, making reservations or planning a vacation. To achieve present moment awareness, we must clear the past and future from our thoughts.

What Are Your Mind's Categories?

To build awareness about the contents of your mind, let's examine which topic groups or subject categories tend to be predominant in your mind. Some categories (or sets of files) are more interesting to you than others due to your experience, talents, needs, and interests. Although you may have a mild level of interest in many topics, one or two of them are typically favorites, and you have likely gathered a lot of content in these areas. Often, more mental energy is dedicated to the topics that interest you, and you will likely choose friends and occupations that align with them. We are attracted to those with whom we have something in common. Which categories interest you the most?

Sentient Beings This category pertains to people, animals, trees, and plants. It is about what living beings do, their activities, their physical attributes (e.g., brunette, tall or short), social characteristics (e.g., extroverted, shy), personalities (e.g., loving, funny), or other characteristics (e.g., gardens). There is content about groups, cultures, friends, co-workers, spouses, children, people, relatives, gatherings, social events and traditions (such as a party), animals such as pets, plants, trees, and flowers. Some individuals may focus more on people to the exclusion of beings like animals.

Places and Locations This is about physical environments, both constructed and natural, locations worldwide and their characteristics, including landmarks, buildings, sights, space, geography, geology, and natural beauty. It could include restaurants, museums, malls, monuments, shopping areas, town squares, clubs, famous buildings, nature trails, hotels, cruises, theatres, or opera houses. It can also include traveling and modes of travel, such as airplanes, trains, homes, and RVs.

Work Tasks and Interests Here the topic group is about doing activities, developing skills and pursuing interests, achieving, and accomplishing a task. The content of this category may include to-do lists, occupational tasks, projects, writing, building, hobbies (sewing, woodworking, knitting, gardening), errands, shopping, running, earning awards, sports, playing games, exercising, martial arts, dance, playing music, racing, performing, singing, talking, meditating, praying, or engaging in group activities (clubs, political or religious groups).

Material Objects Having to do with the ownership of things, this category involves acquiring material possessions such as new technology (the latest iPhone), clothes, handbags, shoes, cars, robotics, drones, toys, books, furniture, paintings, sculptures, computers, appliances, plants, houses, land, or other property. It can also involve collecting hobbies like stamps, coins, baseball cards, art, sculptures, antiques, or vintage clothes.

Information This topic group reflects a great interest in gathering information and knowledge (like a professor, scientist, teacher, researcher, or expert). What information do you gather? There may be an interest in a particular area of knowledge. The person may like to watch, listen, or read to uncover the why-and-how related to topics. The content of this category may include documentaries, clips, books, newspapers, magazines, data, statistics, recent discoveries, facts, news, research studies, complex information, reports, or library research. This category may also have to do with planning and thinking about the future

If you can't decide which categories your mind seems to favor by looking at the list above, try to answer the following questions to see how the answers may fit into the categories above:

- What was one of the most memorable experiences I have had in my life?
- What was my favorite work experience, and why did it matter to me?
- What do I like best about my job?
- What do I enjoy doing in my free time?
- What do I post about the most on social media?
- What did I like the most about my last vacation?

Look at the answers and see if they point to your favorite topic group. The idea is to notice which categories you focus on and where you place attention. As you figure this out, you will become aware of the types of thoughts you invite to stream through your mind. Which emotions relate to these categories? Are they positive or negative? Do they bring joy or pain? Most importantly, they provide vital information about your sense of self—how you and your environment have built and shaped your identity—and how you see yourself.

Are Your Thoughts Egoic or Altruistic?

How many of your thoughts are about you and how many are about others? We are either helping society and the world be a better place or making it worse. It all starts with what we are energizing through our thinking, feelings, and actions.

Some individuals mostly have *egoic* thoughts that are about benefitting themselves. The world is filtered through the lens of their wants, desires, and feelings. Their thoughts focus on getting what they want for themselves at the exclusion of others. This tends to produce behaviors that benefit only them—for example, winning at all costs, cheating, taking advantage of others, littering, or scrawling graffiti on walls and vehicles.

Many people think about how they can be helpful to others, are concerned with how they can improve the environment, and strive to be kind to animals. They want to leave the world a better place than how they found it. This type of thinking is *altruistic,* which is associated with higher well-being, spirituality, and happiness.

How to Stop Having Unwanted Thoughts

Once you have become better acquainted with your mind and thought processes, you will become more aware of how they work. To stop having unwanted thoughts takes practice and awareness. It requires that you learn to still your mental chatter and clear your mind. When a person is in the ongoing process of becoming aware of their thoughts, it is often called an awakening—waking up to what is going on in their mind and their life.

One way of unplugging from particular thoughts is to stop accepting the thoughts as yours and start observing them without emotionally reacting to their contents. Stop taking ownership of the thoughts that are streaming through your mind. They are not yours. They have been personalized through the egoic filter to *seem* like they are yours. If you step back and observe thoughts as an observer, you disengage from seeing them as you and yours. Soon, they will have less power.

People can go through their whole lives never knowing how to still their minds. The more we gain the ability to be aware of our thoughts and become the observer, the higher we can raise our consciousness. Meditation is an excellent practice for learning how to quiet the mind.

Meditate

We know the outer world, our actions, and our feelings, but we know very little about our inner world of thoughts and emotions. Through meditation, we can become aware of our inner world.

When the mind is quiet and observing, we can know ourselves and be the witness to what is going on within us. By knowing who we are and how our inner world operates, we can overcome our weaknesses. Otherwise, we are slaves to what we do not know or understand. Through meditation, the unconscious is brought to consciousness and is dissolved.

You can sit quietly and meditate simply by observing your mind. (See also the meditation discussion in chapter 12.) With eyes closed, imagine looking out your forehead between your eyes. Focus on your breathing as you observe your mind. Every time you begin thinking thoughts, bring your attention back to the center of your forehead. This clears your mind by changing the focus from the content of your thoughts to the center of your forehead. By placing your attention there, you are bringing your mind to the present moment. To help anchor yourself in this space, focus on your breath with a clear and empty mind.

In the beginning, your mind will stray back into the stream of thinking because it is like a magnet that keeps pulling your attention back to it. Keep repeating this process patiently and lovingly, and you will gain more ability to stay focused on the present for more extended periods. Sitting to meditate for 10 minutes every morning and every evening is recommended. Find a time when you won't be disturbed. There is a vast abundance of meditation techniques that I encourage you to explore.

The benefits of meditation to your mind are numerous. You will be able to observe what is going on around you more. It helps you stay focused on the present throughout the day. You will be able to remain calm and emotionally stable when you encounter emergencies or upsetting situations. It helps you be more precise about the thoughts you choose to communicate to your unconscious mind. And, physically, your body will become more relaxed and freer from stress.

As your mind becomes more still with ongoing meditation, it will become more apparent how many people are unfocused, scattered, and unaware. Their thoughts pull them in many directions, and they are easily distracted. They are often critical and complain without looking for a solution; thus, their problems continue. Their thoughts usually jump from one subject to another without purpose or meaning. Once you become more aware, you will notice how different your perspective and clarity become. You will have more control over your actions and what happens in your life.

CHAPTER 8

Beliefs and Attitudes

At this point, you have an idea about the nature of your mind, its mental chatter, your habitual thoughts, and your mind's preferred categories for focus. Now that you have discovered the degree of your negative thinking, we will discuss in more detail how to practice shifting your thoughts to the positive. This involves examining and changing the beliefs and attitudes that have been fueling your negativity.

A belief is a judgment or assumption that we hold. It informs our thinking about everything and incorporates what we like and what we dislike. Attitudes are patterns of beliefs that form our general point of view or outlook about something. Attitudes tend toward black-and-white thinking such as viewing things are good or bad or right or wrong. I discussed attitudes in chapter 3 when I talked about having a positive or negative outlook on life. In life, when something happens, we usually view it according to our beliefs and attitudes.

For example, Edward, 18 years old, lived in Tennessee on a farm over a century ago. He fell off his horse and broke his leg. His family and friends believed it was very unfortunate that Edward broke his leg because he would have to wear a cast on it for a long time and use crutches to get around. He wouldn't be able to engage in activities and games with other young men his age. While he was recovering, all the available young men in town were drafted into the army, including Edward's neighbors and close friends. But Edward's broken leg prevented him from being drafted. All the men who had been drafted were either badly injured or killed in the war. So then people said that it was very fortunate that Edward broke his leg because it prevented him from going to war.

People often believe that an event or situation is bad at one point, only to see the same event as good at another time, as in the example above. When something happens, it can be hard to remain objective and observe the whole picture without taking a position on it. Decisions are often made based on a lack of information—without hearing both sides of the situation, without knowing all the facts, or without closely examining the context in which an event occurs. People may base judgments on past experiences, personal goals and desires, feelings, and limited knowledge.

Beliefs Inform How We See Reality

We form our beliefs at a very early age. Some are taught and others are formed by experience. People adopt beliefs as they go through life, based on what they have seen heard, been taught, and experienced. Some of these beliefs are positive, but others may be untrue and disabling. Our beliefs shape the way we see and react to the world. When a person has a belief, they will tend to focus their attention on what supports their belief.

Johnny dropped out of school during the 12th grade, and his parents and friends thought this was tragic. They wanted him to have an education and believed that he should finish high school and go to college. Johnny had a passion for fashion and the Internet. He went on to build a very successful clothing line of T-shirts sold exclusively at an online store. Within two years of launching his clothing line, he was making a million dollars a year. Johnny's parents and friends now thought that Johnny had done the right thing to drop out of school.

Life is full of experiences like this, but people continue to get emotional about what happens. Their strong beliefs about something cause them to judge it as good or bad, often with no basis in experience or knowledge. This kind of thinking runs rampant in people around the world and even causes wars. We need to gain the wisdom to know we don't have all the answers, and **perceptions of events often change with time**. Thinking in this way can help us become less emotional, judgmental, self-righteous, and opinionated. It is why it is so vital to move out of judgment and become the observer.

Embedded Beliefs

At birth, people begin to experience life. The nature of their experiences from then on determines the kind of beliefs they will adopt, laying the foundation for what they unconsciously expect to happen. A person who was neglected or abused as a child would have very different beliefs than if they had a good caregiver who met their needs and was surrounded by loving people. When a person is repeatedly treated a certain way, it becomes embedded in their unconscious mind and forms matching beliefs, expectations, and emotions. Children and adolescents are particularly susceptible to forming beliefs based on what they are exposed to in their environments.

Adults also accept beliefs unconsciously through what they hear someone say to them or on television or what they read. When these beliefs are accepted, they are acted upon, usually without conscious thought. Once someone accepts a statement, they often make decisions and take action to match the statement.

It is important to consciously examine your beliefs to make sure that they are directing you positively and reflect what you truly want. Start with the list below. How many of these positive beliefs do you hold about yourself?

I can accomplish anything I want to.

I handle time wisely.

I focus on whatever makes me feel grateful.

It is safe to know the truth.

I am kind and loving to others.

I am patient and understanding.

I appreciate the things others do for me.

I can feel secure in my relationships.

I am contributing to making the world a better place.

I am willing to give what I ask to receive.

I take good care of myself, my house, car, furniture, and equipment.

I eat healthy food.

I enjoy my own company.

The world I live in can be safe.

I can relax and feel calm.

I like to leave a person, animal, or thing better off than I found them.

I treat others as I would like to be treated.

I forgive myself and others.

I like to do things to the best of my ability.

I easily let go of the past.

I expect the best each day.

If you didn't find beliefs you hold on the list, write some of your own positive beliefs. Can't come up with too many? Let's look at how beliefs limit us.

Limiting Beliefs

Beliefs have a powerful hold on us. In certain places, when an elephant is small, its leg is chained to a stake in the ground. The stake is large enough that the young elephant cannot pull it out. After numerous attempts, the elephant learns he cannot free himself. Eventually, the elephant gives up trying to get free. Consequently, a full-grown elephant can be confined with a small chain attached to a stake that he could easily pull out. The elephant will not attempt to free himself because the old experience taught him it is impossible. Now he believes that he lacks control over the rope and is completely passive. When humans and animals experience prolonged stress, they believe they cannot change, and they stop trying to help themselves. They also exhibit passivity in future situations. This is one of the major symptoms of depression.

How often do you get annoyed with yourself and put yourself down? Have you ever thought you made a mistake and then became upset? Do you get overwhelmed by a fear of failure? People can internalize negative beliefs about themselves at a young age. These beliefs then form a regular part of our mind's mental chatter about ourselves or self-talk. Our experiences growing up affect how we feel about ourselves and the kind of beliefs we form, which determines how we deal with what happens in life and what we attract.

Below are some examples of such limiting beliefs about ourselves.

I am stupid.

Nothing and no one can be trusted.

I deserve to be treated badly.

I cannot depend on others.

I am unlovable.

I cannot succeed.

I am a failure.

If our beliefs about ourselves are predominantly negative, usually this is because we can't assess ourselves honestly. We often have misconceptions about our actions, thoughts, and feelings. Sometimes help is needed to teach us how to see ourselves as we truly are.

One of our most important beliefs is about how we look at the future. It can make a big difference in dictating our present-day behavior and choices. If someone believes they have no power over their life or the future—*if they have lost hope*—it would be difficult for them to strive to better their life circumstances or learn and grow.

Our beliefs about the past and present are also important. If someone blames other people and circumstances for causing their problems, they are accepting themselves as being powerless and creating barriers to learning from their mistakes. Blaming others is synonymous with believing that others have more power over the person's fate than they do. So, the person goes about life resenting others for their own mistakes and never thinks about what they could have done differently. There's no room to learn or grow.

Notice if you have limiting beliefs that get in the way of your willingness to actualize your potential. Some examples are:

> Others are to blame when things don't work out the way you wanted.
>
> It is difficult to solve problems.
>
> The future is bleak.
>
> I'm not good enough in any way and don't have any talents to develop.
>
> Failure is shameful.
>
> There's no need to consider situations too much, including any consequences.

Now think about negative beliefs that you may have formed concerning your relationships. For example, the belief that:

> No one cares about anyone so don't care what others want, think, or feel.
>
> You have to manipulate and control others to get what you want.
>
> Since you were not treated fairly, you don't have to treat others well.
>
> Being right is more important than being happy.
>
> Other people are stupid or ill-intentioned toward you.
>
> You already know the answers and have nothing to learn from others.
>
> It is acceptable to take advantage of other people.

The ability to take command of your own life and be willing to learn and grow comes from the belief in *hope,* not helplessness and powerlessness. It comes from accepting that you are responsible and can handle any future adversity, including difficult situations and monumental failures. It is having complete confidence in your ability to successfully jump over hurdles. To change your life, first take a deep and honest look at your beliefs about yourself and your relationships.

Lori Becomes Champion

Lori Cole learned firsthand that it's important what we say to ourselves. Lori became a world-champion Armwrestler and maintained that title for several years until she retired, even though her physique is not very large. Lori is slender and not overly muscular, in addition to being beautiful. No one would ever guess that she was an Armwrestler by looking at her.

I knew Lori before she began competing in an arm wrestling because she had attended several of my classes. Lori shared her goal of competing as an Armwrestler with me and asked for my help with her thinking and concentration.

Lori Cole, Champion Armwrestler

It is essential to concentrate in any competition, so Lori began practicing concentration exercises. She also began to learn how to direct her brain through positive self-talk. Each day she practiced saying affirmations such as "I am a winner." She practiced using her mind to direct her strength and energy to her arm to perform her Armwrestling skills.

During her first competition, she was matched with another lady in the same weight class. The referee said "Ready Go!", and suddenly Lori's arm was only a couple of inches from touching the mat. Her mind was racing with thoughts; then, she remembered the affirmations that she had practiced. She began to repeat, "I am a winner," over and over in her mind. Her arm began to rise, and soon, she had her opponent's arm on the mat. Lori had won the match. This was amazing because it is almost impossible to come back and win a match once someone's arm has been forced that close to the mat.

Lori gained confidence from winning that match. She sent on to win many matches, even in heavier weight classes, and become a world champion. She also won many matches, competing with women in much heavier weight classes. Lori's story shows how we can change our beliefs, install new ones, and learn to concentrate. Lori changed her belief to "I am a winner," and she became one.

Preventing Negative Statements from Becoming Beliefs

It is important to be aware of everything that affects us, particularly what we listen to and what we are saying to ourselves. The unconscious mind hears everything and will believe and act on what it is told. Whenever anyone says something negative to us, we must be sure to turn it into a positive statement, which we repeat quietly to ourselves.

For example, if someone says, "You are going to fail this test," immediately repeat to yourself, "I can easily pass this test." Refuse to accept any negative statements someone may say to you or negative thoughts you say to yourself. You don't have to refuse outwardly—just do it inwardly. Here are two stories that illustrate this technique.

The first example is when my son was in the US Army and spent two years in Vietnam. One morning he was with his squad and walking with two friends as they left their patrol base to go to a helicopter. One of the squad members said to two of the guys in a half-joking, sarcastic way, "Charlie is going to get you today."

One of the guys replied, "They are not going to get me today." The other guy said nothing. That day, the guy that said nothing was killed. The guy who replied, "They are not going to get me today," is alive and well.

There is no way to determine whether the soldier's unconscious mind accepted that he would be killed that day or what forces were at work. However, it is true that the unconscious mind acts on what it hears in one way or another. It does not decide based on whether the information is good or bad; it is just information.

The second example is when a girlfriend and I took a fun trip to Las Vegas and kept winning at the blackjack table. We were lucky and won almost four hundred dollars on our first try. Deciding to stop while we were ahead, we cashed in our chips. Twenty minutes later, ready to play again, we returned to the same table and were again ahead by over four hundred dollars. Later, we went back to the table for the third time to play some more and were winning once more. At this point, the pit boss came over to us, pointed his finger at me, and said very harshly, "Don't you know when you are sitting there you are supposed to LOSE."

Because I was familiar with this technique of planting negative words in a person's unconscious mind, the whole time he was talking to me, I kept repeating to myself, "I am a winner, I am a winner, I am a winner." There was no question that the pit boss was serious. It is hard to imagine that a Las Vegas casino would consider someone winning around a thousand dollars significant enough for that kind of mental sabotage, but this seemed to be the case. My friend and I played a while longer, then cashed in our chips and left.

Affirmations Create Positive Beliefs

As discussed, beliefs may be conscious or unconscious, are the foundation of how we see ourselves and the world, and form our attitudes. They filter through every decision we make. Everyone has some negative beliefs. Suppose you have now recognized some of yours. Is it possible to change them? Yes, If you want to change your beliefs, you can do this through affirmations.

An affirmation is a conscious, purely positive statement that we want our minds to accept to change or replace an existing belief or behavior. We employ affirmations to assist us in transforming our minds and how we habitually think. Affirmations can be said within ourselves or out loud, which is more powerful.

Before you can turn to affirmations to help you, practice being consciously aware of your beliefs for a while. You can't change what you don't know about. To become aware of the contents of your mind, learn to observe your thoughts and beliefs and slow them down.

I suggest that the first affirmations you might employ are those to combat any negative self-talk. Here are examples of empowering self-talk affirmations that you could use to replace any disparaging mind chatter you direct at yourself:

> I am capable of success.
> I am a fast learner.
> I desire to be happy.
> I deserve to be treated with respect.
> I am lovable.
> I can easily make positive changes.
> I forgive myself and others.
> I observe my behavior.
> I give up blaming others.
> I am now aware of when I judge others and stop it.
> I am now willing, capable, and able to discover how to be peaceful, understanding, and lovable.
> I am focused on the present.
> I am instantly aware any time I am mistreating anyone.
> I am honest with myself and others.
> I am patient and thoughtful with myself and others.

Next, having improved how you feel about yourself, you can install some new beliefs with affirmations to assist in the transformation process:

> I am now able to appreciate and be thankful for the wonderful things I have in my life.
>
> I now expect good things to happen.
>
> I learn from my mistakes, and life just gets better.
>
> I focus on what I can do and keep my thoughts positive.
>
> When I have negative emotions, I process my feelings.
>
> I am now aware of how I am thinking, and I am consciously learning to think the way I want to think.
>
> I examine who I am and what my purpose is for being here.
>
> I realize that I am connected to every other person in the world, and I am learning to be helpful to them and to love everyone.
>
> I am opening my mind to become more aware of God and spiritual principles.

Transform Your Unconscious Mind

Affirmations can also be used to change your unconscious mind to hold different beliefs on specific topics or areas. Make a list of what you want to change, then use affirmations that align with your new desire.

Then, select three affirmations and repeat them several times each day until you see that your behavior is changing. **Writing down the affirmations is even more powerful than saying them.** After doing those three for a while, select three more and continue to say or write your new affirmations each day until you think and behave the way you want.

Examples of Affirmations

Feelings and Fears

When I feel angry or afraid, I remember to examine and process my feelings.

I can easily get in touch with my feelings.

I practice acceptance every day.

I am aware of my emotions when I am driving.

I am now aware of when I am in resistance.

I take responsibility for my unhappiness.

I evaluate when I am out of balance and process my feelings each day.

I am learning to accept and love myself.

I am keeping my focus on the present.

Character

I now practice telling the truth.

I am open-minded and easily make adjustments in my thinking and actions.

I maintain a good attitude.

I finish what I start.

I make sure to do what I say I will do.

I keep my surroundings and myself neat and clean.

I think positively.

I practice self-care by eating healthy food.

I take responsibility for what I say, feel, and do.

Growth

I can easily remember my dreams.

I am now willing to change what I do not like in my life.

I review my actions daily and make adjustments to improve.

I keep focused on what I can improve in my life.

Each day I am more aware of what I am doing and what is going on around me.

I am aware when I make excuses and stop doing it.

I look for opportunities to be joyful.

It is easy for me to meditate.

I am grateful for the wonderful things I have in my life.

It is easy for me to make changes for the better.

Relationships

I listen and consider feedback from others.

I forgive myself and others.

I make friends easily.

I am kind, considerate, and friendly to others.

I am aware of how I am treating others.

I treat others the way I want to be treated.

I speak in a calm and kind voice.

I take responsibility for any and all conflicts in my life.

I am aware when I am defensive.

I only talk when I have something worthwhile to say.

Success

I easily make plans and complete them on schedule.

I look forward to each day.

I have plenty of time to do the things I want to do.

I now expect my plans to go well.

I am well organized.

I am a lucky person.

An affirmation will have a more powerful effect if you can muster up a sincere desire to align with it and not just say or write it robotically. Coupling emotion with an affirmation gives it life in your consciousness. Put another way, aligning your desires with affirmations nurtures the soil of your mind with the nutrients required to allow the new thought or belief to take root in your mind and grow.

Be aware that some affirmations may strike a chord. If you experience this, it is imperative to pay attention to any resistance, discomfort, or negative feelings that emerge in response to an affirmation. These are signals that you must turn inward and process any fears associated with an affirmation.

For example, if the affirmation "I learn from my mistakes" evokes resistance and someone doesn't want to say it, there may be a fear of failure or not feeling worthy associated with it. They may have had very strict parents, who shamed them for failures during childhood, thereby evoking stress and resistance at the thought of making a mistake. If so, then the person needs to do emotional healing work on the fear of not being good enough so that the affirmation can truly be internalized. Otherwise, the affirmation may not take hold.

To transform your mind, you will be asked to examine every aspect of your life thoroughly. But if you do so, the result will be that your life will change for the better.

Rewiring Janet's Need to Control

Janet was 63 years old and had had two failed marriages when she sought help. Her daughter, Teresa, was 41. One of Janet's ongoing patterns was that she focused on how her sister and daughter did not treat her in a way that made her feel loved and important. Janet also felt that most of her friends treated her the same way. She often felt betrayed and upset, and she dwelled on how badly she was treated. This problem also affected her relationship with her boss and co-workers. She felt exhausted, angry, unhappy, and confused much of the time.

If her daughter spent time with Janet's sister or friends, Janet would feel left out and betrayed. She thought they should have included her. Her ex-boyfriend became engaged and had stopped calling. She kept thinking about what she could do to get him to call her and was very angry with him.

Janet told me many unhappy stories about her family and friends so I realized Janet was trying to change and control other people. I asked Janet, "What gives you the right to say how other people should live their lives?"

They discussed the problem several times, and Janet began to admit that she was trying to control other people to feel loved and accepted. She started changing her behavior.

Janet was a middle child from a large family. Her parents had been so busy that she felt they had never had any time for her when she was growing up. She had felt lonely, ignored, and rejected. She had kept trying to get their attention but was not successful.

Janet finally learned to process feeling unloved and rejected. She stopped trying to make other people do things the way she wanted. She worked on healing her wounds and learned that control is how people try to deal with an underlying fear. Janet forgave everyone and herself. Once she changed, Janet was surprised at how happy she could be and how loving she felt toward others.

Janet created the following new beliefs:

> People can choose where and how they spend their time.
>
> I love and appreciate myself.
>
> It is easy for me to find things to do that I enjoy.
>
> I am learning to be accepting of others.

What Is an Attitude

An attitude is a learned tendency to evaluate things in a certain way and is the basis of how we form opinions about people and what happens in our lives. Attitudes are a function of our beliefs and experience. Because of our attitudes, we may accept and feel good about some aspects of people, situations, ideas, and behavior while there are other things that we reject and are not in agreement with. Attitudes affect the decisions we make, our choice of friends, how we think and feel about ourselves, the kind of career we choose, how we live our lives, and how we act.

People often think or say about someone, "He has a bad attitude." What does that mean exactly? A bad attitude is a colloquial term for an overall tendency to react with negative beliefs and thoughts, feelings, opinions, justifications, closed-mindedness, and defensiveness.

People also say, "He has a good attitude," which means a person usually projects a disposition that responds with harmony, positive thinking and feelings, cooperation, fairness, sharing, friendliness, optimism, hope, open-mindedness, and confidence.

When you come home from work and open the door, your attitude is evident based on how you look, your actions, and what you say. If you are tired, irritable, and upset, your attitude is most likely negative.

Like Attracts Like

People attract the same kind of energy that they put out. When someone greets a person with a negative attitude, things may not go well. If their attitude is positive, they will usually attract a matching response.

Most people are not consciously aware of their attitudinal tendencies. Unless you receive consistent feedback from others, it requires examination and awareness to notice our global tendencies of how we react to the world and what we are projecting out to others based on what we are thinking and feeling.

Do you know what kind of attitude you have:

- When you get up in the morning?
- When you go to work and when you come home?
- When you greet someone?
- When you answer the telephone?
- When you are doing your job?

- As you play a sport?
- On a date?
- With your family?
- When you are alone?

Do It with Positivity

Everything in life has a positive side and a negative side. It is to your benefit (and everyone's around us) to do whatever you have to do with a positive attitude. Before you begin a task or endeavor, first focus on all the positive outcomes associated with it. This can change your attitude toward the task. For example, what are the benefits of cleaning the house? It is better for your health, makes a home a more pleasant place, and feels good when things are in order and easier to find. Cleaning also shows you care, are proud of your home, and take responsibility for what is yours.

It is up to us whether we focus on the positive or the negative side of whatever we are doing in life. Why not focus on the positive to be happier? It is not an accident when people are consistently successful and happy. At some time in their lives, they learned to adopt the frame of mind that aligns with success and happiness. We *can* learn the skills to transform our lives into what we desire.

A good attitude builds positivity and optimism. Contributing to others and being helpful requires a positive attitude toward others. If your mother asks you to get her a glass of water, be happy to get it. It is not about what *she* does for you. It is about how *you* express your love. Be alert to how you can be helpful to others, not just family, but everyone. If someone needs help crossing the street, or climbing stairs, be gracious and assist others whenever you can without expecting anything in return.

Moving Into Harmony

Sometimes, people's beliefs and attitudes are not reflected in their words and behaviors. A person may say they like a sweater they received as a gift but never wear it. They may intend to remain calm in the face of criticism by their boss, but they spurt out angry and defensive comments instead. Contradictions are when your attitudes, beliefs, words, and behaviors do not match. For example, you end up saying one thing but doing another. When contradictions like this *consistently* fill people's lives, it leads to problems and negative emotions. It becomes a barrier to living a harmonious life.

Some people live in contradictions because they may not care about sticking to their word, values, or positive beliefs—they live by the adage that "promises are made to be broken". Others strive to be consistent, but they may be unable to control impulses in an emotional situation. Contradictions may signal the presence of powerful unconscious fears that may need to be faced and healed. If we intend to purchase life insurance week after week but keep putting it off, it may signal a fear of death that needs to be healed. Let's examine where contradictions arise in our lives. The next chapter discusses the idea of awakening to our behaviors. There you will learn about congruency and the important difference between reacting and responding.

CHAPTER 9

Awareness About Behavior

Do your thoughts, beliefs, attitudes, words, and actions match? Can other people one-hundred percent rely on you to do what you say you will do? Are you reliable, dependable, trustworthy, and honest? Have you learned to politely say *no* to requests rather than make empty promises? Do you give yourself permission to stay true to your thoughts and feelings?

Congruency

When thoughts, words, and deeds align, we live in a state of *congruency*. Sometimes, we are not consciously aware when we are not congruent. If someone says they will do something and then doesn't do it, they build negative karma. Their action is producing an adverse impact for themselves that will manifest at some point. Finding the cause of this behavior may require some analysis.

Every time you don't keep your word, it makes you weaker and lessens your self-respect. Excuses are a defense mechanism used to avoid fear. Identify your fear and then process your emotions connected to it. You may feel fear of powerlessness, being overwhelmed, being wrong, or helplessness.

How often do you experience cognitive dissonance? Ask yourself the questions below.

- Why do I say I'll do something I don't intend to do?
- What am I trying to avoid?
- What am I not facing and being honest about?
- What do I need to change to ensure I do what I say I will do?

Friends, spouses, and family members are good people to ask whether we always do what we say we will do. Their feedback can help identify if we are generally congruent. Periodically reviewing our behavior to see if we have congruent thoughts, words, and actions is also a good practice. Another way we can build awareness about the degree of our congruency is to tune into our emotions.

One of the reasons for depression is that thoughts, words, and actions are out of alignment. You can ask in prayer for your thinking to be powerful and your actions to be strong, steady, goal-oriented, spiritual, and congruent with your thoughts. Determine what you need to adjust to be congruent. Once you do what you say you will, the world will respond to the seeming "Golden Bond of Integrity" stamp on your words.

Acting on Impulse

When a person doesn't know why they do what they do, they may be acting on impulse. Many people live their lives this way. It is doubtful whether people incarcerated in prison are aware of the consequences of what they did to put them there. Many people act unconsciously out of pain, desperation, and traumatic pasts. Countless individuals have lost their jobs, marriages, lives, physical abilities, money, children, and even their freedom because they didn't consciously consider their choices and the consequences of their actions.

Reaction or Action?

Most people's behavior is either guided consciously by their minds or is operating on preprogrammed feelings, beliefs, and habits to defend against the outside. To put it another way, people either act or react.

What is the difference? A reaction is an action or thought triggered by something outside ourselves. It is an impulsive act, without thought, in direct response to something said or done by another person. How someone reacts is determined by their feelings, beliefs, and experience. Someone's typical reactions were mainly developed in childhood and adolescence and resulted from imitating those around them.

Acting is when the motivation for doing something comes from inside of ourselves. An action originates in awareness of our thoughts, feelings, and desire. Acting is when we *consciously* choose what we want. We are in charge and our actions are based on our values and desires. A culmination of our experiences also influences our actions. The difference is that action is more thoughtful and deliberate, whereas reaction is less conscious and less under our conscious control.

An example of reacting and acting is when a three-year-old boy has thrown all of his food on the ground, and his mom gets angry and punishes the child. Then she feels bad and wonders if she was too rough. When Mom thinks about what the child has done and what appropriate action to take to address his misbehavior, then she is acting. A reaction is when the mom is emotionally upset at what the child has done and blurts out or acts out punishment without considering it. One is a deliberate, purposeful, and intentional action. This other is an impulsive reaction.

It's important to understand when our actions are conscious or reactive. Most people do not pay attention to whether they are acting or reacting. We need to be aware and observe ourselves closely to discern the difference and become aware of our behavior with others and what fears may or may not be driving us.

Learn to look within and become an observer to gain awareness of your thoughts and emotions so you can move away from being reactive and move into a life of purposeful action.

Being Manipulated

When we are reactive, we may be unaware of the outside forces influencing us. Often, we are being manipulated without realizing it. Some people strive to influence us to get what they want with little regard for what we want. There is a wide array of techniques for doing this—as many as the people who employ them. These strategies are designed to create a cloud of confusion, fear, and upset in others.

When someone is experiencing heightened levels of negative emotion in response to an outside stressor, they may find themselves unable to think clearly and feeling confused. This weaker psychological state makes them more susceptible to others' influence. In this state, they are more likely to react negatively to people's misbehaviors, such as being on the receiving end of yelling, accusations, and demands. At these times, others have control over them because they can dictate the individual's defensive responses by pressing one of their buttons.

When we are reactive, other people are the puppeteers, and we are the reacting puppet.

Ed Reacts to Perceived Criticism

For example, take Ed. At his annual performance evaluation meeting, he learned that his new boss James didn't think that he deserved a raise. Ed became very angry when James mentioned that he needed to improve his communication skills with customers and had had average sales and job performance that quarter. Ed felt unappreciated, betrayed, and picked on. He was so upset that he began to say hateful things and swear at his boss. He slammed the door and kicked over a plant in the office hallway as he left.

This was a strong reaction. Ed is 60 years old. Isn't this behavior more like how an angry four-year-old child would react? Ed's negative reaction was driven by his fear. His mother had always criticized and put him down in front of others when he was a teenager, so he had a hard time facing constructive criticism, even at age 60. Ed thought the problem was caused outside of himself—James was a slave driver who did not appreciate him or value his work. He didn't realize that his fear and anger kept him from resolving the problem calmly and responsibly. There was plenty of room for him to improve his communication skills. But instead, he lived in a whirlpool of reaction after reaction.

Typical Negative Reactions

Here is a list of negative reactions.

Anger is a strong feeling of antagonism and physiological arousal targeted toward someone or something because of a threat, annoyance, or blocked desires. For example, a woman became angry with her boyfriend because she thought he was too friendly with her girlfriend (threat of losing her boyfriend), or a customer was angry with a server because he didn't like how long it took for his food to arrive (annoyance). Anger shows that a person has fear, so they must examine the fear underneath the anger. In these examples, anger-based reactions might be yelling, scolding, or withdrawal from the boyfriend or the restaurant.

Nervousness is based on having fearful thoughts of adverse outcomes related to an anticipated future event and is visible through a heightened physiological response of arousal (e.g., shaking, stomach butterflies, rapid heartbeat, sweating). For example, first dates often evoke nervousness. A woman may feel anxious because she is afraid that the other person might not like her, fearing that she might not be pretty enough or their type. Feeling nervous indicates fear, insecurity, and a lack of confidence.

Defensiveness is feeling the need to defend with words or actions. When someone says something inappropriate or inaccurate, the person on the receiving end may feel the need to protect themselves by defending themselves to show they are innocent. They are reacting to defend their ego. Classic examples of defensiveness are: "It is not my fault she tore her dress," "He should have been more careful," and "I didn't start the fight; he yelled first."

Negative communication, by raised voice, harsh tone, and yelling, happens when someone is out of control due to anger and feeling threatened. An example is when a car hit Harry's bumper at a stop sign. He became enraged and started yelling at the driver who hit his car. Another example is when Emily was told she couldn't go to the party, and she became very upset and started talking to her mother in a loud, angry voice.

Being critical and saying hateful and nasty things is an expression of anger. It is trying to feel better by putting the other person down. For example, a boss was upset with her employee because she disliked how he did his job, so she gossiped about his personal life and made sarcastic jokes. Another example is when Marjorie's husband had a bad day at work and was very critical about how she cooked his steak.

Threats are also an indicator of anger at work. Someone makes threats to another person because they feel vulnerable, out of control, or powerless to influence an outcome in any other way. For example, an exasperated father feels powerless over his son's defiant behaviors. He resorts to angry threats to make his son's life miserable if he doesn't obey the father's rules. Another example is Malcolm. His wife goes out with her friends every weekend and comes home at midnight. Feeling out of control and powerless over her behavior, he angrily threatens his wife that he will get a divorce and kick her out of their house if she doesn't stop going out with the girls.

Blaming other people or circumstances for behavior is about projecting responsibility onto others to avoid being at fault or feeling helpless and powerless. Blame often is accompanied by shaming others, which is a toxic way to engage in relationships. Jerry blamed his wife for causing them to lose some money because he invested in the stock she suggested. Nancy blamed Tom for no one showing up for their party. Tim failed his exam and faulted his professor for the difficulty of the test.

Cheating is a behavior that breaks the rules, regulations, or law to get something valued and desired that is seen as difficult or impossible to obtain through lawful means. People who cheat feel that they deserve what they want and are willing to bend or break the rules to get it. Cheating is reactive because the person loses sight of the cost of this behavior to their integrity and standing in society. They find ways to justify the deception within themselves. People lose their self-respect, and when cheating is discovered, the respect of others is lost as well. The degrees of cheating vary from lying on a tax return, using hidden crib notes during an exam, and being dishonest while playing a board game to win.

Dishonesty is misrepresenting the truth to gain a benefit for oneself or others. It is usually to gain something that is wanted or perceived as needed. In the end, the person engaging in dishonesty loses their integrity and respect. Mason lied about how much money he made on an investment. Jackie didn't tell her boyfriend, Tim, that she was also dating Eduardo. People are also dishonest to avoid feeling the discomfort of hurting or disappointing others in some way. An example of this is saying that an overdue task has been completed when it is still not done.

Irresponsibility is when someone does not forecast the consequences of their behavior and cannot be depended on to make wise decisions. In contrast, to be responsible means being able to be counted on to foresee the consequences of behaviors and taking appropriate steps to ensure the best and safest outcome for all. Sarah was supposed to watch her younger brother for the evening, but instead, she slipped out to have drinks with her boyfriend. Jason was scheduled to be at work at 9 a.m. but didn't show up until noon.

Being unfair means taking advantage of others to gain some benefit, for example, more money, more attention, or more of whatever they desire. People pay the price for being unfair because this behavior is often reciprocated somehow, and they end up losing more than they gained. For example, Jack and Tim pooled their money to invest in buying some fruit for resale, but Jack secretly sold some of the fruit on the side and didn't share the profits with Tim. Tim figured out that Jack had secretly sold the fruit and never did business with him again.

Leg Up on Others is when someone only thinks about their own gain and doesn't consider any harm imposed on others by their behavior. This behavior suggests that their ego is fighting to be seen as more powerful or deserving. Someone thinks that getting a leg up on others will give them what they feel is lacking in themselves. This problem needs to be dealt with on the inside because that is where it comes from. Tracy and Andrea are friends who were both auditioning for the same part in a movie. Tracy got insider information about the role and hid it from her friend to stand a better chance of getting the part. Jeremiah took illegal performance-enhancing drugs to win the race.

Hiding information from another person for self-gain is a more covert way of being dishonest. Jack had a minor accident on his motorcycle and broke a rib, but he hid it from his mother because he was afraid she would make him sell his motorcycle. Tyrone was afraid his parents wouldn't approve, so he hid that he was dating Maria.

Passive-aggressive acts are indirect behaviors intended to harm another person. For example, Jill's husband went out for a night with the boys, so she bought an expensive piece of jewelry as revenge. They are actions and words that are said that do not directly deal with what the person is upset about.

Selfishness occurs when a person feels a lack within themselves and tries to make up for it. They try to make themselves whole at other people's expense. For example, roommates Jordan and

Ryder had to live on a tight budget, and they bought their food together, but Ryder always took more food for himself. Nellie was generous and let Susan borrow her clothes when she needed them, but Susan wouldn't let Nellie borrow anything from her.

Being controlling is an indication of fear. Trying to control others is an attempt to feel more secure and safe. Control drives others away, and in the end, people lose more than they gain. Christopher made his wife keep a list of every dollar she spent and report it to him. Mario secretly put a tracking system on his wife's car so he could keep tabs on her every move.

Negative reactions that aren't consciously dealt with are harmful. They create negative energy inside of us, which attracts more negative experiences. Changing negative behavior does not depend on age. Some people spend their whole lives doing the same thing and not learning from their mistakes. Change occurs when we become aware of what we are doing, take responsibility, process our feelings, strengthen our minds, and engage in positive action rather than reaction.

How Do We Overcome Our Reactive Tendencies?

As discussed, when we are in a reactive mode, we are not in our power. Negative emotions consume energetic resources and distract us from thinking clearly and acting in a way that is for the highest good of all. When reactive, people make poor choices or say and do things that they may later regret.

In a reactive mode, people will argue, resist, and defend their decisions and opinions to convince others that they are right. In response, the other person will insist that they are right. It is a battle about being right. The person with the most power will use it against the other one. The relationship may break up. A person may get kicked out of their apartment or get fired from their job, but the reactivity continues until they are finally ready to examine the pattern and learn how to stop it. Processing feelings so we won't feel upset and angry helps us regain our footing and balance. When we are calm, we have greater access to the knowledge and wisdom that enables us to examine the available choices in each situation with clarity.

Decide to keep yourself from reacting or behaving impulsively. When you are experiencing a negative emotion or feel stressed, take a breath before reacting to anything. Then pause to look within at your inner state. Get in touch with the negative emotions and fears that the situation may arouse and employ the ETT to unpack and release them.

Let's say that you have an impulsive reaction anyway, you can still learn from it. More than anything else, *how* you react can show you *why* you react and what it costs you. If you have been triggered and have reacted strongly by acting out in words or deeds, when you are calm again, take a moment to examine the situation.

1. Take complete responsibility for your upset feelings.
2. What negative emotions did you experience? What were the fears behind them? Process them now.
3. Search to identify what you wanted from the interaction or thought you needed but did not get.
4. Notice if something was said that hurt your feelings or your ego.
5. Check if you are experiencing any fear because of what will happen in the future or if something doesn't happen the way you want.
6. Examine if your thoughts are negative or positive. Do you have any negative beliefs that caused the conflict?
7. Keep asking yourself what part *you* have been playing in creating this upset, and keep focused on what *you* can do to make it better. Figuring out what you can change may take some time.

8. Be willing to set your ego aside and have a humble attitude. Both sides will win if you let go of your negativity.

9. Any ongoing negative thoughts about the situation or people involved indicate there is more processing work to do. Keep processing and peeling back the layers of your negative emotions. Some issues have multiple layers that run deep, requiring multiple processing sessions.

You will grow the most in the long run if you make learning from your reactions and avoiding being reactive in the first place an ongoing process in your life. The most difficult part can be even noticing when you are reacting.

Observing Instead of Reacting

A way to prevent reacting is to double down on developing the ability to observe. Observation enables us to watch what is happening and stop ourselves from reacting. At the same time, it also helps us to notice our emotions and whether we need to process them. It helps to learn strategies that help the mind focus on the present moment. For example, we can meditate consistently. It slows our thoughts, improves concentration, and trains observation. Practicing looking inward and observing what is going on within helps us be more conscious and discerning.

As the observer, we can develop objectivity about negative experiences, which allows us to transcend emotional upset and negativity. The goal is to remain in the observer position no matter the outside influence.

When I was learning to be more observant, I found that I would react to a person's negative behavior without even realizing it. For example, when I perceived that someone was criticizing me (e.g., you drive too fast), I discovered that I would react with a snippy remark. I examined what emotions had been triggered to cause me to behave that way upon engaging in self-reflection.

I also made an effort to avoid thinking about how wrong the other person was for "having made me react." It's not their fault. Perceiving someone else as wrong is just a way to justify my negative feelings and keep me stuck in a negative circular loop. In looking inward, I discovered that perceived criticism often made me feel inadequate and not good enough. I learned to process my feelings whenever I felt criticized and think about whether I needed to respond to the person to address the perceived criticism. After processing feelings, often, there is no need to act at all.

After some time of doing this inner work of transforming your energy, you will realize one day, as I did, that you no longer react negatively to perceived criticism or whatever triggers you. It just won't happen anymore. The person who keeps criticizing you will change and stop making those types of comments.

How to Respond

Processing emotions and observing are *not* suggestions that everyone should become passive in their relationships, let others walk all over them, or suppress their feelings or emotions in any way. On the contrary, everyone can stop and process their emotions *before* taking an action so that, *when* they act, the action is based on inner wisdom and calm instead of pain. This helps individuals make better choices in their interactions with others.

There are times when people do have an opportunity to connect to their feelings before they must respond to someone who seemingly triggered upset in them. For example, if someone received a critical email from a boss about a report they just wrote, they could take the time to do a quick moment of inner work before responding to the email. If they did, their response would be calm, clear, and well-presented.

Other times, though, it may not be possible to take a time-out to do inner transformation work before responding to the external world. Take an individual in the middle of a social situation who became upset due to some trigger. Let's say Jacob was giving a presentation to a group of people and felt attacked by some of the participant's questions. Since a response was called for, he had to act quickly to the perceived stressor without time to process the triggered upset.

If a response is called for in the moment, but you are experiencing negative emotions, make an effort to become aware that you are upset. The best solution is to say as little as you have to and just observe the situation as much as possible. This buys some time to process your feelings and get into balance later.

You cannot make good decisions and resolve a conflict when upset. If possible, take a quick break from the interaction and go to the bathroom. Acknowledge the negative feelings and allow yourself to experience them as much as possible, by letting off some of the steam. This can help you to regain your awareness and footing.

When you return to the interaction, listen objectively, and observe what is going on rather than react, blame, attack, or show coldness or ill-will of any kind. If this is not possible, politely postpone the interaction until a future time when you are calm. If you are interacting with someone close to you, such as a family member, spouse, or close friend, you can say: I need to think about this. Give me a little time to sort this out, and I will get back to you.

A common question is **how does someone know when they are ready to take action?** They are ready when their feelings have been processed, and they feel calm about the issue at hand because then they can think about the situation with a clear mind. They also are fully aware of their thoughts, choices, and consequences regarding the matter.

Do a postmortem after a significant interaction. There is something to be learned when interactions work out successfully. First, there is positive reinforcement in reminding yourself when you have done well. Look at the steps that led to that success. If problems occurred, then examine what could have been done differently. A variety of choices may have led to the failure. Break down the steps to see what happened and what you could have changed to make it better. How did you feel when you expressed your opinion? Angry? Were you only thinking about what you wanted and not what the other person wanted? I have found that I feel the most successful and happy when my responses result in a win-win for all parties involved.

Debra Overcomes Being Reactive

Debra kept getting herself in trouble because she couldn't stop herself from talking back, being defensive, and being angry when she encountered a stressor. She had tried not to answer back, but she couldn't seem to stop herself from blurting things out. She kept getting kicked out of apartments, dropped from relationships, and fired from jobs. She felt that her behavior was other people's fault. Finally, when she had suffered enough, she came to me to find out what she could do differently and how to have a happier life. I became familiar with her history and patterns of behavior.

Debra said, "It is impossible for me to *not* say defensive, angry things when someone accuses me of doing something wrong."

I explained to Debra, "Your ego wants to be right, to be in charge, and to run the show. It wants to be the one to decide what should be done, what should be said, and what the result should be—like what kind of ice cream the other person should have, how much money they should spend, and if the door should be open or closed. Your ego wants to decide what other people should do and even think and believe about you, good or bad."

Then I went on, "Stop trying to defend your ego, feelings, and thoughts. Become willing to allow other people to have their own opinions, beliefs, likes, and decisions. It is all right that they are different than yours. Debra, stop needing to be right. Change your attitude and be willing to accept and allow others to have the freedom to make their choices."

I taught Debra that whatever behavior is going on outside doesn't matter. Debra's job was to get in touch with the fears and negative feelings that caused her to feel threatened when someone didn't agree with her. People can be threatened by any number of things, even mundane things like being told they left the door open or a reminder that they forgot something. Debra learned to stop reacting to the outside and instead process her negative feelings and fears until she was no longer upset about an issue.

Debra also learned that her attitude needed to change by getting to the place where she truly believed: "My job is to accept and allow when other people are making their choices. It doesn't matter what other people do. If it takes the rest of their lives to learn their lessons, then I will accept that. It is all right if they never learn to think the same way I do. My job is to be understanding, kind, and helpful to others."

Debra continued to work on her behavior, stop being defensive and blaming, and accept differences in others. She learned to think about ways to avoid being reactive and look within at her fears, process her feelings, and then consciously choose how she reacts, instead of being played like a puppet by her fears and the will of external actors. This helped her improve her acceptance and understanding if anyone complained to her. She secured a job working at a university coordinating student events, found joy in gardening, and adopted a dog, Mandy, the perfect companion.

Moving from Reaction Toward Forgiveness

Sometimes, people may hold onto fear, anger, and negativity for a long time, particularly about a person or a traumatic event. Examples of these situations can include divorce, fatal car accidents, sexual assault, or abuse.

When helping someone who is upset with others, I ask them if they are willing to forgive whomever has done something to make them hurt, angry, and upset. Sometimes, they will say they cannot forgive. It isn't really a matter of cannot; it's that they *will not* forgive. They may be afraid to let go of their anger because it feels like it is all they have to keep them going.

Forgiveness is a choice. People are afraid that if they forgive, they are saying that the behavior was acceptable. Forgiving a person does not mean that the action was okay or that you agree with what happened. Forgiveness is not about the other person; it is about *you*. Forgiving someone, including yourself, is simply saying that you are willing to stop being the judge and carrying pain, anger, blame, and justifications inside of you.

It is important to forgive because holding onto anger, resentment, and blame creates a heavy burden that poisons everything it touches. The energy of that burden harms your health and damages you and your relationships. When you refuse to forgive, you are being judgmental.

Let's delineate the difference between judging and concluding. Each day, we have to make decisions requiring us to form opinions and draw conclusions about events, actions, people, and ourselves. The difference between drawing a conclusion and being judgmental is that with judgments, emotions are attached. When people merely observe what is happening without negative emotion, it is not judgmental. Conclusions without judgment don't have emotions attached to them.

As long as you hold onto judgment and refuse to forgive yourself or others, there can be no healing within yourself or with the other people involved. Through forgiveness, people lose their enemies, dramas, the fuel for their egos, self-defining stories, and even friends who dwell in the same kind of pain. By releasing judgment, you find more peace and happiness and set a good example for your children and others.

Martha Faced Her Nightmares

Martha had been experiencing pain in the center of her chest and around her throat. Realizing it was emotional she decided she needed to get some help. She started on her quest with a curious mind, open to a path of self-discovery.

Martha didn't know what to expect. Martha felt safe enough to share with me that she had been physically abused by a relative when she was a young child. As Martha talked about her memories, powerful emotions began to surface. They were so overwhelming that she could hardly bear the pain and soon had difficulty breathing. On this day, Martha began releasing her deeply held secrets and facing her pain.

Our next session revealed the buried hate, shame, guilt, anger, and resistance that had a stranglehold on Martha. She began this long journey into darkness, which, at first, blocked out the healing light. Forgiveness was seemingly impossible for her. Martha's fears needed much healing if she was ever going to be able to forgive all the predators of her early childhood and teen years. The closer she got to the truth, the more an onslaught of terrifying nightmares visited her most nights. Martha had been living her life as a spectator. She was not fully connected to her spiritual life and felt separate from God. The blocks to love seemed insurmountable for her.

Martha talked with God and said, "Yes, I am afraid. I am open to your healing energy. Please take these fears from me. My desire for you is stronger than anything else." These were powerful words that took time for Martha to say with full conviction. She learned how her ego played a major role in holding her in pain and resentment. She struggled with feeling like she was a mistake. She had fears of incompetence. The list went on.

The third session was about resistance. Martha learned how to recognize it and what steps she needed to take to deal with it. She had to ask herself, "How do I really want to feel, and what can I do differently to have positive feelings?" Martha knew she had much to learn about stopping her resistance and learning to direct her life.

Months passed, and Martha began to experience the same deep pain in her heart and throat again so she went back for more help. She became very fearful of God. A memory of a priest's robe at eight years old broke through, a memory that Martha had repressed. The priest had raped Martha in the church and then threatened her if she told anyone what he did. He said, "Jesus will hurt you, destroy you, or even kill you." Martha realized how she had connected Jesus with the priest. It was a destructive force in her life.

Martha learned to feel, own, and accept her feelings of hate, fear, sorrow, and depression. Martha's fears kept her disconnected from Jesus. She needed to accept and allow God's healing. It was difficult for Martha to work through the pain of what had happened to her. She learned how to comfort and love the eight-year-old child within Martha, who was very much afraid to open up to more pain. Martha needed to embrace her to make her feel loved and safe, validate her feelings, and accept her pain and all she went through. Martha had to assure her she was not alone and that she was there for her.

Martha continued to seek and work on herself for a long time. Many more traumatic, repressed memories began to surface, and Martha had many more screaming nightmares. As painful as it was, she could feel strength coming from God.

Today, Martha is more open to knowing the truth about herself and to living with a spirit of forgiveness. She better understands her blocks to love and the fears that kept her stuck. Martha's voice is no longer silenced, and the nightmares have ended. She has forgiven herself and everyone else. Martha lives a more peaceful and prayerful life and is open and connected to God's healing love. Jesus has become her friend and companion.

Everyone Teaches Us Lessons

Forgiveness can lead to feelings of understanding, empathy, and compassion for those who hurt us. A wonderful example of forgiveness is Nelson Mandela, the first Black President of South Africa. He had been sentenced to life imprisonment as punishment for his efforts to end apartheid and his advocacy for human rights.

He served 27 years of his sentence. Later writing about when he was released from prison, he wisely said, "As I walked out of the door toward the gate that would lead to my freedom, I knew if I didn't leave my bitterness and hatred behind, I'd still be in prison." Forgiveness is one of the greatest gifts you can give yourself and an act of love toward yourself and others.

Whether you react, act impulsively or respond positively, real change requires that, at some point, you learn how to forgive as you process and accept. This is the path of transformation to a more aware state of being. The next section explores other ways of operating from a higher consciousness.

PART III

Living Our Best Lives: Insights on How to Thrive

CHAPTER 10

Actions for Living in Higher Consciousness

Have you heard the expression, "People are like sheep following other sheep?"

Many actions and thoughts are so habitual that people are unaware of the seeds they sow and the harvest that may result. People have much more power than they realize by becoming aware of their thoughts, the energy they are manifesting, and their actions. Before anyone can take steps to change, they must become consciously aware of what they are doing.

Learning to Make Wise Choices

We make hundreds of choices every day. The question is, will our choices lead to success and well-being? People make poor choices because they lack information or haven't given enough thought to the results of their actions. Many people make decisions based on a whim or impulsively. Few examine their beliefs or motives regarding the decision.

Of course, because we can't predict the future, there will be times we have to make choices without knowing whether they will prove to be wise ones. But we can do as much as possible to make sure we are balanced, informed, and conscious about a choice. It takes practice, patience, wisdom, and time to learn how to make good choices. People master how to make good choices through education, observing others, and learning from their mistakes.

Good choices require some deep thinking, time, research, and analysis. Often, people neglect these steps; and though it's not necessary to think extensively about every decision in your life (like what type of cereal to buy), they should be applied to major life decisions.

Motives Determine End Results

There are situations in life that do require some careful and effortful thought and action. Do we want to date someone, sell our house, buy a new car, change careers, or get married? These major life choices are matters that call for conscious, well-thought-out decisions.

Your motives can determine the outcome of your actions, so know *why* you make a specific choice. Here are a few questions to gain clarity on your motives:

- What is my purpose for taking this action?
- What do I expect to lose or gain?
- What are my feelings regarding making this decision?
- What are the consequences of my action?

My stepfather had Alzheimer's disease for many years. By the age of 90, he was in an assisted living facility and had been on a feeding tube for over a year. Finally, the doctor told our family, "It's going to be necessary to amputate his legs, so I think it's time to take out his feeding tubes." I gave a lot of thought to making the best decision and asked myself, "What is the right thing to do? If I were in his position, what would I want?" I wanted to make sure my decision was for the right reasons, and not about me. My motive for my decision was based on my stepfather's well-being and what I thought he would want.

When we know our motives when planning specific actions, we make wiser choices that benefit everyone.

Planning

When planning an action, it's best to examine some of the following critical factors.

Its cost and benefit to ourselves and others.

The amount of energy and time involved to bring it into fruition.

Whether it aligns with our integrity and purpose.

What risks are involved.

What the foreseeable consequences will be.

Taking time to formulate a well-laid-out plan will be helpful; it will save time, money, misery, and problems, especially regarding large life decisions—a new job, marriage, health, major purchase, or vacation. In these cases, it is not so easy to rectify bad choices.

Sometimes, doubts seep in during the journey, and people get sidetracked by resistance and fear. They may have so much fear that they become paralyzed and refuse to make any decision. For example, Dave bought a new car and then was unhappy about it because he doubted his choice and kept wondering if he should have bought a different car. His doubts weren't about anything in particular with the car he purchased; he just didn't trust in his ability to make the best decision.

Sometimes, no matter how much planning or research is done, we are still not sure about the best option to choose or path to take. We may not have all the information concerning a problem or choice, but we have to make a decision anyway. Remember the story of Snow White who bit into a red apple that was beautiful and shiny on the outside? The apple's appearance was deceiving, and it wasn't until she bit into the apple that she found out that it was poisoned. There are instances when we are surprised by what unfolds after we've made a decision, and it is only then that we know exactly what we are contending with.

It is at this point that many people compound their problems. Instead of looking calmly at the unforeseen issue in front of them, they react emotionally. Then their actions become focused on how upsetting it is, not knowing what to do, and reacting with frustration and anger. When we remain calm and focus on addressing the issue at hand without negative emotion, we can target all of our energy, thinking, and actions toward resolving the problem.

Look at Past Choices

Examine the major choices you have made. Were you pleased with the results? If you were unhappy with a result, look at other options. Professional poker players have it right. They study past games and how they played their hands, going over every detail to see what they would change in the future. This is how they learn and improve their game. In the same way, if you pay close attention to the quality and results of your past decisions, you will also start to make better choices and acquire wisdom.

To help in reviewing past decisions, ask yourself the following:

- What could I have done differently?
- What did I want that I did not get?
- What were the consequences?
- Were my goals reasonable?
- Did I understand what the other person was saying?
- Was I calm and balanced?
- Was I fair?
- Was I irritated or angry?
- Did I complain and blame others?
- Was I clear about what I communicated?
- Did I allow enough time to deal with the situation?
- Did I ask for what I wanted?
- Was I flexible and willing to make adjustments?
- If I could do it over, what would I do differently?

Environmental Influences

Those we associate with can uplift us or bring us down, so it's important to select our friends and acquaintances carefully. We can make good relationship decisions by becoming more consciously aware of our choices about people.

Notice how you feel around the individuals in your social circle. Do they make you feel good or bad? Stop and observe if you are around people who continuously stir negative emotions in you and make you feel defensive and reactive. Ask yourself, what fears are involved? What needs to be healed? If you do the ETT work and the problems are resolved, the issues could have been rooted in your fears.

If problems in a relationship don't resolve after processing, look more closely at your needs and the other person's needs and any patterns in your interactions. Ask whether they are creating negative feelings. Is there anything you can change so that everyone's needs are met or patterns are shifted?

Sometimes when we transform, we grow apart from certain friends who no longer feel in alignment with us. It is all right to let people go lovingly.

Being around some people brings us down. It's best to avoid people who use drugs, abuse alcohol, or break the law. It's best to stay well clear of anyone who abuses people or animals. Find people who have good morals and are uplifting because of their high principles and aspirations. Choose friends and partners of good character before allowing them to join you on life's journey.

It is also important to carefully consider the arena in which we work since it consists of both a physical and social environment, and it's where we spend considerable time and energy every day. Because environment impacts our energy, we can make an effort to choose to work for organizations that operate with integrity or even add value to society and people's lives. In this way, we avoid being exposed to unhappy co-workers and feeling not so good about our work.

Suppose we work for an organization that is dishonest or markets low-standard goods and services. In that case, we may be forced to compromise our values and engage in actions that will lower our standards to match those of the company.

What Are Your Daily Habits?

Most people are not aware of how many decisions they make

each day. Most of our decisions and actions are habitual. A habit is formed by repeating an action or thought until it becomes automatic, which means that it has become ingrained in the unconscious. Once this happens, the behavior or thinking becomes mechanical and occurs without much conscious thought. For example, when someone is learning to drive a car, initially it is a slow process because the person must think about each action— i.e., press on the gas and steer at the same time, or keep an eye on the rear-view mirror and remember to signal—before driving skills become automatic. After enough practice, someone can drive a car without too much conscious thought, and body movements occur automatically, even while the driver is talking to passengers. The unconscious mind has learned to drive the vehicle, enabling someone not to have to think about each step.

In this way, habits can be very useful and, being automatic, conserve our time and energy. They save us from having to make a decision. For example, having a grocery-shopping routine means we don't have to think about where to buy groceries or what kind of toothpaste we want. We can rely on what choices worked for us in the past.

However, repeating negative behaviors, such as when we do anything compulsively, creates bad habits. It is easy to fall into them. One day we skip making our bed, and soon we never make the bed. We tell a white lie or two and then we have a habit of lying. We indulge in a cigarette borrowed from a friend and soon we have a pack-a-day monkey on our backs. We are indulging in negative behaviors automatically, without thought, or unconsciously.

To create positive habits and get out of negative ones, first, you must become consciously aware of your present habits. Analyze your daily actions to determine the habits you would like to add or eliminate. Select one negative one at a time to change. Notice the situations and people that may trigger you to indulge in a negative habit. The ETT method (chapter 5) can deal with any feelings that come up as barriers to changing a habit. Practice affirmations to reinforce your will and change any unconscious beliefs you may have ("I can't do it"). When working on changing habits, also employ self-care methods to provide you with solace and positive reinforcement. When a habit is at the point of addiction, seek help from a 12-step program, treatment center, counselor, or therapist. Always call upon God or your Higher Power to help you transform a habit.

Cultivate Patience

Patience is one of the most important qualities we can cultivate in our everyday lives. It is the willingness to allow ourselves and others the experience of learning and moving about life with ease and without pressure. Patience facilitates kindness and compassion toward everyone. Another word for patience is love. Patience comes from love and is an act of love.

Learning patience is valuable because it puts us in a calm place, enabling us to keep quiet and think about how to reach our goals and what words we can use. Impatience is hurried, annoyed, frustrated, and about "wanting things now." It creates pressure, unpleasantness, and stress. Patience is kind, gentle, loving, empathic, and nurturing.

Impatience comes from the ego because it is based on dissatisfaction and is a form of frustration and anger. Patience comes from the energy of tranquility and acceptance. It is important to have patience with ourselves and others. When being patient, we give up demanding, forceful, pushy, and unreasonable expectations of ourselves and others.

It is easier to learn and study when we have patience because our full attention is placed with ease on what we are doing without being pulled down by a negative feeling. Patience allows us to stick with a task without distraction.

Some other benefits of having patience are that we will become:

Happy

Kinder

More loving

Easier to be around

Able to learn more easily and faster

More successful

Flowing in Positive Energy

When you make an effort to live in higher consciousness, there are many things you can do to help raise your vibrational energy level, such as:

1. Develop your spiritual life and pray to a benevolent Higher Power (i.e., God).

2. Be sorry for hurtful words, negative thoughts, and actions.

3. Make changes in:

    Eating habits

    Sleep

    Work

    Exercise

    Leisure time

    Helping others

    Sharing

    Attitude

    Being kind and generous

4. Be appreciative, grateful, and thankful.

5. Be conscious of what you are doing.

6. Spend time reveling and interacting in nature.

7. Examine your behavior daily and make adjustments.

8. Give to others rather than trying to get even.

9. Use kind words with no intention of hurting anyone.

10. Be kind to all sentient beings.
11. Do what you can to heal the planet.
12. Forgive yourself and others.
13. Live in humility.

CHAPTER 11

Living a Balanced Life

Moving Away from Everyday Pressures

Today, so many people feel stressed from juggling their daily responsibilities of a job, running a household, taking care of their children and their schooling, caring for parents and relatives, and handling the many unexpected things that come up each day. It is difficult for most people to have the time and energy to get everything done. When we feel stress, we usually believe that outside conditions caused it. Other labels we could put on stress are feeling overwhelmed, pressured, uptight, anxious, nervous, and out of control.

There are emotions and fears we carry inside that are causing our stress. For most of us, these feelings have been there most of our lives but have gotten worse as we have aged and life's demands have grown. There are more responsibilities and more restraints, and it feels like we have less time. We still have 24 hours in a day, the same as we have always had. We are just handling how we spend the 24 hours differently.

Ever since I was a teenager, when people would ask me, "How are you?" my automatic answer was always, "Oh, I have been so busy." Many years later, I learned that it made me feel good to think I was busy. I believed working and being busy was positive and meant I was doing well. My mother's favorite thing to tell me was "hurry up." Often, I felt overwhelmed because of all the responsibilities I had to handle. I never had enough time to do all the things I wanted to do.

Finally, I realized that because I was constantly telling myself how busy I was, I was the one creating all the pressure I felt. Also,

I thought about what message I was conveying when I would tell everyone, "I am so busy." I was indirectly telling them that I didn't have time for them. First, when I stopped telling myself how busy I was, the pressure I felt subsided. I started repeating the affirmation, "I have all the time I need to do everything I want to do." It was a huge surprise to realize that my own thinking is what made me stressed. Since that time, I no longer say, "I have been so busy," and the overwhelmed feelings are gone.

Do you believe that it is normal to have nervous pressure inside? The first place to start handling stress is within. Here are some steps to inquire how you may be creating stress for yourself:

1. Ask yourself if you are using responsibilities as an excuse to create pressure on yourself unconsciously.

2. Examine your beliefs about being busy and working. To examine negative beliefs, look for any negative feelings you have. Do you have negative feelings about specific people, certain jobs, some activities, or about politics, religion, marriage, certain foods, and what some say and do?

3. Next, look at your other beliefs about the people or topics you answered in the question above that cause you to be negative. These are the beliefs you want to eliminate and replace with new, positive beliefs that can help you.

4. Make a list of how you are feeling and label your fears.

5. Process your feelings and fears until your energy feels balanced, peaceful, and calm. Sometimes, it may take some time to process your feelings until the point of calm.

6. As you relax more, examine your daily responsibilities with more detachment. See if you have placed more demands on yourself than you can realistically handle. If you have too many things to do each day than you can reasonably do, then become resourceful and set some priorities. Can you let some responsibilities go or get some extra help? It will be easier to do after you have eliminated your fears and negative feelings.

Without handling the pressured energy inside first, it is impossible to find peace and relaxation as a way of life. The energy inside will always cause us to attract a lifestyle that matches what we are feeling. It took a long time to create the stress we have been living with, so be patient since it will also take time to learn to think and act differently to live with balanced energy.

Setting Priorities

Many people are so busy that they cannot accomplish everything they want to do in their day. Several years ago, I wanted to go out for a walk at least three days a week, but I rarely ever found the time to do it. It seemed ridiculous that I desperately wanted to walk but couldn't make it happen. When I went to see a therapist to help solve the problem, he told me that I was not setting a high enough priority on walking.

When I was growing up, I was trained to do my schoolwork and chores. I completed all of them each day, but I didn't do personal things for myself. No one asked me, "Evelyn, what would you like to do today?" Chores and homework were all that mattered because that is what I was taught. There was never enough time left in the day even to take a walk.

The therapist advised me to set a time in her appointment book for taking a 45-minute walk. Following his directions, I made the appointment with myself for two days later. That afternoon a client called asking to see me the day I had set aside time to walk. I stuck to my appointment with myself and gave the client a time on another day. Before going to the therapist, I would have given up the time I had reserved to walk and booked the client, not taking any time for myself. After that, I often walked because I made it a priority.

When you have more activities than time, then learn to set priorities. Analyze which things are the most important and support your life purpose, and schedule the time to do them. Set aside the least important tasks to do another day. Setting priorities allows you to decide what tasks matter the most so you can accomplish them.

What to Do About Worry

It is surprising how much people worry about things they cannot control. Worrying is a fearful way of looking at life. People can train their brains to worry continually by turning life and events into scary stories. People form a habit of viewing life through current negativities and future uncertainties. This mental habit evokes daily nervousness, upset, unhappiness, and tiredness. People who are worriers usually can't articulate one thing that worries them.

During the Covid-19 pandemic, one of my friends called to talk about her anxiety over how tired she felt, her worry about contracting Covid, and her fears for her neighbor's health. She also told me she kept worrying about the 2020 election and who would win. She shared that she worried about what would happen to the country no matter who won. It sounded exhausting.

What is the purpose of worry? People are under the illusion that worry will somehow protect them from harm. Instead, it's damaging and wastes energy. Worrying is a futile mental habit. Someone might as well sit around and think about the sky, whether it will change color, and whether an asteroid might fall out of it. People only let go of the habit of worrying once they wake up and become conscious of the futility of what they are doing.

Here are some points to help evolve past worry. Remind yourself that:

> Worrying does not help; it just exhausts your energy.
>
> Worrying creates more negative energy.
>
> Negativity attracts more negative things.
>
> People don't like being around people who complain and worry, so you are bound to find yourself with fewer friends and companions.

You can't enjoy your own company when you are in a state
of worry and negativity.

When you worry about someone, you send out negative
energy, which only worsens the situation. Instead, wish
the person well and send them positive energy.

Every day, remain aware and focus on noticing whether you
start to worry. Use an affirmation to retrain your brain away from
worrying and into the positive. If you realize that you are a worrier,
decide to stop. Here are some affirmations to use.

I now realize when I start to worry and stop it.

I now focus on what I can do to make the situation better.

I stop thinking about the subject when I have no power to
change the situation.

I find something pleasant and positive to think about.

I focus my mind on things I am grateful for.

If you have fears and insecurities that come up, use this as an
opportunity to process your feelings and fears and bring them
into healing. You will become stronger, more positive, and will
feel better about your life if worry has no place in it.

How to Deal with a Crisis

A crisis is a disruption in the ordinary functioning of life, a
personal tragedy, or something causing severe emotional upset. A
crisis tests our ability to handle the unexpected. Our response to
crisis reveals whether we have emotional stability or not. Having a
crisis is an opportunity to apply knowledge and experience. It can
be a time of learning and gaining more confidence in our ability to
deal with challenges. It is a time of strengthening resilience. Some
people live in a constant state of crisis.

The causes of a crisis are varied: the loss of physical abilities,
money, a job, or a friend; illness; a betrayal; the breakup of
a relationship; being the victim of a crime; an injury due to an

accident; and natural disasters like hurricanes, floods, earthquakes; and death. There are too many types of crises to list all of them here. But they show that it is crucial to be ready for the unexpected as much as reasonably possible. While there are some crises, we may not be able to prepare for, there are still many ways we can empower ourselves to be ready for the unforeseen.

Be Prepared

Everyone needs a plan for what they would do if an emergency came up. For example, we can have extra supplies on hand in case there is a natural disaster. We can keep a flashlight by the bed and know in advance the escape route in the event of a fire. It is prudent to ascertain the location of emergency exits when checking into a hotel or at the movies and to count the rows of seats to the emergency exits when on a plane. We can also practice what routes to take or shelters to go to if authorities tell us to evacuate our homes or an area.

Sometimes being prepared is about considering practical matters like whether we have adequate insurance protection. In some cases, the only preparation we can do is to be as healthy as possible by eating a good diet, exercising, getting enough sleep, and having a good attitude. We can also be sure to take care of our feelings so we are not filled with resentment, old hurts, and fears when a crisis hits, and we keep a positive attitude. The more stable we are, the better we can handle what happens.

Stay Focused

During a crisis, stay focused on the present situation and focus on taking proactive steps to solve problems. Here are some steps you can take:

1. Assess the situation.
2. Deal with your emotions and have a good attitude.
3. Examine your choices.

4. Determine what you can do to help the situation.
5. Ask for help from others if you need it.
6. Visualize and emotionally connect with a positive outcome.
7. Take appropriate and decisive action.
8. Be willing to help others.
9. Stay in the present.
10. *Accept* what you cannot change.

Refusing to accept what you do not have the power to change causes more unhappiness, frustration, and unnecessary problems and prolongs the situation. Blaming anyone (including yourself) is a waste of time. Accept that you do not have the power to control or change many things, and keep your focus on what you *can* change.

There is a saying: "It is not what happens to you, but how you deal with it that counts."

Trusting God

We all have times when we have to deal with an emergency. There are decisions to be made in the moment, and sometimes it takes courage to follow through on them. Here is one time when I had to make a difficult decision and trust that God would help me.

In 1947, I was 16 years old and living on a 180-acre farm in northern Iowa. My boyfriend and I would go to the movies on Saturday nights, driving nine miles into town. One Saturday night, while we were at the theater, there was a severe rainstorm. The dirt road to my family's farm had turned into mud, making it impossible to drive down it without chains on the tires, which we didn't have.

My boyfriend and I discussed how I was going to get home. It was 10:30 at night, and my parents would already be in bed asleep. There was no place for me to go. We decided to drive to another farm two miles to the east of our farm, located on a gravel road. From there, I could walk across some fields to get home.

I hadn't been in those fields, so I didn't know the terrain and had to cross them without a flashlight or umbrella. That particular night, it was still lightly raining off and on, and I couldn't see my hand in front of my face. Not knowing what to expect, I walked across the fields with my arms outstretched. I kept alert in case I ran into a hole, an animal, or a fence. Our farm had a lot of livestock—fifteen milk cows, four horses, and many pigs—and they were in the fields somewhere. I didn't know what livestock the other farmer had and where they were located.

It was very quiet. I listened carefully to tell if I was running into an animal or something. The field was wet and muddy in some places. I kept trekking along slowly and occasionally had to crawl through a barbed-wire fence. I lost any sense of time, but I finally arrived at our farm. I don't know how I found the way to our farm, but luckily, I did. Looking back, I don't think I would have made that same choice because I could have been injured in many different ways, but I will never forget it. I am sure God was walking with me that night.

Grow Stronger through Crisis

We have choices about how we deal with difficult times and threats. When conditions are challenging and painful, it is an opportunity for us to grow stronger or become weaker. At times like these, we are forced to decide how to handle the limitations, new rules, fear, financial hardships, and difficult times. How will we reinvent ourselves? These times can be used to call upon what we have learned from previous difficult experiences. They are also opportunities to do better, acquire new knowledge and experience, and operate from different modalities.

Alternatively, someone can take the path of least resistance and become a victim of circumstances. Some people will become depressed and miserable during crises and unforeseen events.

Like the coronavirus experience, a crisis is a unique opportunity for everyone to find new ways of dealing with things and creating change. Individuals can come out of the experience either stronger or weaker than before it happened. Life is not going to be the same afterward.

In Neuro-Linguistic Programming (NLP), there is a principle: **"The person who has the greatest flexibility has the greatest power."** Think for a minute about what that means. Those who are highly flexible have the best chance of seeking out choices and finding solutions to their problems. A crisis jars people out of their usual routines. They are forced to focus on different things, find new, creative ways of doing things, and set different priorities. People can be distracted from making positive changes in normal times due to their fears of confinement, limitation, sickness, and death. Ironically, it is sometimes easier to be our better selves at difficult times because a person is freed from their regular habits then. Have you noticed how some people are more generous and helpful in times of crisis?

During a crisis or difficult times, how someone directs their thinking and self-talk is especially important. Keep focused on the present and accept the reality of your limitations. Find what there is in your life that you can appreciate and be grateful for.

We can come out of a crisis wiser and stronger if we keep a good outlook, stay in the present, and help others whenever possible. We can appreciate what we do have, accept what we do not have the power to change, make a plan of action for each day, and be as productive as we possibly can be.

Coronavirus, a Recent Crisis

Anyone can experience a crisis at any moment. As I was writing this book, the world was experiencing the onslaught of disease caused by the coronavirus, which brought havoc, tragedy, and panic throughout the world due to the fear of disease and death, people being quarantined at home, stock market losses, and substantial unemployment. Millions of people became infected with the disease, and millions died. It is an experience unlike any we have gone through during our lifetimes.

Many people already live alone or are isolated for some reason. Then with coronavirus, they were spending day after day in even more isolation, which is very difficult for social beings. All the schools were closed so that children of all ages were home and not at school. All except essential businesses were closed.

It was a time when people were forced to experience life differently than ever before. University students expanded to online learning. Mothers and fathers had to balance their jobs—many working from home—while taking care of their children's remote schooling and elderly parents. They also had to manage to complete household tasks and make careful decisions about whom to see in their social circle, how to spend holidays, and what level of risk-taking was acceptable to keep everyone safe. The loss of family and friends was painful for so many.

Some used this time to help others in any way they could. People donated money, volunteered their service, and repurposed machinery to produce needed ventilators, face shields, and masks. Others delivered food to the doors of the elderly and disabled. Retired healthcare workers went back to work to help the sick. Researchers worked around the clock in laboratories to develop a vaccine. Therapists worked remotely to help people cope. And there were groups of people who joined at a set time to pray for everyone suffering from the disease. Observing the capacity of human beings to offer kindness and service to others was inspiring.

The Power of Gratitude

Gratitude can be an empowering force in our lives, particularly during challenging times. Muster up as much appreciation as you can about things in your life. Make gratitude a way of being.

We can be grateful for our relationships, a pet, a tree, the singing of the birds, a good hike, a bed to sleep in, a nice meal, a flower we have seen on a walk, having a comfortable home, heat, water, electricity, telephone, Internet, television, a bed, and a nurturing meal. The list of what can inspire gratitude in us is endless, but the feelings have to be authentic and heartfelt. When we make a habit of living in a spirit of appreciation, we create positive energy, which helps us to feel better and stronger, even in the face of a crisis. We can even feel thankful for the lessons that a crisis will teach us, even when we can't see them yet.

Here is an exercise that helped me to be more grateful, appreciative, and thankful. Each day, I would spend a few minutes thinking about what I was grateful for. Then, for example, I would ask myself, "Why am I grateful for rain?" My answer would be, "The rain gives us water to drink, fills our rivers, and waters the lawns, gardens, and trees. It cleans the houses, streets, buildings, and plants, makes the air feel fresher, and powers electricity." Some days it is hard to feel gratitude, but usually, people can always find something. The power of the exercise is in remembering *why* you are grateful. This exercise trains the mind to appreciate life and remember to see the world in a more grateful and positive way.

Make Time for Fun

Part of living in emotional balance is to have as much fun as possible. Having fun allows us to experience positive emotions and be playful, adding joy and increasing our quality of life. There are plenty of inexpensive ways to have a good time. At the end of life, no one says, "I regret that time I took to have fun."

Everyone has a different opinion of what fun is to them, so figure out what you enjoy, then make time to do it regularly. Here are some things that many people find fun:

Playing card games and board games

Drawing or painting

A car drive

Inviting friends over for lunch or dinner

Taking a vacation
Going to a movie
Shopping
Learning a new hobby
Taking lessons about something interesting
Going out to lunch or dinner
Attending a lecture
Attending a concert
Playing a sport or hiking
Going fishing
Camping
Reading an interesting book
Going to the beach or a park
Spending time in nature
Gardening

Born in a small town in Iowa, I never traveled out of state until I was 18. Traveling was something I had dreamed about and always wanted to do. Between the ages of 20 and 25, I traveled to over 40 states around the US. Then in 1961, at the age of 31, my husband and I went on a three-month trip around the world. That was in the days before there were jets, so we flew on propeller planes.

The world was a different place then than it is today. There weren't nearly as many people, and some countries were not as developed as they are today. One of the biggest impressions on us from that trip was the wall going up between East and West Berlin just when we arrived there. On that trip, the most expensive hotel was $25 a night. The two most expensive countries at that time were Israel and Japan. It was a wonderful experience, and I will always be grateful for that opportunity.

I have returned to many of the same countries more recently. Some of the places have changed so much that I didn't recognize them. The cities have expanded many miles out into the countryside. Israel was barren in 1961 and had far fewer people. Today, it is lush farmland, and there are many trees. It looks like a different country.

In 1984, I started lecturing on cruise ships. The first ship I cruised on was the *Love Boat*. It carried about 650 passengers and seemed large to me then, but it would be considered a very small ship compared to now. I stopped in 2009 when the ships stopped hosting outside lectures. Even so, my husband and I had so much fun cruising that we have continued to take eight or more cruises a year.

What I enjoy about a cruise is the freedom to choose from a vast array of activities throughout the day. My husband and I like to read, watch movies, play cards and games, go to the stage shows, and attend other ship activities. It's nice to be served sumptuous meals and have your cabin cleaned twice a day. Since we have already been on most shore excursions, we usually go off on our own when we go ashore. My husband and I have been all over the world, and we have seen some places many times. I am often asked what is my favorite place, but I can never pick just one.

Find something that you enjoy. Do something wholesome, rejuvenating, and that adds joy to your life. In the modern world, a deliberate effort is often required to make space for fun. It's worth the effort. Engaging in fun activities helps you live a balanced life so you are relaxed and happy. It doesn't stop there. You'll bring and share a happy vibe with you wherever you go. Having fun makes *you* more fun to be around.

CHAPTER 12

Wisdom of the Mind

Navigating through life requires knowledge. Knowledge is related to our intellect and our minds. It has to do with awareness, acquiring skills, or understanding the world around us through facts or objects. Keeping the mind sharp and developing the ability to focus enhances knowledge. Knowledge can be acquired in many ways and from many sources, including our senses, human perception, reason, scientific inquiry, education, and experience. Ultimately, though, knowledge must become wisdom and, once it does, it helps us transcend the mind.

How to Sharpen the Mind

You lose what you don't use.

—Unknown

Some people can fully use their cognitive capacity. They can maintain focus on a task for some time despite distractions. It is not difficult for them to present a thoughtful analysis of a situation and evaluate what is going on at a deep level. They like to contemplate and seek more knowledge about life. For a variety of reasons, not everyone's mental capacities operate at this level, but everyone can take steps to continuously hone their cognitive ability. The first step in this direction is to *reduce and eliminate* factors that dull the mind. Look at your daily life and honestly consider the extent to which you are exposing your body, brain, and mind to harmful chemicals, people, environments, and activities. What activities are you doing that dull your mind? Be careful about what you consume, what you put on your skin, and how foods and different products affect your mind and body.

Drugs, Alcohol, and Other Pollutants Dull the Mind

The biggest culprits in dulling the mind are drugs, nicotine, and alcohol. Eliminate them if possible. If you are shaking your head and have doubts about this, consider how you feel the day after consuming alcohol. Is your mental condition excellent, or do you want to lie down, put a pillow over your head, and wish the world would go away?

Some foods, pesticides, pollutants, chemicals, and surroundings also dull the mind. Become aware of what negatively affects you by paying attention. Consumption of some media and binge-watching television create a passive mental state. Gossip and occupying your mind with meaningless subjects also make it dull—limit what you talk about to only what is essential, inspirational, and useful.

Concentration Creates Alignment and Flow

When someone concentrates, the mind is pinpointed on one particular image, thought, idea, or concept. We are not born with the skill of concentration hardwired in our brains. It takes time, effort, and practice to develop it. As children, people learn quickly. We observed and imitated what we saw from our role models. But the ability to concentrate requires practice.

Concentration is about focusing the mind on the task at hand. It is not about the future or the past; it has to do with focusing on what we are doing right now. From time to time, people go into periods of deep concentration. Some examples include reading a good book, studying a subject that interests them, playing a musical instrument, painting, or focusing on a job.

We have to develop our concentration ability. It takes conscious effort and discipline, some training and practice, to achieve a high degree of concentration. Like any positive habit, once concentrating becomes ingrained in our unconscious through repetition, it can become automatic so we can concentrate when we need to. Some people get help from a teacher or coach to develop their ability to concentrate.

An important reason to learn the skill of concentration is to unite your body with your mind. Once you learn to unite the body and emotions with the mind, you can then align these with your goals. Then you are in flow. When our bodies, feelings, and minds are not in harmony, our thinking is unclear and confused, making it difficult to achieve our goals. (More on goals in chapter 13.)

Joe, Tae Kwon Do World Champion

Joe Alexander lives in Germany and is a Grand Champion in tae kwon do, a type of martial art. Joe mastered both tae kwon do and his ability to concentrate. He trained for four hours a day, seven days a week. It didn't matter which goal Joe set; he believed he could achieve it. According to Joe, the essential

Joe Alexander, tae kwon do champion

ingredients that contributed to his success were an ability to focus, discipline, flexibility, dedication, and a balanced body and mind connection. Joe believes that to be a champion, a person must *want* to do something, not feel they *must* do it. Also, they must genuinely like what they are doing or, even better, love it.

In the beginning, Joe's training was primarily mastering the physical skills of tae kwon do. Once he attained those skills, he began to focus more on developing his mental fitness. Joe explained that he could accomplish more when he incorporated mental and spiritual principles because the body's strength has a limit, but the power of the mind is limitless. If someone sets a course of action in their mind and fully believes it can be accomplished, the body will follow.

One of the incredible goals that Joe set for himself was to break bricks underwater. He said he had to eliminate the idea that this could not be done from his mind. Water is about eight hundred times denser than air, making it impossible to strike bricks underwater with the same force as on the outside.

Joe Alexander and the plaques of his world championships

Joe was invited to be a guest on a television show along with other people from around the globe who had accomplished amazing feats and held world records. For the show, Joe would attempt to break five bricks underwater simultaneously. Due to the water tank size necessary for this feat, it was placed outside the studio building. His performance was scheduled for 3 p.m., but Joe didn't go on then. After waiting for 10 hours in the studio and getting no sleep, Joe was finally called at 1 a.m. the following morning.

When asked how he dealt with the long delay, Joe said, "If something happens, you have to adapt every second. You have to be flexible, keep your mind free, and always work from the middle of your center. Working from your center means having your mind, body, and feelings working in harmony. Joe spent the hours he waited during the afternoon and evening meditating and visualizing being able to break the bricks underwater. He had to deal with tremendous challenges, but he did not let the obstacles get in the way of his goal.

Since the tank was sitting outside, by 1 a.m., the temperature had dropped, and the water in the tank became very chilly. Once again, Joe had to adapt. The water was cold, and the studio lights were very bright as he entered the tank. Joe had to keep his mind and body flexible under these new conditions. He got into position to strike the bricks. Joe broke all the bricks exactly as planned. It was amazing.

A Symbols Concentration Exercise

Symbols are archetypes, which are universal and archaic patterns from the collective unconscious that can activate the personal unconscious. The collective unconscious is the part of the mind containing memories and impulses common to humanity as a whole and inherited as part of being human. Concentrating on an archetypal symbol is another way to direct our unconscious minds to an outcome.

Several years ago, I learned about the work of Dr. Shafka Karagulla. Dr. Karagulla was a psychiatrist who researched why people with the same intelligence did not perform at the same level. She met Dr. Viola Neal, and they began working together to figure out how to help people reach their potential. Drs. Karagulla and Neal called a person not performing up to their intelligence level's potential a "stymied individual." A stymied individual has high intelligence but is confused, lacks confidence, and is scattered in their energy. Although they are talented and capable of doing many things, they often start tasks only to leave them unfinished.

Karagulla and Neal researched techniques to help people actualize their intelligence and concentration. To their amazement, they found that a person who concentrated on certain symbols performed better on various tasks, a finding that aligns with ancient spiritual knowledge and practices in the East. Karagulla and Neal shared this exercise in workshops. Individuals made remarkable progress in concentration by focusing on symbols and performed closer to their IQ level after completing the training.

This Symbols Concentration Exercise for improving concentration is practiced for 15 minutes a day. To benefit fully, the exercise must be done every day for nine months. If a person is inconsistent in practicing it, the full benefit is not achieved. Doing this exercise will help to increase awareness, clarity, flexibility, self-confidence, concentration, and performance level.

Here is the concentration exercise. Every day, practice concentrating on the three symbols below for five minutes each, for a total of fifteen minutes. Use a timer and set it for five minutes before concentrating on each symbol. If you are interrupted at any time, you must start over, so select a time and place when this would be unlikely.

The Symbols Concentration Exercise

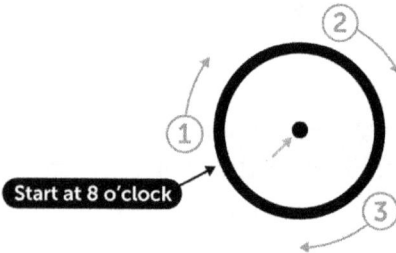

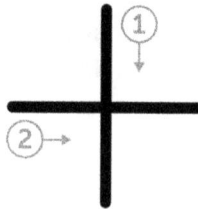

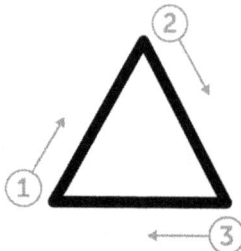

1. Close your eyes and focus on the first symbol. Envision that the circle is in the middle of your forehead, just above your eyebrows. Imagine you are tracing around the circle clockwise one time starting at the eight o'clock position. Then, with your mind's eye, place the dot in the center after you trace the circle.

2. Next, with your eyes still closed, draw the circle with your finger on the palm of your hand and place the dot.

3. Then, sketch the symbol and dot in the air out in front of you with your finger. Repeat this process for five minutes.

4. Now, do a similar process with the plus sign for five minutes. Trace from top to bottom on the vertical axis of the plus sign. Then, from left to right on its horizontal axis. First, draw the symbol in your mind's eye on your forehead, then with your finger on the palm of your hand, and finally with your finger in the air in front of you.

5. For the final five minutes, repeat the process concentrating on the triangle. Start tracing the triangle at the lower-left corner, move upward to the apex, then down the right side, and then over from right to left back to the beginning point on the bottom left.

These shapes hold symbolic meaning. For example, the circle represents the whole, the world, and completion. The triangle represents higher knowledge. The cross represents overcoming obstacles.

Jerry was a gregarious, optimistic, outgoing, and energetic man. He was busy with numerous activities. His optimistic attitude and intelligence, plus his wide range of interests, made Jerry think he could do anything. The large number and variety of Jerry's interests scattered his time and energy so that he couldn't give any one thing the necessary attention. Consequently, he was having trouble reaching a high success level.

Jerry came to me for help. He learned to see how his lack of focus had been a problem. One of his at-home assignments was the Symbols Concentration Exercise. Jerry did the training every day. Within six months, Jerry was setting priorities and eliminating some of his unnecessary activities. Jerry saw what he needed to do and took action. Jerry bought property, built shopping centers, and became wealthy within three years. Like Jerry, various other individuals have positively benefited from this exercise.

Benefits of Meditation

Life is a mystery—a mystery of beauty, bliss, and divinity. Meditation is the art of unfolding that mystery.

—Amit Ray

One of the most powerful ways to improve focus, cognitive faculties, wisdom, and well-being is meditation. Meditation is an essential practice for the mind, body, and emotions.

Meditation is turning the mind inward. Normally, the mind runs rampant with constant thoughts. As long as the mind is full of thoughts, turbulence, and agitation, someone cannot experience what consciousness truly entails. Meditation is a technique to quell racing thoughts and witness the mind by being aware and observing thinking at any moment. Witnessing helps bring the mind to an empty, thought-free state.

One of the ways meditation helps people is that it improves concentration. It enables someone to stay focused in the present because they are more aware when thoughts turn to the past or future. When there is an emergency, they remain calmer and stay focused in the moment to plan their actions. Regular meditation also facilitates more relaxation and less stress.

The first stage of meditation is contemplation. Here the person is a silent observer of their thoughts as they pass through the mind. With observation, the thoughts move more slowly. Someone can't get rid of their thoughts, but the amount and flow can be reduced.

Over time, as the flow of thoughts is reduced, an individual's mind can reach a state of stillness.

It requires time and training to tame the mind to be still and calm. Humans recognize that they need to exercise to build strong muscles and a strong body. It is not as easy to understand that training the mind also requires regular exercise and practice.

I always teach my clients to meditate. Yet some clients meditate a week or two, admit they are calmer and find it beneficial, but find an excuse to quit. They say they don't have enough time for it or forget to do it for some reason. Regular meditation practice requires desire, discipline, and dedication. However, if people truly understood how much it benefits their lives, they wouldn't let anything get in the way of meditating every day. Just as sleep, bathing, and eating are necessary for physical health, a meditation practice is essential for psychological well-being.

Many different types of meditation have been developed— chanting a mantra, concentrating on the breath, focusing on an image or object. A mantra is a word, statement, or sound you rhythmically say during meditation to stop your mind from wandering. It is repeated silently with every breath or as often as needed. Chanting mantras out loud can also be therapeutic. Generally, any technique aimed at quieting the mind is beneficial.

A Meditation Technique

Meditation brings wisdom. Lack of meditation leaves ignorance. Know well what leads you forward and what holds you back and choose the path that leads to wisdom.
    –The Buddha (Dhammapada, verse 282)

I first started meditating in 1965 after taking some classes given by Roy Masters. Based on my experience meditating for 65 years, I recommend meditating a total of 20 minutes a day—10 minutes in the morning, first thing after getting up, and 10 minutes at night just before going to bed. Don't wait until it is too late, or you may fall asleep while meditating. It is also helpful to be alone so you won't be disturbed.

Here is a meditation designed to quiet the mind that I have done consistently for many years. It is an exercise you can do for the rest of your life. A timer is helpful to keep track of time if you are on a schedule. Find a comfortable chair where you can sit with your spine straight and your arms and legs unfolded. Place your palms on your lap face up. Shut your eyes and take a few deep breaths. Now:

1. Relax and become aware of your body while breathing slowly and deeply.
2. Focus on the area between your eyebrows, just above the eyes.
3. Next, focus on the blood circulating through your body. You may feel some tingling as you do this. Start visualizing the blood flowing down your right leg and into your right foot. Then, feel the blood flowing into your left foot and up your left leg.
4. Notice the blood flowing in your intestinal area and the lower part of your back. Next, feel the blood flowing in your stomach, your chest, and then through your upper back.
5. Continue to breathe deeply and slowly and stay focused on the blood flowing around your neck and into your head.
6. Then, feel your blood flowing down your left arm and into your left hand. You may feel some warmth as you put your awareness on the blood flowing throughout your body. Now visualize your blood flowing into your right arm and your right hand. Feel the blood flowing through the fingers of both hands.
7. In your mind's eye, imagine your arms stretched out straight in front of you and place one hand on top of the

other. As you look out from your forehead, notice that you see one hand on top of the other, and you are looking at the back of your hands.

8. Continue to breathe slowly and deeply. In your mind's eye from your forehead, visualize your arms bending and moving toward your face. See the back of your hands slowly get closer and closer and closer until, finally, they are touching your forehead. Your hands and arms are not actually moving, only in your imagination.

9. From this point, become aware of the spot on your forehead in the middle of your eyebrows. You are no longer focused on your hands. Focus on the spot in the middle of your eyebrows.

10. Anytime you begin to have thoughts, once again visualize your arms outstretched before you and observe the back of your hands moving toward your forehead.

The objective is to observe your mind and keep it free of any thoughts. Continue doing this meditation exercise for 10 minutes, and then open your eyes. Repeat the same routine at night for 10 minutes. After you have been meditating for a while, you can shorten your exercise by just focusing on the blood circulating down your arms into your hands and then imagining the back of your hands coming up to your forehead.

Intuition and Driving One Night

Meditation raises the vibration of our energy and improves intuition. However, the mind needs to be still and quiet if we are to pick up intuitive signals. **When the mind is still, insight comes to us in a flash.**

This story illustrates how my longtime meditation practice improved my intuition so much that I have come to trust it. This memorable experience happened late one night while I was driving home on the freeway. Although the traffic was light, I was driving in the fast lane. Suddenly, a thought entered my mind, Move over into the next lane. Fortunately, I have learned to follow my inner guidance system—my intuition—and immediately changed lanes. The oncoming headlights from the opposite lane of traffic and the road's curvature had made it difficult to see that a car driving in the wrong lane was coming toward me until it was very close. The car was going in the wrong direction in the fast lane.

In the past, I might have imagined that avoiding a head-on collision would be a simple matter of swerving one way or the other. That night, I realized more was involved. Avoiding an accident is not simply shifting lanes. First, the fact that the car was going the wrong way on the freeway was a complete surprise. Second, I was going 65 miles an hour, and the oncoming car was driving at an equal speed, which could easily distort my judgment. The speeds of both vehicles showed me that there would have been little time to react.

In reality, because I listened to my intuition, the cars whisked by one another, in different lanes going in opposite directions, with me safe in the right lane. I quickly began honking the horn. In the rear-view mirror, I could see the brake lights come on as the driver realized he was going in the wrong direction. I took a deep breath of relief and said, "Thank you, God." Fortunately, what could have been a tragedy turned out to be two vehicles passing in the night.

CHAPTER 13

Knowing Where You Are Going

Be Clear About Goals

As you sow, so shall you reap.
—Galatians VI

Having clear goals enables us to map out a plan to accomplish our dreams and live a happy life. Time passes by regardless of whether we are working on our goals or wasting our time and energy. Twenty years go by quickly, and we will either be pleased by what we have accomplished or have regrets about what we didn't do. It is our choice. We have the power to choose.

Suppose you find it difficult to know what you want. No one decides to arrive at the last years of life only to think about what they didn't do. A way to help you know what you want and to create goals to get it is to pretend you are 95 years old looking back on your life. From this perspective ask yourself these questions:

- Where are you, and what have you accomplished?
- What would you change if you could?
- What didn't you do that you regret?
- What would you have changed in your life to have been happier?
- Where did you live and why? Was there somewhere you would have liked to live or visit?
- What are the things that you especially like about how your life turned out?

Next, now that your goals have been brought into sharper

focus, it is important to become as specific as possible about them. To help you become clear about your goals, try the following, quick exercise. **Think about something you want in your life and then ask, For what purpose?**

When you have answered that question, ask again, For what purpose? This fleshes out the *why* you think you value a specific goal. This process can help you determine what you value most. Here is an example:

> "I want to make a lot of money."
> *For what purpose?*

> "So, I can have a nice home, furniture, clothes, and a car."
> *For what purpose?*

> "To make my life easier."
> *For what purpose?*

> "So, I do not have to work so hard."
> *For what purpose?*

> "To be more comfortable and happier."

The more specific your goals and reasons for them, the easier it will be for you to take the actions to actualize them. Keep your goals and reasons for them foremost in your mind. Use affirmations about the achievability of what you want. Stay positive about your goals and work out a plan. Having a plan is affirmative and helps you keep track of whether you are moving forward toward a goal. Be sure to include a timeline in the plan.

What Keeps You from Your Goals?

Our goals can get away from us and it can be difficult to understand why. Usually, we are blocking our progress so we need to go within to figure out the problem. It is important to be honest with ourselves. First and foremost, if there is a health problem such as poor habits or an addiction, then goals are nearly impossible to achieve. Address this first. Make overcoming health issues your first and only goal. Some behaviors to change in the health area are:

> Smoking, drugs, alcohol
>
> Poor diet, overeating, or eating the wrong foods for your body
>
> Lack of movement, exercise, or sleep

Also, be aware of these problematic behaviors. They are negative and will keep you from moving forward in a positive manner:

> Lack of discipline and determination
>
> Not setting clear goals
>
> Discrepancies between what you say and what you do
>
> Procrastination
>
> Bad temperament (crankiness)
>
> Dishonesty
>
> Blaming others
>
> Making excuses
>
> Laziness
>
> Not being responsible

To get to the root of what is stopping you, it is easier if you break your goals down into specific life areas such as work, romantic relationships, family, friends, or spiritual life. Look at each goal in a life area and consider these questions to become more aware of your behaviors and habits concerning a specific life area:

- Do you set goals for what you want or let others make your decisions?
- Do you set goals that are possible for you to achieve?
- Do you think about what you want, or do you complain about what you don't have?
- Are you clear about what you have to do to reach your goals?
- What are you doing to actualize your goal and vision? If not, what is the obstacle?

- What are your fears concerning the goal or life area?
- Do you think positively about your goals?
- Do you make excuses?
- Do you rely on others to get you what you want?
- Do you blame other people and other things for the problems in this area?
- Do you give in to immediate gratification and sacrifice your goals?
- Do you have friends around you that live the way you desire to live?
- If you don't know something, are you willing to learn?
- What can you do better in each life area?
- Do you take the time to appreciate and be thankful for what you have?

Clarity from Childhood

Some people are clear about where they are going from an early age. This is a gift. As my next story shows, being clear about what we want and where we are going can be powerful.

When I was five years old, my friend and I were playing in the yard and talking about the future. My friend asked me, "What do you want to do when you grow up?" I answered, "I want to tell people why they keep doing the things they do that cause them problems."

One of the fun things I liked to do was put one knee in my little red wagon and use the other leg to scoot myself along the sidewalk. I would scoot my red wagon to the corner of the block to visit an old lady who lived there. We would sit on the front porch swing and talk about all kinds of subjects. I remember telling her, "Someday, I am going to live in California, in the San Fernando Valley, where they grow the tall palm trees."

I have no idea where these thoughts came from. I lived in a small town in Iowa then and had never traveled more than thirty miles from home. When I became an adult, after traveling around the United States for a while, I ended up settling permanently in California's San Fernando Valley and lived there for almost fifty years.

Before I started traveling, I had gotten my cosmetology license and worked as a hairdresser. After settling down in California, I owned and operated beauty salons for several years. I always had a natural knack to help people with their problems. Twenty years later, I went back to school and got a PhD in psychology. My prediction at five finally came true when my work became helping people deal with their problems. Throughout the years, I continued studying and learning to discover who I am and help my clients.

How Are You Looking for Happiness?

Each goal that a person sets, distilled down, is for the purpose of achieving happiness for oneself or others. People want what they believe will achieve this—and usually, it entails achieving or acquiring things. However, **prestige or things don't necessarily lead to greater happiness.**

To find lasting happiness, we have to look inside ourselves. Getting things on the outside does not create enduring happiness. As soon as we get something we have wanted, we set our sights on something else to want. There is never any real satisfaction. The ego has an addiction tendency that is focused on gaining more things in the world and having more pleasure. It equates happiness with obtaining something that it can possess. It is not aligned with the truth. Once we have found peace and happiness within ourselves, we can be happy with what we already have and will no longer need more and more things.

A Spiritual or Worldly Path?

Ask yourself, Are you living a spiritual or worldly path in each area of your life? Are you looking for happiness outside of yourself—

in the world—or are you seeking happiness within? Figuring out your goals and life vision boils down to one fundamental question: **Do I want a worldly path, or am I searching for a spiritual path?** A worldly path and a spiritual path look quite different. Let's compare them.

Spiritual Seeking Path	*Worldly Seeking Path*
Searches for spiritual information	Has a strong desire for physical things
Learns about spiritual teachings and leaders	Wants more money, sex, and material things
Wants to reach enlightenment (i.e., salvation, illumination, liberation, awakening, self-realization)	Wants to achieve higher status or power, seeks approval from others, aims to satisfy the ego
Feels desire to improve behavior	Keeps doing the same things
Looks internally	Looks outside the self
Seeks to have a close relationship with God	Blames others for problems and mistakes
Has humility and transcends the ego	Is egotistical
Has discrimination	Holds grudges
Has an internal hunger for spiritual knowledge	Is jealous
Prays for greater awareness and understanding	Can be stubborn
Is thankful and appreciative	Feels entitled
Accepts a larger Universal Will (humility)	Often feels desperate and wants to control

Is helpful to others	Usually does not listen to others
Asks for guidance	Can be critical and angry
Asks for forgiveness	Feels guilty
Is accepting, nonjudgmental, responsible	Can be a workaholic

Many people are on the worldly path. They place value on what they think is important and will make them happy. Some have long-term goals they want to achieve, such as being a doctor, architect, lawyer, designer, politician, professional sports player, scientist, homemaker, or parent. On the other hand, some people are only thinking about where they will get their next meal and where they will sleep tonight. Each person is unique and has different ways they want to live their life.

Our Life Purpose

The path we are on—spiritual or worldly—helps determine our life purpose. People often confuse life purpose with the type of work they do. Someone's life purpose is evident in the choices they have made and continue to make.

I've heard people discuss what they believe their purpose is many times. A few people knew what they wanted to do since they were children. Most do not know the answer to that question. I believe that for many people there is more than one path they can choose. Having certain talents and abilities can certainly help someone choose a direction. It could be sports, art, dancing, engineering, science, or just about anything, but there are many opportunities and some choices may result in more happiness than others. Find out what you want your life to be and then use it as a foundation to become the best person you can become.

As I have gained more experience and insight, I believe the greatest purpose that people can achieve is to master themselves by balancing their feelings and thoughts so they can express love from their hearts and share that love with others in each life area. This means that the main importance of the careers you choose or your relationships, friends, and experiences is that they are opportunities to learn and grow spiritually. What is most important is to discover who you are on the inside by becoming consciously aware. In this way, you can learn how to relate to yourself and other people with kindness and love.

We are all at different stages in our development, with a variety of beliefs, desires, talents, and choices. Discovering how to be a loving person, contribute to society, find peace, and joy to share with others is the most meaningful purpose I can imagine. To walk that path, for me, means finding a spiritual understanding and a loving relationship with God. The rewards are well-being, a deep connection to others, and a more profound understanding of yourself. It is well worth the effort.

PART IV

**Actualizing Our Best Social Selves:
Opening the Heart to Truly Loving**

CHAPTER 14

Accept People as They Are

The most powerful, single principle that can transform your social life and relationships is this: **accept and love people where *they* are, not where *you* want them to be.** Be filled with love toward them. Since you can't give what you don't have, love is often confused with need, which is disguised as love. They are not the same thing. Needs have a self-centered element. They focus on filling a void or addressing something lacking within someone. Needs are about getting something from others. It may be attention, compliments, special words, money, or help. Fulfilling needs often requires transactions like bargaining, bartering, or expecting give-and-take in relationships. Fulfilling needs is necessary, but it is not the same as love.

Conditional Versus Unconditional Love

Love cannot be seen. Only the effects and energy of love can be felt. Giving unconditional love involves pure intention, motivation, and action. Unconditional love asks for nothing in return. It comes from a heart filled with love with no strings attached. Therefore, there are no expectations and no disappointments. When giving true love, there is only happiness and fulfillment. Love requires honesty and the ability to see the truth to determine if our love is an earthly conditional love or unconditional love. Few people have the capability to give unconditionally to others and ask or expect nothing in return.

To have positive relationships, practice acceptance, love, patience, and compassion for everyone around us—starting with our family, friends, neighbors, and acquaintances and extending out to everyone we encounter, including the grocery clerk, bank teller, and coffee barista.

It is even important to practice acceptance and love toward the people you do not interact with directly, such as leaders, politicians, people on social media, on the Internet, in an ad, or anyone you see on television. There should be no exceptions—not one—to your practice of love and compassion.

Love Happens When We're Ready

Sometimes, people think they are ready for a romantic relationship, partnership, or marriage, and then things may not go according to plan. As Benny's and my story below illustrates, it is important to trust that things happen when the timing and situation are right. And often this is because the people involved have done some transformation work.

I first met Benny in 1971, and we were together for nearly a year. We had a lot of fun dating, and it was amazing how we liked doing the same kinds of things. He never said anything about how he felt about me or our future together, though. Sadly, we broke up because I didn't think Benny was serious about me. I met someone else and got married a few months later. Shortly after that, Benny phoned to tell me he was also about to get married. My marriage only lasted three years. I dated just one person after that and then stopped dating altogether for 20 years until, finally, in 1996, I started dating again.

By 1998, I had been giving lectures part-time on cruise ships for more than a decade. I was lecturing on a round-trip cruise from Los Angeles to Acapulco. There were more than two thousand passengers aboard that cruise. I was on the trip with my boyfriend, Bob.

Bob and I were seated at dinner the first night with two other people at a table for six by the window, leaving two seats empty. Soon, another couple joined the table. The man had an accent, and I asked Bob, "What kind of an accent do you think that is?" Bob replied, "I think it's an Israeli accent." The man and his girlfriend had been assigned seats in the middle of the room but were moved to our table after asking to be seated by a window.

The following night, the girlfriend of the man with the accent mentioned something about her boyfriend's fire extinguishing business. Suddenly, a light flashed in my head. It must be Benny. I turned to Benny and asked, "I think we know each other. Do I look familiar to you?" He nodded yes. Then, I asked him, "Is it all right if I tell the others how we know each other?" He agreed so I told them about how we had dated for a year in 1971.

Each night during dinner, Benny and I seated ourselves near each other at the table so we could easily talk and become reacquainted. Whenever Bob and I got off the ship in various ports, we kept running into Benny and his girlfriend. One day, we were at the Princess Hotel in Acapulco, Mexico sightseeing, and ran into each other. Bob and I had hired a driver for the day, and, since Ben and his girlfriend didn't have one, they accepted our invitation to join us touring in our

Benny and me when we dated in the 1970s.

car for the rest of the day. When Benny and I were alone, Benny asked me for my telephone number, and I gave it to him.

After the cruise ended, Benny gave me a call, and we started dating. Benny had been dating his girlfriend for eight years off and on. Before the trip, he had told her that they were going because he had promised her a cruise, but he wanted to find a new relationship after the cruise. Meanwhile, my relationship with Bob was not serious, in part, because he lived a long distance from where I lived in Los Angeles. I ended that relationship after Benny ended his, and we started dating and eventually were married.

Ben and I met again during a cruise in 1998.

Benny had told me that he wasn't serious about our relationship in 1971 because he wanted to fulfill his promise to his mother that he would marry a Jewish woman. Since I was not Jewish, he didn't believe he could marry me. After we broke up, Benny did marry a Jewish woman, but the marriage only lasted three years. Benny's mother passed away in 1993, so by the time Benny and I met again, he felt free to ask me to marry him.

I believe that we both were meant to follow our individual paths before we were ready to share our lives with each other. When it was the right time, we met again. Everything happens for a reason, and that is why the experiences that we attract are perfect because they contain the lessons that we need to learn to help us remove the blocks to our full potential.

True Acceptance

When we practice true acceptance, we don't get upset if someone isn't ready to hear us or follow our advice. We are not disappointed if the other person makes a different decision than the one we suggested or wants to take their life in a different direction. We don't judge others, gossip about them, or pity them for their life circumstances. If we experience any of these reactions, it is a blaring signal that it is time to process our own emotions because other people's decisions and lives have awakened and triggered one of *our* fears.

Being a loving person means taking responsibility for our own feelings regarding someone's decisions and allowing them to be free on their life path, even if we disagree. It is not our place to tell others what to do or judge them. Let's begin by learning how to accept others.

Learning to Love People on Their Journey

Sometimes, it is obvious to us when someone is making a mistake. We may lovingly warn them and try to steer them in another direction. Sometimes, the person may be willing to listen to us. Many times, they may choose not to listen to us. Some examples of destructive behaviors follow.

Abusing drugs and alcohol

Unleashing anger at others

Being selfish, bullying, and unkind to others

Smoking

Overeating and eating unhealthy foods

Stealing from others

Being violent in any way, including in our choice of words and thoughts

Overworking and neglecting other aspects of life

Negative thinking

Dishonesty

Being critical

Arguing and fighting

Being unloving and indifferent toward others

Impatience

Nervousness and worrying

Being abusive, physically, emotionally, or mentally

Acting agitated

Being an irresponsible parent

Not working and supporting self and family when capable

Sex addiction

It is important to remember that everyone has their own life path. Loving others means that we maintain our humility and accept that we do not always completely understand a person's life, what they need to learn, and why people make their choices. It is wise to accept the choices of others without judgment. Sometimes, people may need a seemingly negative experience for their evolution. Sometimes, they may veer off course to learn a vital lesson that then accelerates their whole growth process. Jeff is an example of this.

Jeff's Addiction to Excitement

Jeff was a 54-year-old single man with an addiction. He was addicted to dating very young, sexy women, but he soon became tired of them. He liked the excitement of meeting someone new, going on a few dates, and having sex with them. Jeff was successful and wealthy. In his middle 20s, he sold a website for several million dollars. Since then, he has successfully invested his money.

When Jeff was growing up, his parents often fought and bickered. Jeff's mother mainly caused the fights. She complained and always wanted more of everything—more time, more money, more love, more help, and more getting her way. Jeff was present during many of these arguments and yelling matches. When Jeff was 17, his mother left him and his father and started a new family with another man. She would call Jeff on his birthday or send him a card during the holidays but left it to his father to get him through high school and college. He felt abandoned by his mother. This experience shaped Jeff's beliefs and feelings about marriage, and he concluded that marriage was a recipe for unhappiness.

Jeff met most of the women he dated on the Internet. His only requirement was that the women were blonde, aged 20 to 28, attractive, and had slender figures. The dating usually lasted anywhere from one date to a few months. His longest relationship lasted a year.

In the beginning, when he was attracted to a woman, he would be excited and happy. He would treat her very well at first, taking her to nice restaurants and on trips. He showered her with thoughtful gifts. Women were often wowed by his charm, generosity, and sense of humor. They liked his expensive sports car and lifestyle. The new experiences were exhilarating for Jeff, but the exhilaration would only last for a short time. He soon lost interest and started pulling away. Eventually, he stopped returning their calls. As he lost interest, he would find fault with them. They: "are too immature," "are lazy," "no longer turn me on," "interfere with my work," or "keep me from sleeping."

Sometimes, Jeff thought he'd like to have children and be a father, but it remained an empty thought because he never wanted to commit to parenthood or settle down with anyone. The idea was overwhelming. He became lonely and agitated between women, and then the hunt would begin to find someone new to fill the lonely, anxious void quickly.

Jeff had no idea that he was addicted to the excitement of each new fling. He was addicted to the exhilarated feeling of finding a new relationship and a new sexual encounter. He had never looked at how his parents' relationship affected him or how he had an intense fear of getting too close to anyone. He busily avoided intimacy as well as anyone who figured this out and brought it to his attention.

A few of the women in his life genuinely cared about him and tried to reach out to him and work through his inability to commit. He tried to be receptive and hear them out, but in the end, he felt uncomfortable and overwhelmed. He would shut them out to avoid his feelings, unconsciously fearing deep down that he would be abandoned once again. He would tell his friends that he was born to be a bachelor, but he was lonely inside. He would change the subject when people would ask about his love life or interest in having children in the future. He didn't want to hear anyone's advice that he should settle down with a partner.

Jeff's story describes someone stuck in how they live their life. People like Jeff don't know what is causing the problem. Jeff continued to focus outside of himself, criticizing and faulting the women he dated. But it wasn't really about the women he dated. He was never interested in examining his fears and feelings on the inside. He just wasn't ready, no matter what anyone said or did. He was on his own life journey.

If Jeff is ever ready to work on his fears and issues, he may be able to engage in a wonderful relationship. He could also genuinely realize that he is happier by himself. Either way, it would be wise for him to work through his feelings to be free from the pain of abandonment, loneliness, and the inability to commit. This way, he could choose to be in a relationship or not out of true freedom, and not because he is in bondage to his fears.

How to Practice Loving Acceptance

To handle yourself, use your head; to handle others use your heart.

—Eleanor Roosevelt

Are there people in your life like Jeff—who clearly have an issue but are content with how things are and just aren't ready to change? You may have heard the expression: "You can lead the horse to the water, but you can't make it drink."

Loving acceptance must be practiced in every circumstance, even in seemingly incomprehensible situations when a family member or friend is following a dangerous path—adopting an extreme ideology that is harmful, such as joining a cult, hanging out with the wrong crowd, engaging in crime, trying to swindle others, or becoming drug-addicted.

We should speak up and say our truth but be prepared to

accept their choices and deal with our feelings as they arise. It is not always an easy task. It can be painful to watch our loved ones engage in destructive behaviors without heeding our advice and difficult to observe when people are not on the right path and are not ready to listen.

A variety of feelings—rejection, helplessness, and being overwhelmed—may emerge in these circumstances. We will need to take responsibility for them and lovingly process them. It may be difficult to decide that it is time to stop trying to help and allow the person to experience their life. We may have to work hard at getting to a place of acceptance. It may be an ongoing process. It is all right to acknowledge the challenge of finding acceptance. We can only keep striving toward showing acceptance and love, even if we sometimes fall short.

Understand that it is not up to us to judge another person and encourage them to change. It is wise to develop a social awareness of whether someone is ready for our advice, input, or help or not. A good rule to live by is not to provide unsolicited advice or to ask the person if they would like to hear our perspective or not. Suppose a person does solicit advice but resists any suggestions. They are not ready, and we should stop providing any additional advice unless they are ready to follow through. There is no use in continuing to push our point.

Stop fighting, criticizing, demanding, and changing others. Step outside the situation and observe what is going on. If other people are bothering you, or you are feeling pain from their behaviors, focus on what it is about *you* that is getting bothered. What is your fear? It is important to process your fears continuously until there is a place of peace within you. You are not helping the person in distress by being in a state of turmoil and unhappiness because of their behavior. You may be unintentionally adding to their problems. You may even push them further away if they start to rebel against you.

Helping by Letting Go with Love

Randy was an alcoholic and worked for his dad, Jerry. Randy would have periods when he was sober and responsible in his work. Then, he would disappear for days or even weeks on drinking binges. Randy expected his father to have his job waiting for him whenever he would sober up as he had in the past. Jerry needed his son to work for him and was always eager for him to get back to work. Finally, Jerry realized that if his son was going to continue working for him and even run the company one day when Jerry retired, he needed to demand more from his son.

After a three-week disappearing act, Randy returned to work and asked his dad for his job back. Jerry said, "Not right now; let's see how things are in a few weeks." Randy was shocked that he was unable to go back to work immediately. Randy had to go without money, consider how much he wanted his job, and start thinking about his priorities, like having a family one day and his future. He knew that going down the path of drinking was leading him to a dead end. Randy started going to AA, and he stayed sober to have the type of life he wanted.

Randy may have been on the wrong path, but he realized quickly that his life had taken a wrong turn. He was ready to learn. Not everyone is as quick to learn from negative experiences, especially when addiction is at play. It seems like it should be easy to point out a better way for someone, and they would see your truth right away. It can be very tempting to think that if we explain a philosophy, psychological principle, or spiritual exercise to people, they should understand it.

Have you ever tried to explain something to a person, and they didn't understand what you were talking about? This can be because the person is not interested in what you are telling them or is not aligned with the idea. It is as though what you are explaining to them goes in one ear and out the other.

People can only perceive, understand, and accept information they are ready for. Wait until someone is willing, open, and asking for help before reaching out to them.

Someone Must Be Ready for Change

Change takes time and effort. Unless a person is ready and willing to quit a habit or change something, they are not interested in what we have to say about it. They may politely listen, then ignore us. They may argue, get angry, and resist our attempts to help them. They may see it as meddling, annoying, or that we are trying to change them. If we keep pushing them, they may even attack our character, point out our wrongdoings and hypocrisy, call us names or put us down in other ways to get us to back off. At an extreme, they may even shut us out of their lives.

Until someone is ready to open their mind and be receptive, they will not listen or accept unwanted information. It's often the case that people become willing to consider new possibilities only when they have suffered through enough pain and arrived at the conclusion that they can't stand what is going on in their life. That is why it is often not helpful to beg, preach, or demand that someone change their behaviors until they are ready and want to make that change.

When someone is ready to take that step toward change, they will seek answers and accept new knowledge. Until then, any new information will be resisted or rejected, and it will cause tension in the relationship. In the end, all the most helpful intentions may only inadvertently add to someone's pain and suffering.

We should know that we are never helpless. There are times when the biggest help we can offer a loved one is the freedom to learn what they need to learn without judgment and the comfort of knowing that our loving arms will be open when they need us. At these times, we can also offer consistent, positive, loving intentions and prayers for the person when thinking of them. It can be a powerful way to help without interfering in their life choices.

Be a Positive Example

Another way to uplift others is to be a positive example of living up to your highest potential. This is only possible if you continuously deal with your feelings and empty your cups of pain. People who live their highest potential tend to be observers and stay out of judgment. They wish other people well, have compassion for the human experience, and live their lives to serve others.

Shifting our focus from the outer world to our own inner life helps empty our cups, thus allowing positive energy to flow from us to others. In this way, we become a shining example of how change *is* possible. We become a source of inspiration instead of a source of negativity, criticism, blame, and judgment—in short, another source of pain for people.

CHAPTER 15

How to Handle Everyday Problems in Relationships

Every day, situations come up with others that need to be smoothed over. A person gets upset about something someone did. There's a loss of some kind. Someone gets sick. An accident happens. Or a person doesn't like the way their friend thinks or something that was said.

Conflict is a part of life. A conflict can be based on someone being unhappy about something that has happened, someone being frustrated because they can't have something they want, or a bad mood that day. A conflict or problem can result from an unlimited number of unsettling things, but what matters is *how* we react to it. There are a wide variety of responses to conflict that can be distilled down into two categories, positive and negative. Positive reactions are preferable because they help to usher in peace, healing, and progress. A positive response to difficult people or situations flows freely from us when we are balanced in the first place.

Find Balance First

Being balanced means that we are coming from a place of positive well-being. Our thinking and feelings are in harmony and we feel peaceful and calm. We need to take steps every day to keep our energy balanced.

Here is a quick reminder of practices to incorporate into a daily routine to operate at your best. Care for the mind by meditating every day to slow it down and by learning to concentrate to stay focused. Use affirmations to direct your thoughts towards more positivity and away from negativity. Manage emotions by, first, noticing when fear or other negative feelings are present and then processing them until they are gone.

Emotional balance is also made possible by forgiving ourselves and everyone else. Good health is critical to feeling peaceful, stable, and strong—eating healthy food, drinking plenty of water, getting enough sleep, and exercising. Our social lives keep us balanced too. Building strong relationships and surrounding ourselves with people we admire have positive benefits for our well-being. So does practicing compassion, being kind, and being helpful to others.

Always striving for balance is both motivated by and results in our capacity to give love to ourselves and others in our lives. Our well-being is first for ourselves; self-care is self-love. And only when we are in balance can we encourage and enjoy healthy relationships.

Detach and Observe the Situation

From a balanced state, it is easier to observe the whole picture of a situation. The goal is to be helpful and understanding of what is going on—not to win, get our way, or be right. Detaching means being aware of how the other person is feeling and how they are behaving. We recognize *what* we have the power to do in a situation and *when* we don't have any power. Remember, we have no power over another person's feelings and how they choose to act. We only have power over what we do.

With all of the above as a foundation, find out if the other person is expecting something from you when a problematic situation arises. Determine if it is reasonable and viable for you to do. As you become fully aware of what is going on, communicate your ideas with calmness, understanding, helpfulness, compassion, and love. Do only what you can do within the boundary of your positive energy and calm observation.

Do not be manipulated by guilt, anger, or threats. Once you

are knocked off your balanced, positive-energy position, you are in the Pain Pit and are now part of the problem. Here, you've lost your power.

Is Winning All That Counts?

Sometimes, as people talk when they are emotionally upset, they flip from one subject to another without making a point. Something has happened that has triggered resentment or a fear rooted in a similar incident from the past. To "win," they may throw in many topics unrelated to what started the argument. These remarks cause further problems and add fuel to the fire. It doesn't matter that these topics have nothing to do with the current conflict. Winning is more important.

Having a conversation when two people are interacting in this manner is completely futile because the goal becomes about being right or being a winner. Often, the only way to end a negative interaction is if one person admits defeat, which can create distance or harm in the relationship. True communication—the kind that promotes positive relationships and seeks a meaningful direction and purpose—comes from reaching a common understanding. It is about settling the problem and coming to a resolution. It includes considering the other person's viewpoint and cooperating to eliminate arguments rather than focusing on who is right.

Just One Calm Person Transforms a Fight

It takes two people to fight. It is impossible to fight when one of the people in a conflict has a helpful attitude and is free of anger and negativity. Then it will be possible to resolve any problem. It is a matter of making choices and negotiating to reach an agreement. Even if the other person is angry and disagreeable, you can still reach an agreement to resolve a problem if one person can maintain their calm, focus, and center.

Gary had written a check to pay a bill and laid it on the counter, expecting his wife, Barbara, to address the envelope and mail it.

After a couple of days, the envelope was still lying there, so Gary said to Barbara, "Why can't you help me? You haven't addressed the envelope for that check?"

Barbara answered, "I didn't know you wanted me to. You always take care of your mail. If you had asked me to do it, I would have gladly helped you." Then Barbara put the check in an envelope and addressed it. Notice how a fight was averted thanks to Barbara's calm manner.

If a dispute is brewing, adhere to the boundary of understanding what is going on by using wisdom, discernment, and clear thinking. Ask for what you want. You can only come from your calm, powerful center in the dispute if you are balanced, free of negativity, and observing reality. Observe with clarity what is going on and notice your choices of action. Stay in the intention that love is the foundation of your energy, and being helpful to everyone is the goal.

Resolving Relationship Pain

Pain consists of energy caused by our past experiences, thinking, and feelings. I have noticed working with my clients that people often keep themselves in painful situations simply because of how they view them. They may hang onto the pain of relationships long ended in divorce, separation, or death, and dwell on them.

Robert is in love with Jasmine and cannot let go because of the pain of losing the happiness they shared. The relationship ended in a divorce. By dwelling on their former shared happiness and not being able to let go, Robert is blocking new, loving, and fulfilling relationships from coming into his life. He feels lonely and unhappy. When someone has this type of unresolved relationship pain, they may be neglecting the whole picture of the past relationship. They can easily overlook the arguments, times they were unhappy, and problems that caused the rift in the relationship.

If you have unresolved relationship pain and would benefit from gaining clarity, answer the following questions:

- What was the main problem that caused the relationship to fail?
- Would the other person have left you through divorce or separation if they had really loved you?
- What feelings come up in you when you think of the loss of the relationship?
- Do you place attributes and qualities on the person they didn't have?
- Did the person *not* offer you something that you wanted such as:

> The ability to communicate
>
> Honesty
>
> Sexual compatibility
>
> Willingness to share time, feelings, and thoughts
>
> Kindness
>
> Faithfulness
>
> Trust
>
> Fairness
>
> Consideration
>
> Their love
>
> A shared sense of humor
>
> The ability to have fun
>
> Intelligence
>
> Talent
>
> Courage

To fully recover from the pain of past relationships, get in touch with your fear and process your feelings to balance and heal the energy within you.

The energy that causes relationship problems can be due to one or more fears. Search until you identify the fear triggered by the loss of your relationship. Then, go through the process of accepting the fear and any feelings attached to the fear, one at a time, until the painful energy is dissipated. One of the main obstacles to processing deep-seated pain is staying in your head to avoid your feelings.

Other People Cannot Fix Loneliness

Paradoxically, our ability to cultivate meaningful relationships hinges, in part, on how we feel when we are alone.

Loneliness is a common experience. People may try to resolve loneliness by focusing outside of themselves. Someone feeling lonely may think, "If I only had good friends or a partner, I wouldn't feel lonely." For a short time, other people may serve as a source of happiness and a distraction, but loneliness will still be present within them. Soon, fears of losing the friend or partner may settle in, along with jealousy, clingy and overbearing behavior. This may snowball into relationship problems. Using other people to fix the pain of loneliness is like constructing a building on an earthquake fault. It will eventually crumble.

Deep and meaningful relationships are possible when we socialize with others to share love, joy, and life experiences, not to escape our feelings of loneliness.

If someone is experiencing loneliness, then it is time to look inside and address the pain. That will require some work processing fear and loneliness. It is important to examine what other fears may be involved besides loneliness.

Also, look for any beliefs that are contributing to the problem. For example:

> Only certain people are worthy of love.
> I am not worthy of some people's friendship.
> Not everyone needs to be treated with respect, fairness, consideration, and kindness.
> It is not possible to love everyone.
> I am better (worse) than others.

I have little in common with people.

People don't understand me.

When someone faces their fears and addresses their pain, it makes the space for their hearts to be filled with love. Others feel the love emanating from them and want to be around them. They gravitate towards the energy of love. When the mind overcomes negative beliefs that block true friendships, it opens the gates to sharing and receiving love from others. Life becomes enriched through connection and love.

Healing Jealousy and the Need to Control in Relationships

Are you harboring jealousy? Jealousy is an excruciating fear and causes huge problems in relationships.

Someone who is jealous is afraid of loss through competition. This fear causes them to imagine they could lose their significant other or something important to them so they react negatively, emotionally and physically, to the seeming threat of loss. If their partner even smiles at another person, they believe their partner is interested in that person and fear they could lose them. Because people who are in long-term happy partnerships feel secure in their relationships they work to transcend the fear of loss through competition. To heal jealousy, fears must be processed; or if further help is needed, a professional counselor can help to eliminate this fear.

Jealousy is often accompanied by controlling behaviors by the partner, which causes serious problems. Being controlling is an indication of a deep-seated fear that needs to be processed and healed. There is an attempt to control others or situations. They do this because they are fearful and anxious that things will go wrong if they don't maintain control.

Some people employ controlling behaviors to assert dominance. This is a form of abuse. A person may use abuse as a way to force someone into doing what they want them to do, such as hitting them, burning them with cigarettes, taking control of their money, sexual assault, and emotional abuse. Below are some other ways that people try to control others.

Manipulation
Coercion
Threats
Intimidation
Blaming
Creating drama
Irritation
Nit-picking
Keeping score
Need to be the center of attention
Attempting to change you

Additionally, specific behaviors of controlling people toward their partners include:

Demand to know what they are doing all of the time
Monitor their social media, email, and bank account
Tell them what they can do, eat, drink, or wear
Humiliate them in public
Threaten to hurt them to get what they want

Controlling behaviors can occur in friendships, workplace relationships, and family relationships. The problem is that most people don't recognize controlling people. Control can be very subtle; it can be hidden behind the pretense of help, advice, suggestions, or even jokes. It is not a joke. Controlling people want to change you, make you different, and make you fit their reality.

The impulse to control others serves as a protective function against feelings of vulnerability, which the controlling person associates with powerlessness. They want to avoid feelings of weakness. They often create conflict through arguments and engage in behaviors that decrease trust. People who use controlling behaviors are often successful in business because they are goal-driven. They surround themselves with employees that do their bidding.

Some controlling statements:

"Don't interrupt me."

"I didn't ask for your opinion."

"That is none of your business."

"I need you to do this for me."

These are not requests; they are orders. The difference between controlling and cooperative statements is that controlling statements don't reflect that the relationship is valued while cooperative statements do. An example of a cooperative statement is, "I appreciate your opinion. Let's explore the best situation."

Some signs that someone is a controlling person are when they:

Think there is only one right way to do something and are inflexible

Obsess over insignificant details

Get upset when things don't happen according to their plan

Have trouble trusting other people

Have impossibly high standards

Needing to control can result from growing up in families where things were unpredictable, scary, and out of control. It is closely related to perfectionism, which is also rooted in anxiety and fear. Perfectionists crave predictability and are demanding of themselves as well as others.

If you recognize controlling tendencies in yourself, take steps to soften your approach. Examine your anxiety and fears and process them. Be cooperative and learn to give and take. Be willing to work with others and be flexible. Practice acceptance instead of resistance. Keep focused in the present. Affirmations can be helpful, for example, "There are many ways to accomplish a goal."

Helplines, support groups, therapists, and counselors can be helpful resources to deal with control issues.

Setting Healthy Boundaries

How we live our social lives is determined by our boundaries. Boundaries teach people how to treat us. A boundary is an invisible social line we draw around ourselves that communicates acceptable and unacceptable behavior. Boundaries represent structure, rules, and order.

Setting a boundary lets others know what we stand for, how far we are willing to go concerning a topic, and what we will do about it if our limits are not respected. We must first clearly understand our positions vis-à-vis certain situations before successfully communicating where we stand to others. There are many forms of boundaries.

Physical boundaries are about our personal space and bodies, how close we allow people to get to us, and how receptive and affectionate we are.

Mental boundaries relate to our opinions, thoughts, beliefs, and values. Defensiveness, combativeness, and rigidity are all signs of problems in setting boundaries in this area.

Emotional boundaries are about our feelings, ideas, and experiences. We should expect others to accept and respect our emotional boundaries. We do not have to be open to unwanted advice or people trying to change us or how we are feeling. We recognize that other people are not to blame when we are upset. And we don't try to change others to make ourselves feel better.

Financial boundaries relate to how we budget, spend, save, give, and loan money.

Sexual boundaries indicate our ability to control our comfort level around intimacy, physical touch, and sexual behaviors.

Moral boundaries are when we know what our core values are and how they relate to our behavior. We live our lives by a moral code. Weak boundaries here mean we condone the mistreatment of others, turn a blind eye to injustice, or allow ourselves to be mistreated in the form of being lied to, cheated, and abused.

Spiritual boundaries are about being clear about our religious and/or spiritual beliefs and what aligns with them and what does not.

Children who grew up in a home where parents or caretakers were either too strict and harsh or too permissive may have problems setting and respecting boundaries. Also, being subjected to physical or psychological trauma can hamper the ability to set boundaries. For example, a child who was mistreated, beaten, and constantly exposed to their parents arguing and fighting can find it difficult to set and respect boundaries.

When You Don't Set Boundaries

Some people don't realize they have the right to set a boundary or they may not know how to effectively and kindly set a boundary. Often, this is because they suffer from low self-esteem. They may have fears about speaking up because they want to be liked and fear disapproval. For example, helping people with our resources is positive behavior. But if we are too generous and neglect to set boundaries, we can feel taken advantage of, and it robs other people of the opportunity to step up and handle their responsibilities. It's also dishonest.

Be willing to stand up for yourself. You can detect when you are not setting boundaries if you feel taken advantage of, mistreated, abused, or not treated fairly. Look over the situation and see where you need to speak up and set limits.

Ask yourself if any of these experiences and behaviors, which may lead people to struggle with setting boundaries, apply to you.

- Growing up, did you feel you weren't important and that your needs weren't respected by your parents, caretakers, and family members?
- When you were a child, did you have to take care of the needs of others, and your needs didn't get attended to? If you did something for yourself, did it mean you were selfish?
- Are you afraid of hurting anybody's feelings?
- Do you want to be liked?
- Are you a people pleaser?
- Do you feel you don't have a right to speak up?
- Do you fear loss and or that you will be rejected or discarded?
- Do you feel that you don't know how to communicate your feelings?
- Do you make excuses and refuse to see the truth?
- Do you lack self-confidence?
- Are you afraid of other's disapproval of you?
- Are you afraid you'll be punished somehow?

Social Boundaries

There are two common ways someone doesn't set boundaries in social situations. One is when they express their emotions too openly, sharing the intimate details of their lives, wishes, failures, and innermost thoughts with others who may not be trustworthy. Another is when they first meet people and become immediately attached to them. Certain problems typically occur when social boundaries are not defined or expressed. Here are examples of situations where someone would benefit from setting boundaries.

Whenever April went to visit her daughter Mary, Mary would put her mother to work. She would have her do the two weeks' worth of piled-up laundry, clean the house, and do some extra cooking. April arrived home from her daughter's house feeling exhausted and resentful, but she continued to help out over and over without saying anything.

Mabel was in a relationship with Bruce, and he talked down to her. He criticized how she looked and how she dressed. Bruce was disrespectful to Mabel when they were around other people. Mabel had never set any boundaries with Bruce about how he treated her.

When someone doesn't set healthy boundaries, it creates many problems. It allows others to take advantage of them and mistreat them. It may cause resentment to build steadily, turning into psychological, relationship, or physical problems. People may eventually explode and say things they regret.

Learn to Have Boundaries

People who want to take advantage of you by trying to get more out of you—more work or money—may or may not know what they are doing. Some people use and steal everything they can. They start by taking a little and if they get away with it, they will raise the stakes. Beware and say no at the first indication when someone tries to take advantage of you.

Clarify what you want for yourself by being willing to see the truth of a situation. Communicate your boundaries with clear, reality-based communication that is respectful and without criticism, put-downs, or anger. Be consistent and stay on point. **If you do not respect yourself, others will not respect you.**

Setting a boundary requires clear thinking and good judgment. It is crucial to ascertain what is fair and what is in balance when setting boundaries. Having boundaries is healthy and necessary in relationships. Here are some techniques to build boundaries:

1. Know what your boundaries are and stand up for what you believe.
2. Be able to say NO and mean it. Be able to communicate your limits to others.
3. Be able to follow up your communication with actions by being firm and stable.

4. Realize that you may feel fear and guilt when letting others know what you feel and think. Be willing to work through your emotions.

5. Move on if a relationship isn't working. Ask yourself what you want from the relationship and what you are willing to give up. Learn what you can from the experience and let it go.

6. You may feel you need to solve all the problems at work or home. It can result in you feeling taken advantage of and exhausted.

7. Don't go into unnecessary details, overexplain, or defensively justify yourself.

8. Take care of yourself. Be a good role model for your children and others. Teach them about having self-respect, independence, and how to solve problems.

9. Make decisions when your mind is clear, rested, calm, and emotionally stable. Refrain from taking action when you are emotionally charged about a situation.

10. Be willing to walk away without fear or guilt when people disrespect your wishes, are unwilling to negotiate a solution, or mistreat you.

Sarah had difficulty speaking up to her clients when they owed her money and weren't paying their bills on time. Sarah wanted her clients to like her, and she felt that if she asked them for money, they might be offended. Asked if she was willing not to speak up and not get the money owed to her just to be liked, Sarah thought about it and realized she didn't like the feeling that she was begging and groveling to get people to like her. The next day, Sarah got on the phone and began reminding her clients that their bills were due. The problem was eliminated, and Sarah had set a new boundary.

Boundaries are about taking responsibility for ourselves, our values, and our beliefs. We can't blame others because we're not speaking up. People may not be good at mind-reading or guessing what we want. Expectations that another person should know how to treat us put a lot of pressure on a relationship. By setting boundaries, we communicate to others what we want, and how we want to be spoken to, touched, and treated physically and emotionally.

CHAPTER 16

Communication

Good communication is one of the most vital aspects of creating and nurturing positive relationships with ourselves and others. The way we communicate affects our success, our ability to be happy, and the quality of our lives. Let's start with how we talk to ourselves and then move on to how we communicate to others with our bodies and words.

How Do You Communicate with Yourself?

Before discussing tips for communicating with others, let's review what happens when you communicate with yourself (as discussed in chapter 7, "Self-Talk"). How you speak to yourself matters because you're sending messages to your conscious and unconscious minds simultaneously. The words and messages of your self-talk, positive or negative, affect you on a deep level. So, it is essential to learn to stop negative self-talk such as self-criticism. If you make a mistake, rather than beating yourself up over it, find what there is to learn from the experience and leave the negative emotion out of it. The above is also true when you communicate with others. Remember that, in addition to what you say to them, their unconscious minds are also picking up nonverbal messages from you. Taking this into account, below are some communication tips to follow.

What Are Your Face and Body Communicating?

Without verbalizing a single word, we have an amazing ability to affect how others receive our messages and even how we think and feel. In nonverbal communication, our body language (facial expressions, gestures, movements) and attitudes powerfully impart information to others, even without their conscious awareness of it. The sound of a voice—its tone, intonation, loudness or softness, and speed—also communicates volumes.

Sometimes, what people verbalize does not match their nonverbal messages. For example, let's say someone gives a painting to a friend for their birthday. The friend holds it up and says, "This is great," yet shakes his head from side to side as if saying no. The verbal communication is inconsistent with the nonverbal communication of negatively shaking his head. There has been a simultaneous communication of two different and opposing messages.

We can craft our words to please others, but our bodies may give away what we are really thinking and feeling. Often, our nonverbal communication will portray our true feelings. To be congruent in our nonverbal and verbal communication requires our body language to match what we are saying, feeling, thinking, and doing. We need to be aware when congruency is lacking within us and take the time to examine the source of our inner conflict. Otherwise, we will be sending out confusing messages. If you want to know more about how you interact nonverbally, watch videos of yourself with others and focus on your nonverbal communication. Ask yourself if you are being 100% authentic.

How is Your Verbal Communication?

People generally communicate their viewpoints, complaints, and beliefs. They focus on relaying what is on their minds and in their hearts to others. This is where problems often start. According to a study by Microsoft Corp. people now hold their attention on something for only eight seconds. More than ever, it is important to know what we want to say and skillfully use the appropriate thoughts and words to express our ideas. First, ask yourself:

- How often do you say things that you don't mean?

- Do you regularly just try to please people?
- Are you true to yourself and authentic with others?

To improve your ability to have good communication, become more aware of how you communicate. Record some of your conversations—with permission from the other person—and then listen to them. When others fail to understand you, it means you are speaking ineffectively. Learn from this and any other feedback. Avoid assuming that it is the other person's fault. Explore ways to improve your communication. One of the most important insights for improving how you communicate is to take complete responsibility for what you say, both the words and nonverbal behavior. Next are some suggested techniques to employ for more effective communication.

Keep It Simple Speak in a direct manner and get to the point. Use words that someone can easily understand. For example, say to yourself, Today, I am going to complete my to-do list. An example of being direct with someone else is: Are you free to meet at the office at 10:00 a.m.?

Stay in the Present Similar to the discussion in chapter 7 on our thinking, dwelling too much on the past or future in communication does not yield good results. People become defensive when you bring up the past. The past is gone. Talking about the past also often results in the use of words like always and never, which put people on the defensive. Bringing up the past in communication is a waste of time and energy unless it pertains to an accomplishment or improvement in the present.

When discussing the future, avoid talking about fears or the anticipation of negative circumstances or events. This just veers the conversation away from the positive and can magnetize more negativity. We can only make decisions and act in the now. The future is not here yet, so focus on the future only as a necessary act in the present, such as making appointments or talking about practical details surrounding coming events such as plans for outings or vacations.

State It in the Positive If someone were asked, "Do not think of a pink elephant on the street," their mind thinks about a pink elephant on a street. If we are tired or not paying attention, the not in the statement will be ignored.

If a child is told not to play in the street, they will first think about playing in the street. Playing in the street can be easily visualized, but not playing in the street cannot be visualized. The five senses process information about what they see, hear, feel, touch and smell. There is no way for the senses to process not seeing, or not feeling something. The word not creates an empty vacuum. The child first visualizes playing in the street. If she gets distracted while processing the statement, her thinking may stop at playing in the street.

A better way to communicate is to use affirmative statements and avoid not. Instead of saying, "Do not play in the street," it is better to say, "I want you to stay in the yard and play in this green grassy area." Do the same when talking to yourself. Keep focused on what you want, not on what you don't want to reinforce accomplishing what you want to achieve.

Avoid Non-Directive Words It is best to stop using the words probably, hope, maybe, wish, might, perhaps, and try. These words do little to direct the unconscious mind or that of other people into action. People mistakenly believe they are making a meaningful statement when using these words, but they are not. None of these words are taken as a directive or instruction by the unconscious mind. For example, if someone asks their friend to go to dinner with them next week and the friend answers "maybe," does the person know if their friend will come to dinner? The same is true with all the other words. There is no commitment in a statement using these words.

When people use the word "try" in a sentence, it also means nothing.

I Versus You The use of I statements is essential to good communication. If someone uses a lot of you statements in a potentially negative conversation, the other person may become defensive because they feel they are being blamed. Take, for example, the statement, "You don't return my calls." The tone and the message will be instantly transformed by changing it to an I statement. State your feelings. Say instead, "I felt hurt when I didn't hear back." This I statement will be met with less resistance.

Ask Questions When communicating, ask yourself, what does the other person want from me in this communication? Many times, people just want to blow off steam and feel better. They aren't looking for answers or advice on what to do differently.

It is essential to understand what people want. For example, if someone just wants to vent and we begin to tell them how to solve what we consider their problem is, they'll become defensive, not hear us, or feel like we don't understand. They could be caught up in their emotions and unable to communicate their thoughts clearly.

As listeners, it is our job to ask questions to bring out what the other person may be leaving out. In addition, if we're not sure we understand what someone is saying, we can repeat back to them what we heard them say in our own words and ask if our understanding is correct. This is very helpful in making sure we do understand the person.

As we listen, we can also pay attention to many other factors. Is the person blaming or taking responsibility for what is going on? Have they looked at both sides of the issue? Are their emotions blinding them to reality? Is the person open to finding understanding and solutions? What are their nonverbal cues saying?

Review these tips for good communication and incorporate them into your daily life as much as possible.

Summary of Helpful Communication Tips

Be congruent with your words, emotions, and actions.

Know your motive for what you are saying and doing.

Keep it simple. Be direct, concise, and clear.

State it in the present (unless talking about a specific project in the future or the past that relates to the present in some way).

Make statements in the positive. State what you do want, not what you do not want.

If you are not sure you understood what the other person said, then repeat it back to them to see if your understanding is accurate.

Think and speak with integrity.

Stop blaming others and take responsibility.

Be a good listener and pay attention to the feedback.

Be consistent and supportive.

Be flexible, open, and make necessary adjustments to be a better communicator.

How Much Do People Listen to You?

When speaking with others, it is important to be able to tell if the other person is listening to what we're saying. If they're not, then why continue to talk? If they're not listening, it's our job to find out why. Is the subject not interesting to them? Do they disagree with our viewpoint? Do they obviously not understand what we're saying? Could it be that they simply don't care? Is the person focused on something else? If any of these are true, the other person will tune out and stop listening to us.

Ask for feedback when you aren't sure if the other person understood what you've said. Notice when people have stopped listening because you're talking too much, for example if they aren't looking at you anymore. Some people talk just to be talking. They ramble and seem to have no purpose for what they are saying. It is a waste of time and energy and accomplishes nothing.

Are You Nagging?

If your message is falling on deaf ears, ask yourself if you have been focused on the problem rather than the solution. Are you complaining, criticizing, and nagging about what is wrong? Simply ask for what you want instead of focusing on the problem and why the person is wrong, guilty, or should be blamed. Most people aren't willing to listen to constant complaints about themselves. Communicate what you do want in the affirmative and focus on fixing the issue at hand with an agreed-upon *solution*. As always, stick to discussing the present and avoid bringing up the past.

Being Ghosted

It can be frustrating or provoking when someone doesn't return our calls and emails. We also could feel disappointed, not cared about, disrespected, or angry. People have a right to decide if they want to call us or not. They may have good reasons. Situations such as these can trigger our need to control, so we become defensive. The only path forward is when we accept their decision and deal with our feelings about it. Once we are in balance again, we can weigh our options.

Disrespect and Verbal Abuse

Some people allow others to be disrespectful and even verbally and physically abusive. Verbal abuse is when someone is making angry criticisms, accusations, creating arguments, and trying to put people down. When someone is verbally abusive, it does not help to be defensive. It will usually energize the person to continue the abuse. The person bearing the abuse may be hurt and upset but may have a hard time standing up for themselves. Later, the abuser may say how sorry they are and apologize profusely. They may deploy their charm to keep the abused person confused and prevent them from leaving. The abusive behavior and the tolerance of it by another person may be because of unresolved trauma from the past. It can also come from low self-esteem, fears, never having learned how to love and be loved, failing to stand up for oneself, or not feeling worthy enough to require respect.

When someone displays abusive behavior, first, determine if it is safe to communicate with them. If it isn't, refrain from saying anything more than is necessary. Once there is a time of calm, talk to the person and tell them how you feel and what you would like to change. Set some boundaries. Often the person will not listen to you and will continue to find fault with you. If the abusive behavior continues, know that the person is not hearing you and may not be ready for change.

It is up to you to decide whether you are willing to live this way or if you need to find other ways to change what is going on. Going to see a counselor could be helpful. If you don't want to tolerate the abusive behavior and have tried other solutions, it may be in your highest good to leave the situation.

Diarrhea of the Mouth

Have you ever talked with someone who does all the talking?

This is a common problem. I have had phone conversations with someone that lasted an hour, and during that time, I said six words. The person continuously talked the whole time. I knew what to do to change it, but I chose to listen instead. It happened more than once. One time, I fell asleep while the person was talking. I'm not sure they even noticed.

Some people don't know how to have a back-and-forth conversation. Their need to talk is so strong that they don't realize how thoughtless and inconsiderate they are. Several years ago, I frequently went out for dinner with my friend Fred. He would do almost all of the talking. It made me uncomfortable. I felt as though I was being treated like I didn't have anything worthwhile to say. Sometimes I felt bored. I liked Fred, so I didn't want to stop seeing him. I gave a lot of thought to the problem and started figuring out what I could do to address it. Soon, I realized that I was contributing to the situation by listening so intently and asking Fred so many questions. The next time Fred and I went to dinner, I listened to Fred for a while, commented on what he had been saying, and then changed the subject to something I wanted to talk about. It worked very well, and I no longer had the problem with Fred.

It's not enjoyable to have someone talk *at* you rather than *with* you as in a back-and-forth conversation. I realized that I stopped enjoying my meetings with Fred because he only wanted to talk about himself and wasn't really interested in what I had to say. I call when someone wants to do all the talking "diarrhea of the mouth." Some choices in dealing with this problem are: let the person talk, be more proactive and interject your ideas into the conversation, or you can just stop seeing the person.

Facing the Fear of Public Speaking

At some point in our lives, we may be called to share our ideas or teach in front of an audience. It can feel like a full-blown crisis to be put on the spot in public—the kind where your breathing gets faster, your blood pressure shoots up, and sweat beads form. The fear of public speaking is widespread. I know first-hand about this fear from when I took a public speaking class in junior college many years ago. The first time I stood in front of the class to deliver a five-minute prepared lecture, I started trembling, and my neck and face turned beet red. In those days, I knew nothing about identifying fear and processing feelings.

A couple of years later, I started giving lectures about handwriting analysis to groups all over Los Angeles, delivering an average of two to three lectures per week. The fear of being boring and not good enough was a strong motivator for me to work diligently at preparing the material. As I gained more experience, there was a noticeable decrease in my fear and, gradually, I became much more comfortable lecturing. It began to feel more natural, and soon I barely had any anxiety.

I had been giving lectures for many months already, when I was invited to lecture to the largest group of people yet. The audience members would entail individuals with powerful positions who were well known. Intimidated by this new challenge, my fear level went through the roof.

I faced the challenge by doing everything possible to ensure the lecture would be successful. Rather than outline it, as usual, I decided to write out the entire speech word for word. After meticulously writing the lecture, I had another person check the grammar and wording to ensure it was correct and professional. Then in the hopes of guaranteeing that I wouldn't make a mistake, I decided to read the talk instead of speaking spontaneously. Every night, I prayed that God would guide and help me give a good, informative lecture.

At the lecture, I was seated on stage with 10 men on either side of me. Before the program, I checked my notes carefully to be sure they were in order and then went up to the podium and placed them near the microphone.

Following an introduction, I walked to the podium, feeling very nervous and fearful, and looked out at the sea of faces. As I had practiced numerous times, I started to read the lecture. After reading page two, I turned the page only to realize there was no page three.

My heart started racing. I stopped talking and began looking through the papers, around the podium, and even on the floor, but there was no page three. So, I took a deep breath and said to myself, "Well, they are just going to get me."

It must have looked strange to the audience to see this controlled speaker and serious person stop reading to look around for a piece of paper, only to suddenly come out from behind the podium with the microphone and begin talking spontaneously with no notes. Fortunately, I had done this numerous times before. I interacted with the audience, brought several people up on stage, and sprinkled in several jokes. The group had some good laughs and a lot of fun. That night was a huge lesson. I vowed never to read a lecture again. I never did find page three and suspected that this was how God had answered my prayer.

Share What You Know

Do you have valuable knowledge, talents, or skills that could help others? Why keep these hidden? People can forgo developing a talent or actualizing a dream because of fear.

The fear of public speaking can be about the fear of making a mistake, forgetting what to say, being vulnerable, getting disapproval from others, and not being perfect. The ego also gets involved and wants to make a good impression. It is natural to lack confidence if someone is not an experienced speaker or unfamiliar with a subject. Generally, the more often we have done something, the more comfortable we will become doing it.

Strive to surmount your fears. Use the ETT in chapter 5 to process your feelings. Also, examine your beliefs to see if they are telling you anything negative like, "I am not a good speaker." Process your fears and emotions about public speaking every time they come up before a public-speaking event, then be sure you are fully prepared by taking some additional steps.

First, know the material well and rehearse your talk until you deliver it the way you want. Think about possible audience questions and be prepared to answer them. If it turns out you don't know the answer to a question, then admit it and tell the asker that you will find out the answer and get back to them.

Second, in the beginning, you need to be willing to give speeches even if you are afraid, anxious, and uncomfortable. How can you have faith you'll give a wonderful speech if you lack experience? That will come with practice. Have the courage to be vulnerable and give the speech regardless of how you feel.

Moving from Ego to Serving Others

Taking the time to develop your public speaking skills is very important. In the end, however, *intention* is paramount to successful public speaking. If your intention is to glorify yourself in any way, then you may be susceptible to fears because you can and will sometimes fail at being a well-received public speaker. When this is the case, you may find yourself occasionally going home, feeling weary about your performance.

However, someone's emotional landscape changes completely if their intention is **not about making themselves look good but rather about contributing something helpful to others.** They tune out fear and into a more caring, altruistic vibration. When we are singularly focusing on helping others, there is no space to focus on imperfections, what type of image we are projecting, or what others think about us. If we have helped others in any small way, our job is done. Fears are irrelevant in this space.

This means that instead of intellectually talking to the audience in a matter-of-fact way that lacks feeling, you let your voice and words carry your energy and emotions to them. In this way, they know how you feel about your subject. Get your listeners involved so they respond to what you are saying. Add some humor and fun. If you are having fun, your audience is having fun. Allow participants to ask questions. If there's no question-and-answer period scheduled during the lecture, then meet with them on the side after the program is over and talk with them about their questions. Remember to review your performance so you can do better next time.

What matters most is striving to reach every person in the audience and give them something of value in a way that can be received. Every time I engage in public speaking events, I focus on making myself a vehicle through which the energy of love, wisdom, and peace can flow to the audience. It requires accepting myself, connecting with the energy of universal love, and asking to be a conduit of positivity to share with others.

To reach an audience in this way, take even five minutes to be still and meditate right before your talk. Do some exercises to wake up your body right before talking as well. When preparing the materials, do so with the sole intention to help and bring positivity to someone. Ask at each stage of the preparation process and during the talk:

- How can I maximally uplift the audience with new information and positivity right now?
- How can I be a conduit of light, love, and peace?

One helpful technique that actors employ before going on stage is to send their energy to the four corners of the room. It makes everyone in the audience feel like the actor is talking just to them.

Do this by first visualizing the room and audience. Next, feel your energy moving throughout your body from the top of your head down to your feet and back up to the top of your head. Stomp your feet on the floor a few times and wiggle your body to help your energy move. Then take in a huge breath, bend over at the waist, and stretch your arms out while pointing your fingers to the farthest corners of the room while exhaling. Do each corner separately. Visualize your energy expanding to fill the entire space. Imagine everyone in the room being able to feel your energy.

Learning from Experience

Public speaking will get easier every time you do it. Be open to improvement. Each time you perform, review the performance, then work on those areas that need improvement. Solicit feedback from trusted, more experienced individuals whenever you can. It is your choice as to how much you want to perfect your talents, skills, and abilities.

When you review your public speaking style after a talk, ask yourself some of the following questions.

- Was your voice strong and confident?
- Did you have enough volume?
- Did you send your energy to the four corners of the room?
- Did you look at the audience?
- Did you talk *with* the audience and not *at* them?
- Did you make the content of the talk interesting and informative?
- Did you make sure the microphone was working correctly before the talk?
- Was the lighting appropriate?
- Did you make sure the equipment you would use was working properly ahead of time (laptop projector, blackboard, flip chart, and handouts)?
- Did you answer questions from the audience?
- Did you allow participants to speak to you after the talk?

Bring Awareness to Communication

Just as we discuss elsewhere on other topics in this book, growth and understanding will come when we stay aware. Bringing our awareness when we are engaged in any form of communication will teach us a lot about ourselves and others.

For example, when communicating, we can look within and ask ourselves what we are trying to say. Do we need to express a story or an idea and need someone to lend an ear? Are we venting emotions or upset? Are we striving to connect with someone and have fun socially? What value is this conversation or other interaction adding to the lives of those involved, ours and theirs? What is the quality of our listening during this interaction? What is theirs?

In summary, to cultivate more awareness when engaged in an interaction, ask the following questions:

- What effect are you having on them?
- Are you speaking affirmatively?
- What nonverbal cues are you giving and receiving?
- Do they understand what you said?
- Did they agree with you or disagree?
- Do they offer a different opinion?
- Are they friendly or irritated?
- Are they respectful?
- Are they talking *at* you?
- What do they want?
- Are they open to other ideas and solutions?
- Are they defensive (making excuses or getting angry)?
- Are they controlling or judgmental?
- Do they keep repeating what they are saying?
- Are they being affected by drugs or alcohol?
- Do they have the ability to understand?
- Are you truly listening or distracted?
- Can you find ways to reflect back to the person?
- Are you expressing love and caring?

PART V

Reaching Out to Spirituality

CHAPTER 17

Discovering Our Spiritual Selves

The Big Questions

Living day-to-day, we sometimes find ourselves searching for answers to the many mysteries of life that we have. Some of the big questions are, "How can I stop feeling so much pain?" "How can I make the right choices?" and "Why am I here?" We also ask ourselves how we can find peace and happiness and make a difference in the world. These are important questions and the people that find the answers to them are very fortunate indeed.

The exercises and techniques in this book will set you on a path of finding answers. Emotional pain can be a strong motivator to seek out what you need to know. As someone heals their fears and negative feelings, they gain the freedom to walk on a spiritual path. Doors are opened when they learn to look within to heal and release negative energy. And room is made for love to fill the space where negativity once dwelled.

Perhaps life's biggest questions are, "Why death?" and "What happens after death?" There are a variety of beliefs about the subject. The only thing we know for sure is that at some point we will die. Knowing that a day will come when we will pass away can be positive. It can motivate us to realize our time is limited and we need to learn how to have good character, obey the law, and be the best we can be in all circumstances. If we fear death, it helps to deal with it by processing the feelings, learning how to accept death, and getting on with living life.

Our concept of God, or not having any concept, is another one of life's mysteries. People relate to God in different ways.

Some don't believe in God. There are many different beliefs and viewpoints about what God is. We have the freedom to choose what we believe, but often that belief comes from what our families believe. Most of the major religions have similarities in their tenets. Many embrace spirituality and the mystical. Because everyone is on their own journey, it's important to accept other people's choices and beliefs even though they may be different than ours.

As you progress spiritually, you will move past your pain and may also start asking yourself, Am I the best person I can be? Am I conscientious and doing what I can to support people, the environment, and animals? Helping others can be as simple as being supportive with kind words, giving physical help, emotional support, and donating money. Animals and nature need our support also. Each day there are opportunities to help others. We need to recognize those opportunities and act upon them as part of our spiritual journey.

When your journey of transformation has brought you to this point, you will be able to become the observer of your life even while living it daily. Since we are not our body and not our mind, we do not have to identify with our body and thinking. Even when we are faced with stressful situations, we can observe ourselves going through the experience and not emotionally react to what is happening. With objectivity, we just do what we have to do with good behavior.

Peace and happiness come from the work of looking within to identify our conflicts and confusion. We need to heal our fears and negative energy and learn to be grateful, thankful, and appreciative each day. But we don't have to be alone on this journey of transformation, Spirit is there for you. You just have to reach out.

Splitting a Banana

One of the big questions that I have pondered in my life is about what happened to my stepsister Marie and me. The many *whys* I have asked about this story have helped me on my journey.

When my family lived in Burlington, Iowa, my two stepsisters, Marie and Doris, would visit us for a few weeks in the summer. Marie was just a year younger than me, so we became close.

Marie, Evelyn's stepsister, age 12

Both girls were deaf and couldn't speak. They lived at a school for the deaf in Nebraska. I learned to sign at seven years old. Marie and I would lay in bed in the dark, signing into each other's hands, talking. It all seemed very natural to me. I was amazed at all the things Marie and Doris learned at school. Even though they couldn't hear the music, they learned to dance by feeling the vibration of the music on the floor. Marie was very talented and an excellent artist. When she drew someone, it looked just like them.

One day, as Marie and I were having lunch together, we split a banana. A couple of days later, Marie became sick. She laid in bed for two days and only became sicker so my stepfather drove her to the hospital late on the second day. On the morning of the third day, as I came downstairs, I started to vomit. My mother was on the phone with my stepfather, who was calling from the hospital to say that Marie had just died. She'd had a temperature of 108 degrees. So as soon as my mother saw that I had vomited, she rushed me to the hospital.

Once there, because of Marie, the doctors, having a better idea of what to do for me, took my case very seriously and treated me very quickly. In 1942, penicillin had only recently been invented, but the doctors gave it to me right away. Even so, by noon, my temperature climbed to 106 degrees, and the next day, the doctor told my parents that they didn't think I would live.

This happened during World War II. Government officials

were very concerned that, because of the munitions plant in town, the city was being food-poisoned by foreign spies. Some high-ranking Army officials came to the hospital to question me. I told them what Marie and I had eaten during the previous few days, including how we had shared a banana. The Army officers went to my home to take our food and garbage to the University of Iowa in Iowa City to be tested. It was determined that the banana contained Streptococcus bacteria, which is what had poisoned Marie and me. Streptococcus is one of the deadliest bacteria. The officials told us bananas are the perfect food for it to grow in since they are warm, dark, and moist inside. The banana Marie and I had shared had a broken, dark peel.

Since I was not expected to live, my mother asked a priest to come to the hospital to pray for me. I remember praying with the priest; however, I didn't know I wasn't expected to live. The penicillin, excellent care, and, I believe, God saved me. After five days in the hospital, I was sent home to finish my recovery.

Today, I am very thankful to Marie for helping to save my life. If Marie hadn't gotten sick first, my mother wouldn't have rushed me to the hospital right away, and the doctors wouldn't have known to give me penicillin immediately. We all have our time when we give our bodies back to the earth. I have always believed that that time in 1942 was not my time to die.

Ask to Align with Spirit

To discover who you are, fan the burning desire inside to find answers instead of pushing it away or covering it up with distractions. Energizing this desire will light the path toward a spiritual life. Align with spirit through prayer or meditation and ask for guidance and to be shown the way. Make it your main priority by putting it above everything else.

You will be guided to read certain books and meet special people. You may have a meaningful dream, mystical experience, a near-death experience, or experience miracles. As the spiritual connection grows, you will continue to learn and experience more, and your faith will grow stronger. Your vibrational energy will increase, and your intuition will open to receive guidance.

There are many ways to seek spiritual answers to the difficulties in your life. Even when things appear hopeless, opportunities exist to make changes. Hopelessness can be turned into an opportunity to align with the spiritual. Ask yourself: What can I learn from this experience? What do I need to change in myself? How can I align with spirit here? Open your heart to change. Keep asking and looking, and help will come. It may come in the form of a person, book, minister, rabbi, priest, counselor, a 12-Step program, friend, stranger, or even an intuitive flash. It can appear in any number of ways and is different for everyone. Have patience because this is a gradual process that demands a whole-hearted desire and willingness to do what is required.

Your actions and thoughts reflect how you are doing on the spiritual journey. Examine each day if you respect and like the person you are. Let the light and love radiate from your heart and share your joyful spirit with others. Ask to be shown the way. Stop thinking you have all the answers. Be open and patient regardless of how long it takes, learn to be humble, kind, considerate, helpful to others, respectful, generous, understanding, honest, and willing to learn.

Spirituality Freed Jim

I met Jim sometime during the first half of 2005 because his girlfriend was a friend of mine. Jim and his girlfriend were in a relatively new relationship and had some problems. They visited me hoping that I could help them get the relationship on track. Unfortunately, Jim and his girlfriend didn't end up together, but one of the gifts that emerged from the relationship was our working together.

When Jim and I first met, he was an ardent atheist and had been that way since he was 12 years old. One day when we were talking, out of the blue, I surprised Jim when I asked him, "Carol tells me you don't believe in God. Is that true?" After confirming this was correct, Jim then shared that he had grown up in the Catholic Church as a boy, but since he was 12, he had fully closed himself to the idea of the existence of God. He had lived as a strict atheist from then on for the next four decades.

Jim, having learned to trust me, asked me to describe the God I believed in. My response was brief as I described a God very different from the one that the Church had taught Jim. I explained that there is a God among us and everywhere. I asked Jim to look around at the world, and who did he think created the land, plants, ocean, animals, and people? I answered a God that gave us free will and allows us to experience life, learn, and develop ourselves as we choose.

Jim listened intently and could feel his mind open as he contemplated what I told him. It was a concise and perfectly reasonable explanation of how the universe was created and how it all works. He remembers the conversation as much for the shortness of the exchange as for the simplicity and power of the words.

In this way, the door to spirituality was opened for Jim, which facilitated a new course in his life. At our next appointment, Jim was able to tell me that he now accepted God. Jim hadn't been looking for it, but for reasons Jim couldn't understand at the time, he had found acceptance. He was surprised at how agreeable he felt to the ideas I had shared. They made sense to him.

Jim's acceptance of the existence of God brought him emotions of relief, discovery, and liberation. There was a feeling of joy and satisfaction for having found something so valuable, which he hadn't even known he was looking for. It was like finding a map to a hidden treasure. Jim realized there might be an entire dimension that he had been missing in his life by not having considered other possibilities. He began to explore the metaphysical, and this was the first step on a new path and new life for him.

Jim had been a daily abuser of alcohol when we met, even though he managed to live a functional life with some control over liquor. Jim says that my definition of an alcoholic rings true in his ears today, many years later, as if I'd said it to him yesterday, "You know you're an alcoholic if alcohol is affecting your life."

Jim began drinking alcohol at 22. In New England, where he had grown up, alcohol was a part of the environment. After being discharged from the Marine Corps, he felt a bit lost. This was ironic because the urge to find himself was why Jim had enlisted in the first place.

Then Jim met a wonderful girl and married, and they had problems early on, which was mostly his fault, so they moved to California for a new start. Unfortunately, he rediscovered his fondness for alcohol about a year after moving to California. Jim always managed to earn a decent living, but alcohol was not a good element to add to the bright future of a young married couple. Even so, they had two wonderful daughters, a beautiful home, well-paying jobs, excellent private schools for the girls, and fun excursions. In short, they were living the dream.

Several years after moving to California, Jim, now 26, began to recognize that his drinking was causing problems in his marriage, so he decided to stop drinking. He was alcohol-free for a month until he and his wife went to a party. There was plenty of booze, and he found himself craving a drink. Giving in, he got busy drinking. It was like he was trying to catch up on thirty days of lost time. He was utterly out of control. He could still recall an awareness that hit him that night, this must be what it feels like to be an alcoholic. It made him feel surprised, frustrated, and even deeply sad.

However, for the next 37 years, the lust for alcohol accompanied Jim. The addiction and craving overpowered everything his heart desired. Willpower didn't have a chance in his decades-long battle with the bottle. His desire for alcohol consumed his days as he continued to drink and attempted to function as well as possible. On the weekends, he would let loose and allow his desire for alcohol to have its freedom.

When Jim thinks of his angry actions, arguments, insecurity, judgments, jealousy, fears, resentments, poor decisions, lack of empathy and compassion, and what he put others through, he feels sad that he couldn't change it. To have permitted his life to be controlled by alcohol seems silly now. But he allowed it. Despite hundreds of attempts to quit, he could not stop the craving—until the last time.

Eventually, Jim was shown how to reform his behavior—through the gift of a spiritual path. For the first time in many years, after gaining a new understanding of spirituality, he noticed the craving loosening its hold. That hadn't happened before. In the past, when he quit drinking, it wouldn't be long before the yearning and feelings of need would reappear, expand, and intensify.

Jim after recovery

Jim accepted that willpower alone wasn't enough; he needed God in his life. He became honest about what he was doing and surrendered his old ways. He started to believe that he deserved to live an enjoyable life without alcohol.

Now Jim is traveling in a wonderful new direction, one that he cherishes every day. His newfound gift of spirituality helped him achieve a solution for a problem that had been haunting him for 37 years. He has been able to eradicate alcohol and its effects from his life.

Spirituality helped Jim to be able to finally live a normal life. **He learned the real reason he was drinking in the first place: he had been unable to accept his fears, feelings, and pain.** He had fallen into the trap of trying to escape. Certainly, it was his fault. The change began the day I helped him question his life and change some of his beliefs.

It seems obvious now to Jim that addressing his inner world through spiritual work brings gifts that make for a good life. Before, Jim didn't know how to change because he didn't have the tools, knowledge, or ability. With a genuine belief in God and a foundation of spirituality, Jim was finally free from alcohol. Once he accepted sobriety, he was given the freedom to live an unimpaired life and realized that God was there to help him. Jim is forever grateful for the peace, strength, and confidence that comes from the path that he found.

Some things Jim has realized about drinking alcohol:

1. He can feel happy about his life every day without alcohol.
2. Alcohol robbed him of the wonderful things he could have enjoyed and benefited from. For example, the ability to love and be loved, personal development and growth, quality relationships, stable finances, good health (physical, mental, emotional), an enjoyable career, ambition, contributing to the welfare of others, and more.
3. Most importantly, when he was drinking, he hadn't cared about how other people felt. He lacked empathy and compassion and never got to experience the benefits of giving to others.
4. Jim learned that Carl Jung was onto something when he said that people can stop drinking through the cultivation of spirituality.
5. Believing in a Higher Power helped Jim in every way. He learned to value life more, and he started understanding and experiencing what love is.

Evolving Past the Ego

The old question, "Would you rather be right, or would you rather be happy?" has been around for a while. Many people answer, "I would rather be right." The part of you that fights to be right is our ego. It is not really who you are. The ego wants power and control and isn't interested in integrity, justice, and love. Ask yourself, why is being right, at the expense of everything like your relationships, important to the real you?

Eventually, everyone will find their spiritual path. The question is, how much suffering is someone willing to go through to get there? **One of the hardest things for the ego to admit is "I am my own worst enemy."** It is up to us to choose the path that we want.

I think everyone is entitled to be happy, deserves to have a joyful life, and has the power to transform. If someone wants to live a more spiritual life, an ongoing examination of the ego's effect on their life is necessary. The spiritual path is one of reflection and contemplation.

What humans see in the world is constantly changing and is an illusion. The desire and struggle to get more things, financial gain, or control leads to pain and unhappiness. Have you ever told yourself that if you get something you want in the future, then you'll be happy? The future never gets here, you are always in the present. If you can't be happy now then you will never be happy. Lasting happiness is a state that emanates from within, not the outside.

The ego has no interest in spiritual matters unless these avenues serve to show off its superiority. The ego is only attracted to the distractions that pull people away from the spiritual path. When the ego is in charge, moments of satisfaction and happiness are only fleeting and there can be no lasting happiness. The energy of desire and superiority associated with the ego attracts many problems. Here are examples of when the ego is speaking:

> Don't they know who I am?
>
> I want.
>
> I am special and people should treat me that way.
>
> I belong on a pedestal.
>
> I deserve.
>
> My needs are all that count.

Only my point of view matters.

You must acknowledge and adore me.

Why am I not always being considered?

Each problem created by the ego's desires can be looked at as a learning opportunity. An outlook focused on growth and learning instead of self-pity, despair, and guilt is an antidote to the ego.

Living a Spiritual Life

Many people are living their lives surrounded by unconscious, ego-based body armor to shield them from what they fear. It is created by their minds—confused with wrong ideas, craving gain, and fearing loss—which cause suffering and frustration. This limits people's movements, choices, freedom, and growth and keeps them from realizing their full potential.

For those desiring to transform and expand their lives, the journey is a spiritual one. The way is to turn inward by releasing their focus on the outer world. Human senses have been created to look outward. But to transform means to go inside of ourselves.

Observing and accepting our fears lets go of negative energy. As we release our negativity, we can become quiet and peaceful. Meditation enables us to be observers, increase our awareness, and get to know who we are.

We stay on track by keeping our focus on the spiritual journey steady and by being consciously aware every day. We practice observing what we are doing and how we are thinking and feeling. Without a watchful eye, it is possible to fall back without even realizing it.

Once we come through the long process of learning what is within us, we begin to understand **our most heartfelt desire is to break out of the cocoon that has limited us for so long**. Upon unveiling our spiritual selves, our desires and goals often change. Our lives become dedicated to self-knowledge, and the focus becomes to free ourselves from the self-imposed limitations of the ego. Then we experience more happiness and manifest more love.

When our main goal is to develop spiritually, with sincerity, honesty, and dedication, we have a steady purpose. Our actions become based on awareness, humility, love, and nonviolence. The heart is purified and in alignment with our thoughts, desires, and behaviors. By strengthening our minds, our feelings, words, and actions come into harmony with our wills.

Those of us on a spiritual path know there are no accidents. The obstacles and challenges that we face in life are opportunities for us to learn. Without obstacles, we would be stuck where we are. What counts is how we deal with our challenges. It is important to accept what we are dealt in life without resistance, strive to find solutions, and learn from each experience. Spiritual knowledge comes from this understanding, and from listening and being aware.

People with a spiritual orientation have a mindset of cooperation, nonjudgment, and hope as we face the issues that come up. We strive to come from a place of humility in our thinking and actions, which includes a willingness to know we don't have all the answers and may have been looking in the wrong places. Being spiritual means being willing to adopt new thinking and different actions to bring about a new way of living. Once someone lets go of the old, they can enjoy the birth of the new. It requires courage to make changes. And change is what transformation is all about.

CHAPTER 18

My Journey of Walking with God

Everyone's life is different, and people want different things. But what we have in common is that everyone wants to be loved and happy. Spirituality is a pathway that can lead you to the fulfillment of happiness and being able to love yourself and others. Discovering how other people have found peace, happiness, and love on a spiritual path can help you understand what is possible. In this chapter, I share my spiritual journey.

How I Found Spirituality and God in Life

Since I was a young child, I have been trying to find what makes life meaningful. In the small town in Iowa where I was born, I started going to the Baptist Sunday school every week by myself at the age of six. My parents didn't go to church. I found the stories at church about Jesus and the Bible characters very interesting.

One Sunday, the teacher talked about sin and showed us one glass of water with clear water and another glass with black water to indicate what happens when someone sins. Sometimes, I would attend the church service to listen to the preacher's sermons.

When I was thirteen, we moved to a city about thirty miles away with a population of 30,000. It seemed like a large city to me at the time. Our neighbor and her daughter attended an Episcopalian church, so I started going with them to

Evelyn, age 16

their church. Then things became confusing to me because the priest there said different things from what the Baptist preacher had said. One said it was all right to smoke and have some drinks, and the other said they were sins. I didn't know which one was right, but I knew they couldn't both be right. Through the years, I attended many other different denominations of churches, and most of them gave some different messages. The good part about it is that I continued to search for more answers.

After I moved to California in 1955, I started going to spiritual churches. I went to Science of Mind, Unity Church, and some others. The messages in these spiritual churches made a lot of sense to me. I didn't throw out what I had learned from the other churches. I just continued learning more about God, spiritual principles, truth, and living life.

Searching for Knowledge

My search for more knowledge continued for the next 45 years as I kept attending various classes. I studied Psychology, Astrology, Numerology, Reincarnation, Palm Reading, Handwriting Analysis, Dreams, Intuition, Spirituality, Hypnosis, Muscle Testing, Dowsing, Buddhism, Eastern Philosophy, Kinesiology, Meditation, and Healing.

In 1965, I learned to meditate at the Foundation of Human Understanding in Los Angeles. Roy Masters was the teacher and leader of the Foundation. I attended his lectures three nights a week and on Sundays. At the Foundation, I also learned about hypnosis and spiritual principles. From that time on, I have meditated every day, in the morning and evening, and believe it is one of the best things I have ever done. Meditation teaches us how to still the mind; it raises our vibrational level and our intuition. Meditation is a great tool to train the mind. By learning to stay focused in the present, we know how to stay calm if there is an emergency, an accident, or an upsetting condition.

In my early forties, I decided to become a minister, not to

become a preacher—I wanted to learn more about God. The church where I studied was a spiritual church that used the King James Bible. In class, we had to read and study the whole Bible. Everyone also had to write a thesis on another religion, anyone we wanted. I chose to do my thesis on Judaism. The church had no special denomination but basically believed in Christianity and healing work. After several years of study, I became an ordained minister and have conducted a few weddings.

A Dark Night of the Soul

When I was studying, I had some deep spiritual experiences and went through tremendous pain. About a year after the ordeal was over, I recognized the experience as "a dark night of the soul." During that year, I suffered from extreme emotional pain and sadness. I cried nearly every day for no special reason and couldn't make any plans because I never knew if I'd manage to go out. Yet, also at this time, a great deal of information about God was being given to me spiritually. Later, I learned that the teaching that I was receiving was like the Course of Miracles. On one occasion, I was told by Jesus, "Evelyn, you will have to walk through the ring of fire." I saw a huge ring, taller and wider than me, and the entire ring was on fire. I didn't know what it meant at the time. Later, I discovered that it meant I would have to learn many lessons and that the fire represented purifying my lower vibrations. The purification process was emotionally painful.

Suddenly, one day the sadness and crying stopped. I couldn't believe it was over and kept wondering if it would return, but it didn't. I went back to school and got my PhD in Psychology. After that, I studied Neuro-Linguistic Programming (NLP) for five years and received my Certified Teachers Training for Advanced NLP. NLP teaches how the brain learns and operates and how this affects behavior. I also learned how to use language to reach a deeper level of communication with myself and others to be more effective. This involves using subtle hypnosis, physical techniques such as vocalizations, and connecting various strategies, such as rapport, with spoken words.

In the meantime, I continued working on eliminating my negative energy and letting go of my fears. Every day, I prayed to God and asked for his help. I had many experiences that increased my faith, including situations where my life was saved due to a silent voice in my head providing information on what to do. I also had dreams that came true exactly as I had dreamed them. I couldn't share most of what was going on in my life because other people wouldn't understand.

A time came when life was getting better. There seemed to be less pain, and I was feeling happier. I continued my search for God. For the next 25 years, I did coaching, teaching, and lecturing, which I loved. It was rewarding to see other people make improvements in their lives. I also used my NLP Training in my work. During this time, I continued reading self-help, spiritual, and psychology books. I also regularly lectured on cruise ships.

Many years later, I semi-retired from my work and had more free time. My hunger for more spiritual knowledge was always there. I kept praying and asked to be shown how I could live that would be pleasing to God.

Meeting Sai Baba

In 2016, after praying to gain more knowledge, I noticed a book titled *Sai Baba: Man of Miracles* by Howard Murphet on my bookshelf and had a feeling to pick it up and read it. The book is about Sri Sathya Sai Baba. Back in 1984, after I bought the book, someone told me that Sai Baba, who lived in India, could make gold, silver, and diamond jewelry appear miraculously in his empty hands for people. I lost interest in reading the book and let it collect dust on my shelf for years after hearing that.

When I finally did read *Sai Baba Man of Miracles* in 2016, it touched something inside me very deeply. I started reading more and more of his books, and I felt like I was finally learning things that I had asked about my whole life. It was like being nourished after being hungry for a long time.

Sai Baba said many of the same things as Jesus. Born in India in 1926, Sathya Sai Baba was a teacher and philanthropist. During his life, more and more people from within and without India went to learn from and pray with him and be healed. By 1995, millions of people were going to see Sai Baba in southern India from over 150 countries. Some people lived in his ashram for long periods. That year when his followers celebrated his birthday, a million-and-a-half people attended. He had to fly over them in a helicopter to enable all of them to see him.

I read more than 300 books by or about Sai Baba during the next three years. His teachings emphasized that it didn't matter what religion someone aligned with; any of the main religions in the world were acceptable. He wanted people to be of service to and love one another. Sai Baba wanted people to build their character and solve their problems rather than focus on what is wrong with other people. He wanted people to be kind to each other and treat others as they would like to be treated. He did not want anyone prophesizing for him.

Sai Baba felt right to me because he only wanted to give to people. He fed those living at his ashrams for free and treated the poorest people the same as he treated the rich and famous. He built large hospitals that were some of the world's most modern and staffed them with the finest doctors. On the first day the largest hospital opened, several open-heart surgeries were performed. No patient was ever charged for any of the services. He built large schools for students from the first grade through college. All these schools were free for the children who lived on the ashrams. Sai Baba furnished them with rooms, clothes, food, and everything they needed. He also built new water systems in areas of southern India so residents could have easy access to water instead of having to walk long distances carrying water to their homes. He did all of this for free.

Sai Baba was able to perform some of the same miracles as Jesus. He helped the disabled to walk, the blind to see, and healed numerous illnesses. He could take a pot of food and make it stay full, so there was enough to feed thousands.

I had been taught that we are all connected and to love everyone, not just our family and friends. It was hard for me to understand how to love strangers and people across the world that I had never even met. Sai Baba helped me know that there is a part of God in everyone, even though everyone does not acknowledge it and some may not experience it. Sometimes, this part of us is called the Soul.

We are all a part of one another and affect each other in everything we do. Gradually, I was able to see everyone as a part of God and expand my world to include everyone in it. I realize that many do not acknowledge or believe in God. That doesn't matter. They are still connected to God so I can love them for that. I don't have to like a person's actions, but I can still love them for who they truly are underneath.

CHAPTER 19

The Fruits of a Spiritual Life

Authenticity

Authenticity involves the courage to stand up for the truth and what we believe no matter what the cost. If we don't rationalize our behavior, give in to defenses, or conform to get approval, then others have no room to intimidate us. We are not afraid to stand up for our principles even if we lose friends, money, and prestige. It means we have learned the lesson of how high the cost is if we sell out our integrity to the highest bidder.

As challenging as being authentic may sound, once you choose to align spiritually with God, the universe, or your choice of a higher being, you will be nourished and supported. This will give you strength and endurance. Ultimately, there is great joy in being true to yourself.

Good Character

Have you ever noticed how satisfying and good it feels to help someone? It seems society's focus today is more about getting stuff than building character. Developing honesty, dependability, trust, honor, love, kindness, generosity, friendship, valor, and the willingness to share with others should be what is most important. Adults know right from wrong, but for many, this becomes unimportant compared to getting what they want, and they will sacrifice honesty, truth, and their characters to do it. It is as easy to tell a lie as it is to tell the truth for many people. Often, lying becomes such a habit that the person doesn't even know they are lying. It's just another way to get what they want.

Negative emotions like anger, hate, and rage are some of

the biggest problems humans have to deal with. Anger causes wars and fights with family members, friends, co-workers, and strangers. It is also directed at the self. Until people learn how to deal with their anger, it is impossible to have lasting peace and happiness. Most people go through their whole lives never learning how to give up anger or even where it comes from. They may learn to hide it better or deflect it by focusing on other things, but not many know how to give it up completely.

Once you are committed to a spiritual journey, you will regularly process your feelings and thoughts, manage how your mind works and commit to transcending your ego. The result will be that a new character will emerge in you—one based on kindness, compassion, and justice for all. The journey of spirituality can teach a person the value of cultivating a stellar character and how good it feels on a spiritual level to do so. Peace, joy, and lasting happiness are available to those who value this rather than being right and getting what they want.

Manifesting Love

Love is a very high vibrational energy. You can only manifest love when your energy has reached a high level. Walking a spiritual path can lead you to the higher vibrational energy of love. Only you can choose the path you want to have for your life.

Love manifests when you release the negativity of guilt, shame, despair, anger, rage, fear, jealousy, greed, and hate. You will develop more loving energy and become repelled by vile behavior, such as violence, anger, and negativity. Then loving yourself and others proceeds naturally. Cultivating spirituality will expand your compassion, devotion, empathy, understanding, and patience for yourself and other people. Your desire to help others will increase. The loving energy you give out comes back to you in many ways. Even animals, flowers, plants, and all of nature respond positively to the energy of love.

When you are filled with love, you are *unable* to give love to only certain people. It would be like only being able to turn on a water faucet for some. Faucets don't work that way. When you turn on the faucet, the water comes out regardless of who the water is for because the water is there for all. In the same way, if you are filled with love, it will be expressed to everyone and everything.

The Power of Prayer

Praying to God for guidance and help is a powerful source of well-being for millions of people. To free yourself from the ego, pray for everyone consistently, without discrimination about who they are. A prayer is a form of meditation. Praying for others is a way to wish them well. It is a form of goodwill. It seeks to empower them. Once we have made our life purpose a spiritual one, prayer comes as naturally to us as breathing.

To pray presumes the interconnection of all that is because, otherwise, how can prayer help? There must be a force connecting us. Prayer treats people we may not know like close kin or family and as worthy of receiving our good intentions. Prayer benefits both the well-intentioned person praying and the recipient. When we pray for others, we become the funnel through which positive energies go out into the world, thus the person who prays receives as much as the person who is prayed for.

Suggestions on How to Pray

There are many ways to pray, as evidenced by the wide range of practices in the world's religions and spiritual traditions. Many of these paths are powerful and worthwhile. Especially powerful prayer includes certain components.

First, prayer should be offered to the universe with a spirit of true humility. End each prayer with "if it is in the highest good" because we know that we cannot see the entire picture of the highest good in the universe and the true depth of each situation and why things occur the way that they do.

Second, offer prayer with full authenticity and full depth

of emotion. Prayer devoid of emotion will not hold vibrational weight in the universe. It is just like wanting anything in life. We need to dig deep down to the recesses of our spirits and really, deeply want something to energize its potential to manifest in our reality. It is the same with prayer. We should pray from our hearts and deep down from the pit of our stomachs, not simply recite words without offering any genuine emotions.

Third, what is prayed about and the words used can be powerful, so they should align with goodness and a positive intention of uplifting others.

Here is a powerful way to pray every day. Begin by envisioning the globe encircled with light and praying for every single sentient being on earth. Pray to uplift the consciousness of humanity and to fill their hearts with love. In addition to praying for humanity, add a prayer for all those in positions of power who have the potential to affect people with their actions and choices. Add a prayer for friends and family who you know need help in any area. Here are some more examples of people to keep in mind for prayers.

Worldwide leaders of corporations, for royalty, presidents in the world and their families, cabinet members and advisors, politicians in the Congress and Parliaments, judges, military leaders and soldiers, government employees, and lawyers in government. Pray that they give up their anger, judgment, greed, and selfishness and raise their consciousness so they will work toward the highest good of all the people in the world and be of service and kind to everyone.

All people in helping professions such as healthcare work-ers, healers, researchers, scientists, professors, teachers, educators, religious leaders, and counselors.

All the workers in the world.

All parents, children, and families.

Those who are experiencing illness, prejudice, abuse, pain, addiction, poverty, rejection, and being outcast by others.

Anyone affected by natural disasters, such as earthquakes, volcanos, fires, tornadoes, hurricanes, floods, diseases, and the many other disasters in the world today.

What about ourselves? Should we pray for ourselves? Of course. Every day, we can ask to gain a deeper understanding of life, that our spiritual development is nourished, to let go of the ego, and to be a vehicle of light in the world. Regularly, we can also offer more specific positive intentions to improve our lives.

Intuitive Experiences and Miracles

As you continue your spiritual journey of untangling the ego's hold and transforming your mind and emotions, you may find that you become more intuitive and that you notice the miraculous more in your life.

My mother and a friend had driven up from Orange County to Sherman Oaks, California, to visit me for the day. When they were ready to go back home, I also had to leave for an appointment. We drove our separate cars up to a T where one street runs into a boulevard. My mother was in front of me, and we were both going to make a left turn. The light turned green, and my mother made the left turn.

I started to accelerate into the turn, but I felt a very strong feeling in the palm of my left hand that felt like someone was rubbing it hard. It was so strong that I stopped the car and looked at my hand. At that moment, a car, speeding on the boulevard, going from my left to right, went through the red light. If I hadn't stopped to look at my hand, I would have been turning into the intersection and the path of the speeding car only to be hit. I have always believed that the distraction of my hand was protection. Intuition and guidance have saved me at least six other times in my life.

You Can Do More Than You Think

As your intuition develops, you may notice you are willing to try new things or can do what you couldn't do before. A few years ago, a girlfriend and I attended a seminar about how to do an intuitive reading on someone and their life. I wanted to leave early because, as I explained to my friend, I already knew how to do it. Then I suggested an experiment to her. When we got home, my friend would give me the name of someone she knew, and I would meditate and tell her about that person.

My friend got a pad and pen to write down what I was going to say, then gave me the name of a man who lived in New York City. As I meditated, I told myself to go to New York, to the man's address. I began describing what I saw: "The man is sleeping now, and the sheets on his bed are light pink with small roses on them. There is a white fireplace in the living room with photos on the mantle. The man weighs 191 pounds and, when he was younger, injured his left leg in a skiing accident. He is very creative, has a great sense of humor, and works in an office. He lives with a friend, and they get along very well."

My friend called the man the next day to see if the information was correct. Everything was accurate, except he weighed one pound more. I never tried to repeat this exercise because I haven't had any reason to. It taught me that it is possible to do this, and it made me wonder how many other things we can do that we do not know we can do.

Intuition in Dreams

Dreams are an essential way to process our thoughts, memories, and the day's events and sort out and express our deep-seated fantasies and desires. They are how our unconscious relays information to us. There are different types of dreams. Some dreams express emotions. Other dreams can be about things going on in the person's life. There are also prophetic dreams about the future.

If you want to know more about your dreams, before you go to bed, tell yourself, I am going to remember my dreams. Have a pen and paper beside the bed so you can write the dreams down as soon as you awaken. You may think, I don't need to write the dreams down; I'll remember them. You won't remember them unless you write them down. You could also keep your phone by the bed to record your dreams on a voice memo or note app.

As soon as you wake up, don't move your body. Go over any dreams in your mind, and then write them down. If you get up before reviewing the dreams, you may forget them.

I have had a few important dreams that have come true. In one dream, I was driving on a freeway and got off on the ramp I always get off to go home. At the bottom of the ramp, when I went to step on the brakes, they weren't there. A police car was parked across the street, but there was no police officer around. The garage I used for car repair was a mile up the road. In the dream, I decided to drive very slowly to the garage using the emergency brake and got safely to the garage. Three months after I had that dream, the exact thing happened in real life at the same off-ramp as in the dream. There was even an empty police car parked exactly as there had been in the dream. When the brakes failed in reality, I thought, this is familiar, and I know what I am going to do.

It has always surprised me when a dream has come true in real life. Before the above dream happened, I didn't know someone could have a dream that would come true down to the smallest detail. I had another dream that the kitchen door to the outside of my home was open a couple of inches. At night, as security, I would intentionally block that door from being opened from the outside by leaving the oven door down, making it impossible to open the kitchen door more than a few inches. When I got up the morning after the dream, the kitchen door was open a couple of inches, just like in the dream. Someone had tried to get in during the night.

Trust Your Intuition

One evening in 1968, I was getting dressed to go to a large party with many people. There would be an orchestra and dancing, but I felt despondent. It was unusual for me to feel this way. I drove to the party, started conversing with others, and danced a few times, but I couldn't shake off the heavy feeling. Finally, I found a quiet corner and sat by myself in my gloom and doom. After the party, I went home still feeling sad.

The next day, while I was doing some work in the apartment, there was a knock on the door. When I opened it, there was a soldier in an army uniform standing there. He asked my name and then told me that my son, Mike, had been wounded in Vietnam. That was the only information he gave me, so I didn't know how seriously Mike had been injured.

A week later, I received a letter from Mike. He wrote that he had been wounded and filled me in on what had happened. Mike and his platoon of 15 men had just been dropped off by a helicopter and started moving out. The men made a wedge formation, and Mike was one of the point men. As they walked, Mike came upon a small bush

My son, Mike, serving in the US military in Vietnam.

about two feet high, so he went right to walk around the bush and then forward again to get back in formation. The squad leader was directly behind Mike. Only the squad leader went to the left to walk around the bush.

At that point, there was a massive explosion that killed four of the soldiers and wounded six others. Mike got some shrapnel in his arm near the elbow. The wounded men were medevacked back to the rear area. Mike's wounds were cleaned and bandaged, but the shrapnel in his arm couldn't be removed. He was off duty for the arm to heal for two weeks and then went back to duty.

A team of soldiers immediately examined the location of the explosion when they picked up the bodies. They discovered it had been booby-trapped with artillery rounds. A tripwire was found wrapped around the foot of the soldier who had died stepping on the booby trap.

Mike served four years in the US Army, and two years of that was on active duty in Vietnam. Thankfully, he came home without having any more physical injuries.

Mike and I had always had a close intuitive connection. There was no way for me to know why I felt so gloomy that night of the party. But it turned out that that night was when the explosion happened and Mike was injured. I had learned to pay attention whenever I am having strong unexplained feelings and realize my intuition might be telling me something.

Consciousness

Everything offered in this book is to help you to become conscious: all the tools for examining and releasing your negative thoughts, feelings, fears, and resistance; the stories that show you the way; the information on how the unconscious operates and how to deal with it; and the ideas and concepts you have learned about your inner world. Consciousness is the greatest gift and ultimate aim of entering into a life with a spiritual focus.

Consciousness is the part of you that is able to observe the thoughts, feelings, and actions that are the real you. The I AM. When you are performing an action, who is it that is observing you doing it? There has to be something separate within you that is the observer. This is consciousness, the I AM.

Without the I AM there can be no perception or imagination. The I AM (observer) does not react or get involved with action. The I AM is not the doer, it is not the experiencer. The I AM quietly and peacefully observes what is going on. The I AM is free of memories and anticipation.

Consciousness is the observer, stillness, and silence.

There is a spectrum of frequencies in human consciousness. All people are at different levels. Some, who are still mired in negativity and ego, vibrate at low levels. Others, those expressing love and kindness to all, are at high levels. Everyone sees life through different perspectives because their consciousness level, understanding, and wisdom are different. Someone with a lower-frequency consciousness relies solely on their five senses to get information from education, science, medicine, and the media. They miss out on the flashes of insight arising from being in tune with universal consciousness that can be real turning points. Becoming higher and more expanded in consciousness is the goal of any spiritual path because that is what happiness is.

The ego is engaged in limiting awareness and lowering consciousness. When consciousness is lowered, it is difficult to feel inspiration and guidance or even to stay authentic in ourselves and true to our spirituality. When we are operating from programming, emotional responses, and egoic perceptions we are not in a higher conscious state.

The higher the frequency of your consciousness, the more awareness and information that is available to you. People can only become aware of the deeper mysteries of life by developing their consciousness. I encourage you to expand your awareness away from all limitations and toward acceptance so that you reach all possibilities.

When we live life in a state of acceptance, we can realize we are a part of Infinite Consciousness. Regular meditation helps us become more conscious by quieting the mind and encouraging acceptance. Consciousness makes us more aware of Truth. **Infinite love is the only Truth.**

Notice how you behave and the results of your actions. Study the person you have become. When you are no longer obsessed with the body and mind, you can be spontaneous and living can be effortless. You can discover the I AM by having a sincere attitude, searching, and wanting to know. Each day examine your motives and actions. Strive to learn how to *be* and have an attitude of witnessing and observing events without becoming involved.

Becoming conscious means, it is not enough to know about truth and spiritual principles, we must live them. Knowledge and action must be one. Be invincible and unaffected by the ups and down in life. Be willing to give a helping hand whenever possible. And above all else let yourself be the conduit through which Infinite Consciousness flows love.

So, on your journey of transformation to consciousness, open your heart, let it be filled with love, and share it with everyone. This is the greatest gift of life.

Epilogue of Gratitude

I am thankful to have shared this journey and communed with you, the reader, through this book. If you have found some insight that has awakened and uplifted your spirit here, then I would have my heart's desire.

May this book help you become more consciously aware and find what you are seeking.

May it help you learn to understand how to live with more peace, joy, and love for yourself and others.

May it inspire you to love the people in your life more deeply and extend that love to serve all of humanity.

I pray that you will be able to accomplish what you came into life to do and that the world is a better place because you are here.

May your path be blessed and filled with love and light.

God Bless You.

Acknowledgments

I give thanks to God for his grace, guidance, and love in helping to write this book.

I want to thank my husband, Benny, for sharing some of his life experiences and allowing me to write about them. His emotional support and understanding are most appreciated. My son, Michael, I thank you for sharing your experiences when you were serving in the military in Vietnam.

The testimonial stories that Jim and the other people contributed to the book are most appreciated and I give a heartfelt thank you to each of them. I also want to thank Lori Cole and Joe Alexander for contributing their stories to this book.

I deeply appreciate the wonderful and insightful work of my talented editor, Marie Timell. Thank you, Marie, for your generosity, time, and effort in making this book what it is today. I would also like to express my deep gratitude to Fran Grace and Rodger for reviewing an earlier version of this book and offering feedback before publication.

Recommended Further Reading

The Astonishing Power of Emotions, Esther and Jerry Hicks

Between You & Me, Prof. Anil Kumar Kamaraju

A Catholic Priest Meets Sai Baba, Don Mario Mazzoleni

Change Your Thoughts, Change Your Life, Wayne W. Dyer

Dissolving the Ego, Realizing the Self, David R. Hawkins

Emotional Intelligence: Why it Can Matter More Than IQ, Daniel Goleman

The 5 Love Languages, Gary Chapman

Here and Now, Anil Kumar Kamaraju

How to Remove Conditioning, Catherine Kapahi

The Intuitive Way, Penney Peirce

Letting Go, David R. Hawkins, MD, PhD

The Miracle of Change, Dennis Wholey

The Most Powerful Book of Affirmations Ever Written, Sheldon T. Ceaser, MD

My Dear Students, Volume 3 Sri Sathya Sai Hostel for Senior Students, Sri Sathya Sai Vidyagiri

Mystic Secrets Revealed: 53 Keys to Spiritual Growth and Personal Development, Edwin Harkness Spina

Negative Self-Talk & How to Change It, Shad Helmstetter, PhD

A New Earth, Eckhart Tolle

Positive Affirmations, Rachel Robins

The Power of Love, Fran Grace, PhD

Power vs. Force, David R. Hawkins, MD, PhD

A Practical Guide to Vibrational Medicine, Richard Gerber, MD

Sai Baba Man of Miracles, Howard Murphet

Sai-Chology, Anil Kumar Kamaraju

Secrets of a Parallel Universe: Facing Our Deepest Problems is the Key to Ultimate Personal Success & Happiness, Roy Masters

Stillness Speaks, Eckhart Tolle

Why Walk When You Can Fly? Isha Judd

Appendix of Detailed Contents

About the Author

Evelyn Budd Michaels

For most of her life, Dr. Evelyn Budd Michaels has searched for solutions that enable her and people to live healthier, happier, and more prosperous lives. She has discovered many principles and techniques that help accomplish these goals, which she has drawn on while working with her clients.

Dr. Evelyn Budd Michaels has a PhD in Psychology and is certified as a Practitioner, Master Practitioner, and Trainer in Neuro-Linguistic Programming (NLP). Her training in kinesiology techniques includes certified training in Total Body Modification (TBM), Holistic Energy Restructuring, Bio-Energetic Synchronization Techniques (BEST), Emotional Complex Clearing (ECC), Neuro-Emotional Technique (Net), and Personal Development techniques. Dr. Budd Michaels is a certified member of the American Board of Hypnotherapy. She is also a renowned expert on Handwriting Analysis. Her experience in this field allows her to use handwriting as another diagnostic tool to assist her clients.

Dr. Evelyn Budd Michaels has been coaching people for over 35 years. She has reached millions of people throughout the world through TV, radio, and seminars. She also produced and was the hostess of her cable television show, *Synergy 4 Success*. This talk show presented new and unique information to assist viewers in achieving personal and professional success. Guests included world champions, artists, celebrities, and interesting people from many walks of life.

She has sailed all over the world on cruise ships, and, from 1984 to 2009, regularly lectured to passengers on the subjects of Handwriting Analysis and Self-Improvement.

Her magazine and journal articles include "Stress Reduction," "Creating Happier Relationships with Yourself and Others," "Secrets Revealed in your Handwriting," "Dynamic Communication," and "Walking the Spiritual Path."

If you would like more direct help with applying the information in this book or have any questions, please go to the website: www.insightsforselftransformation.com

Or email me at **EvelynBuddMichaels@gmail.com**

If you want to contact me and are interested in attending Internet classes, then please email me a note and your email address. Or you may go to the website.

Address for Vital Verite Press is:
P.O Box 359
4804 Laurel Canyon Blvd
Valley Village, CA 91607

www.ingramcontent.com/pod-product-compliance
Lightning Source LLC
Chambersburg PA
CBHW052030090426
42739CB00010B/1845